Commentary on the

POSTERIOR ANALYTICS

of Aristotle

BY ST. THOMAS AQUINAS

Translated by
F.R. Larcher, O.P.
College of Santa Fe
Santa Fe, New Mexico

With a Preface by
James A. Weisheipl, O.P.
Pontifical Institute of Mediaeval Studies
Toronto, Canada

 **AGI BOOKS, INC.**

33 Buckingham Drive   Albany, New York 12208

This translation of the Commentary on the Posterior Analytics is based on the Leonine Text.

It has been correlated with the text of the Posterior Analytics as found in The Oxford Translation of Aristotle by W.D. Ross, by permission of the Clarendon Press, Oxford.

Manufactured in the United States of America by the Hamilton Printing Co., Rensselaer, New York.

CONTENTS

CONTENTS   V

BOOK II

PREFACE

The purpose of logic is to provide an analytic guide to the discovery of demonstrated truth and all its various approximations throughout the philosophical sciences. In the words of St. Albert the Great, logic "teaches the principles by which one can arrive at the knowledge of things unknown through that which is known" (*De Praedicab.*, tr. I, c. 5, ed. Borgnet I, 8b). St. Thomas defines logic as an art "directive of the acts of reason themselves so that man may proceed orderly, easily and without error in the very act of reason itself" (Foreword). Logic is thus a construct based on the natural processes of the mind invented for a very specific use, namely, scientific reasoning. Because it is a construct, logic is said to deal with "second intentions," that is, deliberate constructs of the mind, existing solely in the mind, of ideas based upon the way human beings know reality ("first intentions"), such as predicables, subject, predicate, major premise, minor premise, middle term and conclusion. The analysis and construction of this guide is the scientific, or theoretical, aspect of logic. Under this consideration, logic is itself a science and it is this aspect that modern logicians seem to be interested in. Nevertheless the purpose of this construct is that it be *used* by thinkers who want to get on with the discovery of truth in the various sciences. In this way the whole of logic is a methodology, solidly established by analysis, to guide the mind in its quest for answers to problems raised in scientific inquiry. The general name given to all of Aristotle's logical treatises is *Organon*, the instrument. For this reason Boethius, the 6th century translator of most of Aristotle's *Organon*, says that logic is "not so much a science as an instrument of science" (*Comm. super Porphyry*, ed. 2a, I, c. 3; see St. Thomas, *In Boeth. de Trin.*, q. 5, a. 1 ad 2; St. Albert, *Post Anal.* I, tr. I, c. 1, ed. Borgnet II, 2b).

It must be noted, however, that logic is only a general methodology common to all scientific knowledge (See J.A. Weisheipl, "The Evolution of Scientific Method," *The Logic of Science*, ed. V.E. Smith (New York:

St. John's Univ. 1964) 59–86). There is over and above this a particular logic peculiar to each field of knowledge. That is to say, the proper method of natural philosophy is not at all identical with that of mathematics, metaphysics or moral philosophy. Logic, or general methodology, must be understood before any of the particular sciences are investigated and organized systematically. This, at least, was the common view accepted by all scholastic thinkers, even though this was not the actual procedure followed in medieval universities (see J.A. Weisheipl, "Classfication of the Sciences in Medieval Thought," *Mediaeval Studies*, 27 (1965) 89).

In studying methodolgy, or the common logic of all the sciences, Aristotle and those after him followed a logical order which considered problems arising from each step of logical thinking. The scholastics thought they had found this order in the various books of logic. Thus according to St. Thomas (Foreword) the predicables (in the *Isagogy* of Porphyry) and the categories (in the *De praedicamentis* of Aristotle) deal with universals that are begotten by the first act of the mind. Propositions, or enunciations (in the *Peri hermenias* of Aristotle) deal with constructs of various types of judgement in the second act of the mind. These two areas of logical investigation are prior to the analysis of reasoning itself, the third act of the mind. St. Thomas recognized that there are two types of analysis, or resolution, to be considered: the formal structure of reasoning, which Aristotle discusses in the *Prior Analytics,* and the material structure of the premises, which can be of three kinds, namely necessary and scientific (considered in the *Posterior Analytics*), probable and dialectical (considered in the *Topics*), and erroneous and false (considered in the *Sophistici Elenchi*). Of all these branches of logic, the most important is the *Posterior Analytics,* the only logical book commented upon in full by St. Thomas Aquinas. St. Albert clearly states that the *Posterior Analytics* is the apex, the most perfect and only absolutely desirable (*simpliciter desiderabile*) study among the logical works of Aristotle (*Post. Anal.,* I, tr. 1, cap. 1, ed. Borgnet II, 2b). And the Leonine editors of the works of St. Thomas state that "the posterior analytics deal with demonstration and thus are the ultimate goal of the whole science of logic" (Praef. ed. Leon., I, p. 131).

No one has ever doubted that the *Posterior Analytics* is an extremely difficult work to understand. Even Themistius, paraphrasing the Greek text, found much to complain about (*Paraphrasis in lib. Post.,* praef.). According to John of Salisbury, after the text was translated into Latin, there was scarcely a master willing to expound it because of its extreme subtlety and obscurity; "there are almost as many stumbling blocks as there are chapters" (*Metalogicon* IV, c. 6, ed. Webb 171). However, John blames most of this on the bungling mistakes of scribes and he proceeds to give the Latin West the first paraphrase of Aristotle's difficult work.

Part of the difficulty seems to be that this is an early work of Aristotle, for the terminology is not yet fixed and especially in the First Book, Aristotle seems to approach the same point from many directions, giving the reader the impression that many different points are being made. The best guides for understanding Aristotle are St. Thomas Aquinas, St. Albert the Great, Averroes and Robert Grosseteste.

When reading St. Thomas' commentary one must not only read the text of Aristotle first, but one should have a pencil and sufficient paper to outline the text as understood by St. Thomas. Division of the text was always one of the basic tools of the scholastic method. Therefore it is important to keep in mind this outline in order to understand the point about to be made and to appreciate it in the context of the work as a whole. Clearly Aristotle himself wrote according to a systematic order, and it is up to the reader to appreciate this order.

Since St. Thomas did not know Greek, he had to rely on one of the many Latin translations of the *Posterior Analytics* available to him. At the time St. Thomas wrote his commentary, around 1270, there were four Latin translations from the Greek and two from the Arabic. Even though it seems that Boethius himself translated the work, the *Posterior Analytics* had to come into the Latin West anew in the 12th century as part of the *logica nova*. The common text in the Middle Ages was the version made by James of Venice before 1159; it was the "vulgate text" (*Arist. Lat.*, IV.2) in use during the second half of the 12th century and the earlier part of the 13th century. A very influential version from the Arabic was made by the translator, probably Michael Scott, of the works of Averroes together with the Commentator's views between 1220 and 1240. St. Thomas was undoubtedly familiar with these two translations, but he most likely relied on the revised version made by William of Moerbeke in the second half of the 13th century (*Arist. Lat.*, IV. 4; cf. De Rubeis, *Diss.* XXIII, c. 1–2, ed. Leon., 1, cclix–cclxii).

The *Posterior Analytics* of Aristotle possesses a remarkable unity from beginning to end. The first chapter of Book I is a propaedeutic to the entire work; it poses the fundamental problem concerning the possibility of learning, that is, of demonstrative knowledge. Its point of departure is the problem posed by Plato in the *Meno* (80 D-86) where Socrates attempts to inquire into the nature of virtue, a subject about which he admittedly does not have full knowledge. Meno intervenes and objects that all inquiry is impossible, for "a man cannot inquire either about that which he knows, or about that which he does not know; for if he knows, he has no need to inquire; and if not, he cannot, for he does not know the very subject about which he is to inquire." Either we already know what we seek to learn, and this is not learning, or we do not know what we are seeking, and hence cannot know when we have found it. Plato solves this dilemma by his doctrine of remembering ideas already innate in the mind. The Sophists and nominalists of the Academy took an opposite view and claimed that all learning is simply an aggregation of individual observations. In other words, the Sophists maintained that there can be no demonstrations, but only the acquisition of a totally new fact. Aristotle took a middle course between these two extremes that would have all knowledge in act or no knowledge in act by his ingenious doctrine of potentiality. Instead of saying that all knowledge is actually in the mind or actually not in the mind, Aristotle insists that all knowledge is potentially in the mind and the business of learning is to draw this potentiality into actuality. Basically it is the same solution Aristotle offers in the *Physics* to explain the possibility of real change.

In the very question posed for inquiry there is already some knowledge in the mind from which inquiry begins. The all important starting point for inquiry is the question or problem posed. Already we have some idea, if only tentative, of the subject of inquiry, and some knowledge of the predicate; otherwise the question would never have arisen. The purpose of inquiry is to find the definitive medium or middle term that will provide an answer to the question raised. This middle term must be one or all of the physical causes in reality; the mind will not rest until it has found a causal reason for the conclusion. However there are many different kinds of scientific questions that can be raised: whether something exists (*an sit*), what is it (*quid sit*), does it have this or that property (*quia sit*), and why is this so (*propter quid*). For Aristotle and for St. Thomas only a true, objective, invariable cause can produce demonstrations worthy of the name scientific. This cause or middle term cannot be found outside the area in question, for this would give only a probable view. In other words, if a question is raised concerning the physical world, then only an answer found within natural philosophy will do. One cannot, in this case, appeal to harmony, morals or metaphysics for the right answer. The cause must be found within the context of the question. The answer is not found despite the question or problem, but because of it.

Nothing could be farther from the truth than to think of all demonstrative knowledge as "deductive." This is only rarely the case. Most scientific inquiry requires the reverse process of analysis or breaking down. Once a middle term, a true medium of demonstration, has been found in whole or in part, the result may be expressed in the form of a syllogism that can be tested according to all the rules described in the *Prior Analytics* and *Sophistici Elenchi*. Thus the syllogism is not a means of discovery, but rather a means of exposition of the truth acquired by analysis. In fact the syllogism itself can be expressed in a definition that explicitly states the reason. Aristotle calls such a definition a statement "which differs from the syllogism only in position."

Although the *Posterior Analytics* is a scientific work that can be studied and understood in its own right, it cannot be fully understood until one can see this kind of process at work in the various Aristotelian sciences. The scholastics themselves did not grasp the significance of this work until they could see it at work in the other writings of Aristotle. The *Physics* and *Ethics* of Aristotle in particular helped to instruct the scholastic in its use. Only then could Albert the Great and St. Thomas apply this methodology to such new branches as theology. St. Thomas' *Summa theologiae* is the crowning glory of the use that can be made by applying the methodology to a new realm of knowledge. The very first question of the *Summa* is a masterpiece of Aristotelian methodology.

Although the present English translation of St. Thomas' commentary may seem to many to be excessively literal, it has the merit of following the procedure of William of Moerbeke, who rendered, apparently at the request of St. Thomas, a literal translation from the Greek lest any nuance be lost. It is hoped that those who are able will also consult the Latin text in difficult passages.

James A. Weisheipl, O.P.
Pontifical Institute of Mediaeval Studies
Toronto, Canada

FOREWORD OF ST. THOMAS AQUINAS

As the Philosopher says in *Metaphysics* I (980b26), "the human race lives by art and reasonings." In this statement the Philosopher seems to touch upon that property whereby man differs from the other animals. For the other animals are prompted to their acts by a natural impulse, but man is directed in his actions by a judgment of reason. And this is the reason why there are various arts devoted to the ready and orderly performance of human acts. For an art seems to be nothing more than a definite and fixed procedure established by reason, whereby human acts reach their due end through appropriate means.

Now reason is not only able to direct the acts of the lower powers but is also director of its own act: for what is peculiar to the intellective part of man is its ability to reflect upon itself. For the intellect knows itself. In like manner reason is able to reason about its own act. Therefore just as the art of building or carpentering, through which man is enabled to perform manual acts in an easy and orderly manner, arose from the fact that reason reasoned about manual acts, so in like manner an art is needed to direct the act of reasoning, so that by it a man when performing the act of reasoning might proceed in an orderly and easy manner and without error. And this art is logic, i.e., the science of reason. And it concerns reason not only because it is according to reason, for that is common to all arts, but also because it is concerned with the very act of reasoning as with its proper matter. Therefore it seems to be the art of the arts, because it directs us in the act of reasoning, from which all arts proceed. Consequently one should view the parts of logic according to the diversity among the acts of reason.

Now there are three acts of the reason, the first two of which belong to reason regarded as an intellect. One action of the intellect is the understanding of indivisible or uncomplex things, and according to this action it conceives *what* a thing is. And this operation is called by some the informing of the intellect, or representing by means of the intellect. To this operation of the reason is ordained the doctrine which Aristotle hands down in the book of *Predicaments*, [i.e., *Categories*]. The second operation of the intellect is its act of combining or dividing, in which the true or the false are for the first time present. And this act of reason is the subject of the doctrine which Aristotle hands down in the book entitled *On Interpretation*. But the third act of the reason is concerned with that which is peculiar to reason, namely, to advance from one thing to another

1

in such a way that through that which is known a man comes to a knowledge of the unknown. And this act is considered in the remaining books of logic.

It should be noted that the acts of reason are in a certain sense not unlike the acts of nature: hence so far as it can, art imitates nature. Now in the acts of nature we observe a threefold diversity. For in some of them nature acts from necessity, i.e., in such a way that it cannot fail; in others, nature acts so as to succeed for the most part, although now and then it fails in its act. Hence in this latter case there must be a twofold act: one which succeeds in the majority of cases, as when from seed is generated a perfect animal; the other when nature fails in regard to what is appropriate to it, as when from seed something monstrous is generated owing to a defect in some principle.

These three are found also in the acts of the reason. For there is one process of reason which induces necessity, where it is not possible to fall short of the truth; and by such a process of reasoning the certainty of science is acquired. Again, there is a process of reason in which something true in most cases is concluded but without producing necessity. But the third process of reason is that in which reason fails to reach a truth because some principle which should have been observed in reasoning was defective.

Now the part of logic which is devoted to the first process is called the *judicative* part, because it leads to judgments possessed of the certitude of science. And because a certain and sure judgment touching effects cannot be obtained except by analyzing them into their first principles, this part is called *analytical*, i.e., resolvent. Furthermore, the certitude obtained by such an analysis of a judgment is derived either from the mere form of the syllogism—and to this is ordained the book of the *Prior Analytics* which treats of the syllogism as such—or from the matter along with the form, because the propositions employed are *per se* and necessary [cf. *infra*, Lectures 10, 13]—and to this is ordained the book of the *Posterior Analytics* which is concerned with the demonstrative syllogism.

To the second process of reason another part of logic called *investigative* is devoted. For investigation is not always accompanied by certitude. Hence in order to have certitude a judgment must be formed, bearing on that which has been investigated. But just as in the works of nature which succeed in the majority of cases certain levels are achieved—because the stronger the power of nature the more rarely does it fail to achieve its effect—so too in that process of reason which is not accompanied by complete certitude certain levels are found accordingly as one approaches more or less to complete certitude. For although science is not obtained by this process of reason, nevertheless belief or opinion is sometimes achieved (on account of the provability of the propositions one starts with), because reason leans completely to one side of a contradiction but with fear concerning the other side. The *Topics* or dialectics is devoted to this. For the dialectical syllogism which Aristotle treats in the book of *Topics* proceeds from premises which are provable.

At times, however, belief or opinion is not altogether achieved, but suspicion is, because reason does not lean to one side of a contradiction unreservedly, although it is inclined more to one side than to the other. To this the *Rhetoric* is devoted. At other times a mere fancy inclines one to one side of a contradiction because of some representation, much as a man turns in disgust from certain food if it is described to him in terms of something disgusting. And to this is ordained the *Poetics*. For the poet's task is to lead us to something virtuous by some excellent description. And all these pertain to the philosophy of the reason, for it belongs to reason to pass from one thing to another.

The third process of reasoning is served by that part of logic which is called *sophistry*, which Aristotle treats in the book *On Sophistical Refutations*.

BOOK I

Lecture 1
(71a1–10)

THE NEED FOR PRE-EXISTENT KNOWLEDGE
IN ALL LEARNING

a1. All instruction given

a3. The mathematical sciences

a4. and so are the two

a8. Again, the persuasion

Leaving aside the other parts of logic, we shall fix our attention on the judicative part as it is presented in the book of *Posterior Analytics* which is divided into two parts. In the first he shows the need for the demonstrative syllogism, with which this book is concerned. In the second part he comes to a decision concerning that syllogism (71b8) [Lect. 4].

Now the need for anything directed to an end is caused by that end. But the end of the demonstrative syllogism is the attainment of science. Hence if science could not be achieved by syllogizing or arguing, there would be no need for the demonstrative syllogism. Plato, as a matter of fact, held that science in us is not the result of a syllogism but of an impression upon our minds of ideal forms from which, he said, are also derived the natural forms in natural things, which he supposed were participations of forms separated from matter. From this it followed that natural agents were not the causes of forms in natural things but merely prepared the matter for participating in the separated forms. In like fashion he postulated that science in us is not caused by study and exercise, but only that obstatcles are removed and man is brought to recall things which he naturally understands in virtue of an imprint of separated forms.

But Aristotle's view is opposed to this on two counts. For he maintains that natural forms are made actual by forms present in matter, i.e., by the forms of natural agents. He further maintains that science is made actual in us by other knowledge already existing in us. This means that it is formed in us through a syllogism or some type of argument. For in arguing we proceed from one thing into another.

Therefore, in order to show the need for demonstrative syllogism Aristotle begins by stating that some of our knowledge is acquired from knowledge already existing. Hence he does two things. First, he states his thesis. Secondly, he explains the character of prior knowledge (71a11) [Lect. 2]. Concerning the first he does two things.

5

First (71a1), he asserts a universal proposition containing his thesis, namely, that the production of knowledge in us is caused from knowledge already existing; hence he says, "Every doctrine and every discipline . . ." He does not say, "all knowledge," because not all knowledge depends on previous knowledge, for that would involve an infinite process: but the acquisition of every discipline comes from knowledge already possessed. For the names "doctrine" and "discipline" pertain to the learning process, doctrine being the action exerted by the one who makes us know, and discipline the reception of knowledge from another. Furthermore, "doctrine" and "discipline" are not taken here as pertaining only to the acquisition of scientific knowledge but to the acquiring of any knowledge. That this is so is evidenced by the fact that he explains the proposition even in regard to dialectical and rhetorical disputations, neither of which engenders science. Hence this is another reason why he did not say, "from pre-existent science or intuition," but "knowledge" universally. However he does add, "intellectual," in order to preclude knowledge acquired by sense or imagination. For reason alone proceeds from one thing into another.

Then (71a3) he employs induction to prove his thesis; and first of all in regard to those demonstrations in which scientific knowledge is acquired. Of these the best are the mathematical sciences because of their most certain manner of demonstrating. After them come the other arts, because some manner of demonstrating is found in all of them; otherwise they would not be sciences.

Secondly (71a4), he proves the same thing in regard to disputative, i.e., dialectical, arguments, because they employ syllogism and induction, in each of which the process starts from something already known. For in a syllogism the knowledge of some universal conclusion is obtained from other universals already known; in induction, however, a universal is concluded from singulars made known in sense-perception.

Thirdly (71a8), he manifests the same thing in rhetorical arguments, in which persuasion is produced through an enthymeme or example but not through a syllogism or complete induction because of the uncertainty attending the matters discussed, namely, the individual acts of men in which universal propositions cannot be truthfully assumed. Therefore, in place of a syllogism in which there must be something universal, an enthymeme is employed in which it is not necessary to have something universal. Similarly, in place of induction in which a universal is concluded, an example is employed in which one goes from the singular not to the universal but to the singular. Hence it is clear that just as the enthymeme is an abridged syllogism, so an example is an incomplete induction. Therefore, if in the case of the syllogism and induction one proceeds from knowledge already existing, the same must be granted in the case of the enthymeme and example.

Lecture 2
(71a11–24)

EXTENT AND ORDER OF THE PRE-EXISTENT
KNOWLEDGE REQUIRED FOR
OBTAINING SCIENCE

71a11. The pre-existent knowledge   a16. Recognition of a truth

After showing that every discipline is developed from knowledge already existing, the Philosopher shows what is the extent of this pre-existing knowledge. Concerning this he does two things. First, he determines the extent of pre-existing knowledge in regard to the things that must be known in order to attain knowledge of the conclusion, of which scientific knowledge is sought. Secondly, he determines the extent of pre-existing knowledge of the conclusion, of which scientific knowledge is sought through demonstration (71a24) [L.3]. Now two things are included in pre-existing knowledge, namely, the knowledge and the order of the knowledge. First, therefore, he determines the extent of pre-existing knowledge so far as the knowledge itself is concerned. Secondly, so far as the order of the knowledge is concerned (71a16).

In regard to the first it should be noted that the object of which scientific knowledge is sought through demonstration is some conclusion in which a proper attribute is predicated of some subject, which conclusion is inferred from the principles. And because the knowledge of simple things precedes the knowledge of compound things, it is necessary that the subject and the proper attribute be somehow known before knowledge of the conclusion is obtained. In like manner it is required that the principle be known from which the conclusion is inferred, for the conclusion is made known from a knowledge of the principle.

Now the extent of pre-existent knowledge of these three items, i.e., of the principle, of the subject, and of the proper attribute, is limited to knowing two things about them, namely, *that* each is and *what* each is. But, as stated in *Metaphysics* VII, complex things are not defined. For there is no definition of "white man," much less of an enunciation [proposition]. Hence since a principle is an enunciation, there cannot be pre-existing knowledge of *what it is* but only of the fact *that it is true.* But in regard to the proper attribute, it is possible to know *what* it is, because, as is pointed out in the same book, accidents do have some sort of definition. Now the being of a proper attribute and of any accident is being *in* a subject; and this fact is concluded by the demonstration. Consequently, it is not known beforehand *that* the proper attribute exists, but only *what*

7

it is. The subject, too, has a definition; moreover, its being does not depend on the proper attribute—rather its own being is known before one knows the proper attribute to be in it. Consequently, it is necessary to know both *what* the subject is and *that* it is, especially since the medium of demonstration is taken from the definition of the subject of the proper attribute.

This, therefore, is why the Philosopher says (71a11) that it is necessary to know beforehand in two ways; because two items are known beforehand concerning things of which we have pre-existing knowledge, namely, *that* it is and *what* it is. [Then he goes on to say] that there are some things concerning which it is necessary first to know *that* they are, such as principles, concerning which he then gives examples, citing as one example the first of all principles, namely, "There is true affirmation or negation about everything." Again, there are other things, namely, proper attributes, concerning which it is necessary to know *what is said to be predicated*, i.e., what is signified by their name. And he does not say unqualifiedly, "what it is," but "what is said to be predicated," because one cannot properly know of something *what* it is before it is known *that* it is. For there are no definitions of non-beings. Hence the question, *whether it is*, precedes the question, *what it is*. But "whether a thing is" cannot be shown unless it is known beforehand what is signified by its name. On this account the Philosopher teaches in *Metaphysics* IV that in disputing against those who deny principles one must begin with the meanings of names. An example of this is "triangle," concerning which one must know beforehand that its name signifies such and such, namely, what is contained in its definition.

But since accidents are referred to their subjects in a definite order, it is not impossible for something which is an accident in relation to one thing to be a subject in relation to something else: for example, a surface is an accident in relation to a bodily substance, but in relation to color it is the first subject. However, that which is a subject in such a way as never to be an accident of anything else is a substance. Hence in those sciences whose subject is a substance, that which is the subject can never be a proper attribute, as in first philosophy and in natural science, which treats of mobile being.

But in those sciences which bear upon accidents, nothing prevents a same thing from being taken as a subject in reference to one proper attribute, and as an attribute in reference to a more basic subject. Nevertheless, this must not develop into an infinite process, for one must arrive at something which is first in that science and which is taken as a subject in such a way that it is never taken as a proper attribute, as is clear in the mathematical sciences, which treat of continuous or discrete quantity. For in these sciences those things are postulated which are first in the genus of quantity; for example, unit and line and surface and the like.

Once these are postulated, certain other things are sought through demonstration, such as the equilateral triangle and the square and so on in geometry. In these cases the demonstrations are said to be, as it were, operational, as when it is required to construct an equilateral triangle on a given straight line. But once it has been constructed, certain proper attributes are proved about it; for example, that its angles are equal, or something of that sort. It is clear, therefore, that in the first type of demonstration "triangle" behaves as a proper attribute, and in the second type as a subject. Hence the Philosopher is using "triangle" as a proper attribute and not as a subject when he says by way of example, "We must assume that triangle means so and so" (71a14).

He says, furthermore, that there are certain things about which we must know beforehand both *what* each is and *whether* it is. And he uses the example of "one," which is the principle in every genus of quantity. For although it is somehow an accident in reference to substance, yet in the mathematical sciences, which treat of quantity, it cannot be taken as a proper attribute but only as a subject, since in this genus [quantity] it has nothing prior to it.

The reason for this difference is shown by the fact that the manner in which the aforesaid, namely, principle, proper attribute and subject, are manifested is not the same. For the way in which they are known is not the same: for principles are known through the act of composing and dividing, but subject and proper attribute by the act of apprehending the essence. And this, too, does not belong in similar fashion to a subject and to a proper attribute, since a subject is defined absolutely, for nothing outside its essence is mentioned in its definition; but a proper attribute is defined with dependence on the subject which is mentioned in its definition. Therefore, since they are not known in the same way, it is not surprising if they are not foreknown in the same way.

Then (71a16) he determines the extent of foreknowledge on the part of the order which foreknowing implies. For something is prior to another both in the order of time and in the order of nature. And this twofold order must be considered in regard to pre-existent knowing. For something is known before something else in the sense of being known prior in time. Concerning such things he says that someone could know certain things by knowing them prior to the time when he knows the things to which they are said to be foreknown. But certain others are known at one and the same time, although one is prior by nature to the other. Concerning these he says that one acquires a knowledge of some of these foreknown things at the same time that knowledge of the things to which they are foreknown is acquired. He indicates what these are when he adds that they are the things contained under certain universals of which we have knowledge, i.e., of which it is known that they are contained under such universals.

Then he clarifies this with an example. For since two propositions are needed for inferring a conclusion, namely, a major and a minor; when the major proposition is known, the conclusion is not yet known. Therefore, the major proposition is known before the conclusion not only in nature but in time. Further, if in the minor proposition something is introduced or employed which is contained under the universal proposition which is the major, but it is not evident that it is contained under this universal, then a knowledge of the conclusion is not yet possessed, because the truth of the minor proposition will not yet be certain. But if in the minor proposition a term is taken about which it is clear that it is contained under the universal in the major proposition, the truth of the minor proposition is clear, because that which is taken under the universal shares in the same knowledge, and so the knowledge of the conclusion is had at once. Thus, suppose that someone should begin to demonstrate by stating that every triangle has three angles equal to two right angles. When this is known, the knowledge of the conclusion is not yet known. But when it is later assumed that this figure inscribed in a semicircle is a triangle, he knows at once that it has three angles equal to two right angles. However, if it were not clear that this figure inscribed in the semicircle is a triangle, the conclusion would not be known as soon as the minor was stated; rather, it would be necessary to search for a middle through which to demonstrate that this figure is a triangle.

In giving this example of things which are known at a time prior to the conclusion the Philosopher says that a person obtaining a knowledge of the conclusion through demonstration foreknew this proposition even according to time, namely, that every triangle has three angles equal to two right angles. But inducing this assumption, namely, that this figure in the semicircle is a triangle, he knew the conclusion at the same time, because this induction shares in the evidence of the universal under which it is contained, so that there is no need to search for another middle. He adds, therefore, that "some things are only learnt in this way" (71a23), i.e., learnt in virtue of themselves, so that it is not necessary to learn them through some other middle which is the ultimate reached by analysis in which the mediate is reduced to the immediate. Or it can be read in such a way that the "ultimate," i.e., the extreme, which is subsumed under the universal middle does not need a further middle to show that it is contained under that universal. And he manifests what those things are which always share the knowledge of their universal, saying that they are the singulars which are not predicated of any subject, since no middle can be found between singulars and their species.

Lecture 3
(71a24–b9)

PRE-EXISTENT KNOWLEDGE OF THE CONCLUSION

a24. Before he was led on to   b1. yet what they know
a28. If this distinction   b5. On the other hand
a30. for we cannot

Having shown the manner in which certain other things must be known before knowledge of the conclusion is obtained, the Philosopher now wishes to show how we know even the conclusion beforehand, i.e., before knowledge of it is obtained through a syllogism or induction. Concerning this he does two things:

First (71a24), he establishes the truth of the fact, saying that before an induction or syllogism is formed to beget knowledge of a conclusion, that conclusion is somehow known and somehow not known: for, absolutely speaking, it is not known; but in a qualified sense, it is known. Thus, if the conclusion that a triangle has three angles equal to two right angles has to be proved, the one who obtains science of this fact through demonstration already knew it in some way before it was demonstrated; although absolutely speaking, he did not know it. Hence in one sense he already knew it, but in the full sense he did not. And the reason is that, as has been pointed out, the principles of the conclusion must be known beforehand. Now the principles in demonstrative matters are to the conclusion as efficient causes in natural things are to their effects; hence in *Physics* II the propositions of a syllogism are set in the genus of efficient cause. But an effect, before it is actually produced, pre-exists virtually in its efficient causes but not actually, which is to exist absolutely. In like manner, before it is drawn out of its demonstrative principles, the conclusion is preknown virtually, although not actually, in its self-evident principles. For that is the way it pre-exists in them. And so it is clear that it is not preknown in the full sense, but in some sense.

Secondly (71a28), in virtue of this established fact, he settles a doubt which Plato maintained in the book, *Meno*, which gets its title from the name of his disciple. The doubt is presented in the following manner: A person utterly ignorant of the art of geometry is questioned in an orderly way concerning the *per se* known principles from which a geometric conclusion is concluded. By starting with principles that are *per se* known, to each of which this person ignorant of geometry gives a true answer, and leading him thus by questions to the conclusion, he gives the true answer step by step. From this, therefore, he would have it that even

11

those who seem to be ignorant of certain arts really have a knowledge of them before being instructed in them. And so it follows that either a man learns nothing or he learns what he already knew.

In dealing with this problem he [Aristotle] does four things. First, he suggests that it cannot be settled unless we grant the truth established above, namely, that the conclusion which a person learns through demonstration or induction was already known, not absolutely, but as it was virtually known in its principles concerning which a person ignorant of a science can give true answers. However, according to Plato's theory the conclusion was pre-known absolutely, so that no one learns afresh but is led to recall by some rational process of deduction. This is similar to Anaxagoras' position on natural forms, namely, that before they are generated, they already pre-existed in the matter absolutely, whereas Aristotle says that they pre-exist in potency and not absolutely.

Secondly (71a30), he shows that the way some have answered Plato's problem is false, namely, by saying that a conclusion is not in any sense known before it is demonstrated or learned by some method or other. For they might face the following objection based on Plato's problem: If an unlearned person were asked by someone, "Do you know that every duo (pair) is an even number?" and, if upon answering that he does know this, he were presented with a duo which the person interrogated did not know existed, for example, the duo which is one third of six, the conclusion would be that he knew one third of six to be an even number, a fact which had not been known by him but which he learned through the demonstration proposed to him. And so it seems to follow that he either did not freshly learn this or that he learned what he already knew. To avoid this dilemma, they would answer that the person who was questioned and who answered that he knew every duo to be an equal number did not say that he knew every duo absolutely, but those he knew to be duo's. Hence, since that duo which was proposed was utterly unknown to him, he did not in any sense know that this duo was an even number. And so it follows that when one knows the principles, the conclusion is not in any sense pre-known, either absolutely or in a qualified sense.

Thirdly (71b1), he refutes this solution in the following way: That is known, concerning which a demonstration is had, or concerning which a demonstration is for the first time received. And this is said on account of those learners who begin to know scientifically. But learners do not obtain a demonstration touching every duo they happen to know but every duo absolutely; and the same applies to every number or every triangle. Therefore, it is not true that he knows something about every number which he knows to be a number, or of every duo which he knows to be a duo, but he knows it about every one absolutely. And that he knows it not only of every number he happens to know is a number, but of every number absolutely, is proved at (71b4) on the ground that the conclusion agrees with the premises in its terms. For the subject and predicate of the conclusion are the major and minor extremes in the premises. But in the premises no proposition concerning number or straight line is stated with the addition, "which you know," but it is stated of all without qualification. Neither, therefore, is the conclusion of the demonstration asserted with the aforesaid qualification, but it is asserted of all without reservation.

Fourthly (71b5), he presents the true solution of the problem under discussion in terms of the truth already established, saying that there is nothing to prevent a person from somehow knowing and somehow not knowing a fact before he learns it. For it is not a paradox if one somehow already knows what he learns, but it would be, if he already knew it in the same way that he knows it when he has learned it. For learning is, properly speaking, the generation of science in someone. But that which is generated was not, prior to its generation, a being absolutely, but somehow a being and somehow non-being: for it was a being in potency, although actually non-being. And this is what being generated consists in, namely, in being converted from potency to act. In like fashion, that which a person learns was not previously known absolutely, as Plato preferred; but neither was it absolutely unknown, as they maintained whose answer was refuted above. Rather it was known in potency, i.e., virtually, in the pre-known universal principles; however, it was not actually known in the sense of specific knowledge. And this is what learning consists in, namely, in being brought from potential or virtual or universal knowledge to specific and actual knowledge.

Lecture 4
(71b8–72a8)

NATURE OF THE DEMONSTRATIVE SYLLOGISM

b8. We suppose ourselves	b19. a syllogism, that is
b10. when we think that	b20. Assuming then that my thesis
b12. Now that scientific	b22. Unless these conditions
b14. Consequently the proper	b23. Syllogism there may indeed
b16. There may be another	b24. The premises must be true
b17. What I now assert	b27. The premises must be primary
b18. By demonstration I mean	b29. The premises must be the causes

After indicating the need for the demonstrative syllogism, the Philosopher now begins to settle questions concerning the demonstrative syllogism itself. And his treatment is divided into two parts. In the first he determines concerning the demonstrative syllogism. In the second he determines concerning the middle from which the demonstrative syllogism proceeds (89b21) [Book II]. The first is divided into two parts. In the first he determines concerning the demonstrative syllogism in itself. In the second he compares demonstration to demonstration (85a12) [L. 37]. The first is divided into two parts. In the first he determines concerning the demonstrative syllogism. In the second he shows that one does not proceed to infinity in demonstrations (81b10) [L. 31]. The first is divided into two parts. In the first he determines concerning the demonstrative syllogism through which we acquire science. In the second he shows how we also acquire ignorance through a syllogism (79b23) [L. 27]. Concerning the first he does three things. First, he determines concerning the demonstrative syllogism by showing what it is. Secondly, he determines concerning the matter of the demonstrative syllogism, pointing out the nature and character of the matter out of which it is formed (73a21) [L. 9]. Thirdly, he determines concerning the form of the syllogism, pointing out the figure in which it is chiefly presented (79a17) [L. 26]. Concerning the first he does three things. First, he shows what the demonstrative syllogism is. Secondly, he clarifies certain terms that appear in the definition of the demonstrative syllogism (72a8) [L. 5]. Thirdly, he excludes certain errors that could arise from his doctrine on the nature of demonstration (72b5) [L. 7].

In regard to the first it should be noted that in all things which exist for an end, the definition which employs a final cause is both the explanation of the definition which expresses the material cause, and is the middle which proves the latter. For the reason why a house should be made of stone and wood is that it is a structure protecting us from the cold and heat. Along these lines, therefore, he gives two definitions of demonstration, one of which is expressed in terms of the end of demonstration, which is to know in a scientific manner. And from this one is concluded the other, which is drawn from the matter of a demonstration. Hence he does three things in regard to this. First, he defines what it is to know in a scientific manner. Secondly, he defines demonstration in terms of its end, which is to know in a scientific manner (71b18). Thirdly, from these two definitions he concludes to that definition of demonstration which is expressed in terms of the matter of demonstration (71b19).

Concerning the first he does five things. First (71b8), he determines what the scientific knowing, which he intends to define, bears upon. And in regard to this it should be recognized that we are said to know something in a scientific manner absolutely, when we know it in itself. On the other hand, we are said to know something in a scientific manner qualifiedly, when we know it in something else in which it exists either as a part in a whole (as we are said to know a wall through knowing the house), or as an accident in its subject (as in knowing Coriscus we are said to know who is coming toward us), or as an effect in its cause (as in the example given earlier, we know the conclusion in the principles), or indeed in any fashion similar to these. To know in these ways is to know incidentally, because we are said to know that which is somehow accidental to what is known of itself. However, what the Philosopher intends to define here is scientific knowing in the strict sense and not according to an accident. For this form of knowing is sophistical, since Sophists use a form of argument typified by the following: "I know Coriscus; Coriscus is coming toward me: therefore, I know the person coming toward me."

Then (71b10) he presents the definition of scientific knowing in the strict sense. Apropos of this it should be noted that to know something scientifically is to know it completely, which means to apprehend its truth perfectly. For the principles of a thing's being are the same as those of its truth, as is stated in *Metaphysics* II. Therefore, the scientific knower, if he is to know perfectly, must know the cause of the thing known; hence he says, "when we think that we know the cause" (71b10). But if he were to know the cause by itself, he would not yet know the effect actually—which would be to know it absolutely—but only virtually, which is the same as knowing in a qualified sense and incidentally. Consequently, one who knows scientifically in the full sense must know the application of the cause to the effect; hence he adds, "as the cause of that fact" (71b11). Again, because science is also sure and certain knowledge of a thing, whereas a thing that could be otherwise cannot be known with certainty, it is further required that what is scientifically known could not be otherwise. To repeat: because science is perfect knowledge, he says, "When we think that we know the cause"; but because the knowledge through which we know scientifically in the full sense is actual, he adds, "as the cause of that fact." Finally, because it is certain knowledge, he adds, "and that the fact could not be other than it is (71b11)."

Thirdly (71b12), he explains the definition he laid down, appealing to the fact that both those who know scientifically and those who do not know in that way but believe that they do, take scientific knowing to be as above described. For those who do not know in a scientific manner but believe that they do, are convinced that they know in the manner described, whereas those who know in a scientific manner do know in the manner described. Furthermore, this is the proper way to manifest a definition. For a definition is the notion which a name signifies, as it is stated in *Metaphysics* IV. But the signification of a name must be based on what is generally meant by those who employ the name. Hence it is stated in *Topics* II that names must be used as the majority of people use them. Again, careful consideration would indicate that this explanation seems rather to show what the name signifies than to signify something directly. For he does not explain science, concerning which a definition could, properly speaking, be formed, since it is a species of some genus; rather he explains scientific knowing. Hence at the very beginning he said, "We suppose ourselves to possess unqualified scientific knowledge" (71b8) and not that scientific knowledge is such and such.

Fourthly (71b14), he draws a corollary from the definition, namely, that that of which there is unqualified scientific knowledge must be something necessary, i.e., which cannot be otherwise.

Fifthly (71b16), he answers a tacit question, namely, whether there is another way of knowing scientifically in addition to the way described here. And he promises to discuss this later. For it is possible to know scientifically through an effect, as will be explained below (cf. L. 23). Furthermore, there is a sense in which we are said to know scientifically the indemonstrable principles to which no cause is ascribed. But the proper and perfect manner of knowing scientifically is the one we have described.

Then (71b17) he defines the demonstrative syllogism in terms of its end, which is to know in a scientific manner. In regard to this he does three things. First, he asserts that scientific knowing is the end of a demonstrative syllogism or is its effect, since to know scientifically seems to be nothing less than to understand the truth of a conclusion through demonstration.

Secondly (71b18), he defines demonstration in terms of the end, saying that a demonstration is a sciential syllogism, i.e., producing scientific knowledge.

Thirdly (71b18), he explains, "sciential," saying that a sciential syllogism is one according to which we know scientifically insofar as we understand it, and not in the sense of a syllogism yielding knowledge to be put to use.

Then (71b19) he concludes from the foregoing a definition of the demonstrative syllogism that is based on its matter. Concerning this he does two things. First, he concludes it. Secondly, he clarifies it (71b24).

Concerning the first he does three things. First (71b20), he sets forth the consequent in which the material definition of demonstration is concluded from the premises laid down above. And he says that if scientific knowing is what we have stated it to be, namely, knowing the cause of a thing, etc., then it is necessary that demonstrative science, i.e., science acquired through demonstration, proceed from propositions which are true, first, and immediate, i.e., not demonstrated by some other middle, but clear in virtue of themselves (they are called "immediate," inasmuch as they do not have a middle demonstrating them, but "first," in relation to other propositions which are proved through them); and which, furthermore, are better known than, prior to, and causes of, the conclusion.

Secondly (71b22), he justifies himself for not adding another element which, it might seem, should be added, namely, that demonstration proceeds from *proper* principles. But he says that this is understood in virtue of the elements he did state. For since the propositions of a demonstration are causes of the conclusion, they must be its proper principles. For effects require proportionate causes.

Thirdly (71b23), he manifests the necessity of the aforesaid consequence, saying that although a syllogism does not require these conditions in the premises from which it concludes, a demonstration does require them, for otherwise it would not produce science.

Then (71b24) he explains this definition as well as the subsequent statement that unless these conditions are fulfilled in a demonstration it cannot beget science. First, therefore, he shows that a demonstration must proceed from true principles in order to beget science, because there cannot be scientific knowledge of that which does not exist, for example, that the diagonal is symmetrical, i.e., commensurable with the side of the square. For those quantities are said to be incommensurable which lack a common measuring unit. These are quantities whose ratio to one another cannot be expressed in terms of one number to another number. That this is the case with the diagonal of a square and its side is plain from Euclid's sixteenth proposition. Now what is not true does not exist, for *to be* and *to be true* are convertible. Therefore, anything scientifically known must be true. Consequently, the conclusion of a demonstration which does beget scientific knowing must be true, and *a fortiori* its premises. For the true cannot be known in a scientific way from the false, although something true can follow as a conclusion from something false, as he will show later (cf. Lecture 13).

Secondly (71b27), he shows that the demonstration is composed of first and immediate or indemonstrable principles. For no one can possess scientific knowledge unless he possesses the demonstration of things that can be demonstrated—"and I am speaking *per se* and not *per accidens*." He says this because it would be possible to know some conclusion without having a demonstration of the premises, even were they demonstrable; because one would know it through other principles, and this would be accidental.

Suppose, therefore, that a demonstrator syllogizes from demonstrable, i.e., mediate, premises. Now he either possesses a demonstration of those premises or he does not. If he does not, then he does not know the premises in a scientific way; nor consequently, the conclusion because of the premises. But if he does possess their demonstration, then, since one may not proceed to infinity in demonstrations, principles immediate and indemonstrable must be reached. And so it is required that demonstration proceed from principles that are immediate either straightway or through middles. Hence it is stated in *Topics* I that demonstration is composed of first and true statements or of statements made credible by these.

Thirdly (71b29), he proves that the propositions of a demonstration are the causes of the conclusion, because we know in a scientific manner when we know the causes. And in virtue of this he shows that they are prior and better known, because every cause is by nature prior and better known than its effect. However, the cause of a demonstrated conclusion must be better known not only with respect to the knowledge of *what it is,* but also with respect to the knowledge *that it is.* For in order to demonstrate that there is an eclipse of the sun, it is not enough to know that the moon is interposed; in addition it is necessary to know that the moon is interposed between the sun and the earth. Again, because prior and better known are taken in two ways, namely, in reference to us and according to nature, he says that the things from which a demonstration proceeds are prior and better known absolutely and according to nature, and not in reference to us.

To elucidate this he says that "those things are prior and better known absolutely," which are farthest from sense, as are universals; but "the prior and better known in reference to us" are nearest to sense, namely, the singulars, which are opposed to universals in the way that the prior and the later are opposite, or in the way that the nearest and the farthest are opposite.

However, it seems that the contrary of this is found in *Physics* I, where it is stated that universals are prior in reference to us and later according to nature. But it should be said that there [in the *Posterior Analytics*] he is speaking of the order of singular to universal absolutely; and this order must be taken according to the order of sensitive and intellectual knowledge in us. Now in us sensitive knowledge is prior to intellectual, because intellectual knowledge in us proceeds from sense. For this reason the singular is prior and better known in relation to us than the universal. But in *Physics* I he is not speaking of the order of the universal to the singular absolutely but of the order of the *more* universal to the *less* universal, for example of animal to man. In this case the more universal is prior and better known in reference to us. For in every instance of generation, that which is in potency is prior in time but is later according to nature; whereas that which is complete in act is prior by nature but later in time. Now one's knowledge of a genus is, as it were, potential in comparison to one's knowledge of the species in which all the essentials of a thing are actually known. Hence, too, in the generation of our science, knowledge of the more common precedes knowledge of the less common.

Again, in the *Physics* it is stated that it is natural for us to proceed from what is better known to us. Therefore, it seems that a demonstration is composed not of things that are prior absolutely but in reference to us. But it must be said that here he is speaking according to the fact that what is in the sense is better known in reference to us than what is in the intellect; but there he was speaking according to the fact that what is better known in reference to us is also in the intellect. But demonstrations do not proceed from singulars which are in the sense but only from universals, which are in the intellect.

Or it might be said that in every demonstration one must proceed from things better known to us, provided they are not singulars but universals. For something is made known to us only by that which is more known to us. But sometimes that which is more known in reference to us is also more known absolutely and according to nature, as happens in mathematics where on account of abstraction from matter the demonstrations proceed from formal principles alone. In this case the demonstrations proceed from things which are more known absolutely. But sometimes that which is more known in reference to us is not more known absolutely, as happens in natural sciences where the essences and powers of things are hidden, because they are in matter, but are disclosed to us through the things which appear outwardly. Hence in these sciences the demonstrations are for the most part made through effects which are better known in reference to us but not absolutely. But he is not now speaking of this form of demonstration, but of the first.

Finally, because in his explanation he neglected to point out that demonstration should proceed from proper principles, he hastens to add that this fact is easily ascertainable from what he did say. For from the fact that he stated that demonstration is from things which are first, it follows that it is from proper principles, as he stated above. For "first" and "principle" seem to be the same: for that which is first and highest in each genus is the cause of all the things that are after it, as it is stated in *Metaphysics* II.

Lecture 5
(72a8–24)

FIRST AND IMMEDIATE PROPOSITIONS

a8. A 'basic truth' in a

a9. A proposition is

a10. If a proposition is dialectical

a11. The term 'enunciation'

a15. I call an immediate

a19. If a thesis assumes

Because the Philosopher had stated above that demonstration is from "first and immediate principles," but had not yet identified them, he now sets out to identify them. And this is divided into three parts. In the first part he shows what an immediate proposition is. In the second part he shows that such propositions must be better known than the conclusion (72a25) [L. 6]. In the third part he excludes certain errors which arose from the foregoing (72b5) [L. 7]. Concerning the first he does two things. First, he shows what an immediate principle is. Secondly, he divides them (72a15).

With respect to the first he proceeds this way. First (72a8), he recalls what has been said above, namely, that a principle of demonstration is an immediate proposition, for he had also stated above that a demonstration is composed of things which are first and immediate.

Secondly (ibid.), he defines the immediate proposition and says that an immediate proposition is one which has no other one prior to it. And the reason underlying this description is clear from what has been said. For it has been said above that demonstration is composed of things that are prior. Accordingly, whenever a proposition is mediate, i.e., has a middle through which the predicate is demonstrated of its subject, it is required that there be prior propositions by which this one is demonstrated. For the predicate of a conclusion is present in the middle previously to being present in the subject; in which, however, the middle is present before the predicate is. Therefore, it follows that that proposition which does not have some other one prior to it is immediate.

Thirdly (72a9), he shows what is the nature of the proposition which is mentioned in the definition of an immediate proposition. Concerning this he does three things:

First, he defines absolutely what a proposition is, saying that it is the one or the other part of an enunciation in which one thing is predicated of one thing. For the enunciation has two parts, namely, affirmation and negation. For anyone who syllogizes must propose one or the other of these parts but not both, for this latter procedure is characteristic of one who first raises a question. (Hence it is on this basis that a proposition is distinguished from a problem). For just as one and only one thing is concluded in one syllogism, so the proposition which is a principle of the syllogism should be one—and it is one if one thing is stated of one thing. Hence in asserting that it is "one of one," he distinguishes the proposition from the enunciation which is said to be "of several," whether sundry things are said of one thing or one thing of sundry.

Secondly (72a10), he lays down the difference between the dialectical and the demonstrative proposition, saying that whereas the demonstrative proposition takes one definite side of a question, the dialectical takes either side indifferently. For since dialectic begins with the probable, it can lead to each side of a contradiction. Hence when it lays down its propositions, it employs both parts of a contradiction and presents them in the form of a question [Is an animal that walks on its feet a man, or not?]. But a demonstrative proposition takes one side definitively, because a demonstrator never has any other alternative but to demonstrate the truth. Hence in forming its propositions he always assumes the true side of a contradiction [An animal which walks on two feet is a man, is it not?]. On this account he does not ask but posits something as known in the demonstration.

Thirdly (72a11), he defines the term, "enunciation," which appeared in the definition of a proposition, saying that an enunciation embraces both sides of a contradiction, as is clear from what has been said.

Then he shows what contradiction is, saying that contradiction is a form of opposition between whose parts there is of itself no middle. For although between privation and possession and between immediate contraries there is no middle in a given subject, nevertheless, absolutely speaking, there is one; for a stone is neither blind nor seeing, and something white is neither even nor odd. Furthermore, whatever immediacy they have in relation to a definite subject is traced to their participation in contradiction, for privation is negation in a definite subject; and of two things that are immediately contrary, one has some of the marks of privation. But contradiction in the full sense lacks a middle in all cases. And this belongs to it of its very nature and not in virtue of something else. Hence he says that of itself it has no medium.

He then explains what the parts of a contradiction are. For contradiction is an opposition of affirmation and negation; hence one of its parts is affirmation, which asserts something of something, and the other is negation, which denies something of something.

Then (72a15) he divides immediate principle. Concerning this he does two things. First, he divides. Secondly, he subdivides (72a19).

He says therefore first (72a15), that there are two types of immediate principles of a syllogism: the first is called a "position" [thesis] and is said to be immediate because one does not demonstrate (neither is it required that the student, i.e., the one being instructed in the demonstrative science, have it, i.e., advert to it or assent to it); the other is called a "dignity" or "maxim," which anyone who is to be instructed must have in his mind and assent to. That there are such principles is clear from *Metaphysics* IV, where it is proved that one such is the principle that "affirmation and negation are not simultaneously true," for no one can believe the contrary of this in his mind, even though he should state it orally. To such principles we give the aforesaid name of "dignity" or "maxim" on account of their certainty in manifesting other things.

To clarify this division it should be noted that any proposition whose predicate is included within the notion of its subject is immediate and known in virtue of itself as it stands. However, in the case of some of these propositions the terms are such that they are understood by everyone, as *being* and *one* and those other notions that are characteristic of being precisely as being: for *being* is the first concept in the intellect. Hence it is necessary that propositions of this kind be held as known in virtue of themselves not only as they stand but also in reference to us.

Examples of these are the propositions that "It does not occur that the same thing is and is not" and that "The whole is greater than its part," and others like these. Hence all the sciences take principles of this kind from metaphysics whose task it is to consider being absolutely and the characteristics of being.

On the other hand, there are some immediate propositions whose terms are not known by everyone. Hence, although their predicate may be included in the very notion of their subject, yet because the definition of the subject is not known to everyone, it is not necessary that such propositions be conceded by everyone. (Thus the proposition, "All right angles are equal," is in itself a proposition which is immediate and known in virtue of itself, because equality appears in the definition of a right angle. For a right angle is one which a straight line forms when it meets another straight line in such a way that the angles on each side are equal). Therefore, such principles are received as being posited or laid down.

There is yet another way, and according to it certain propositions are called "suppositions." For there are some propositions which can be proved only by the principles of some other science; therefore, they must be supposed in the one science, although they are proved by the principles of the other science. Thus the geometer supposes that he can draw one straight line from one point to another, but the philosopher of nature proves it by showing that there is one straight line between any two points.

Then (72a19) he subdivides a member of the original division, namely, "position," and says that there is one type of position which takes one side of an enunciation, namely, either affirmation or negation. He refers to this type when he says, "i.e., asserts either the existence or non-existence of a subject." Such a position is called a "supposition" or "hypothesis," because it is accepted as having truth. Another type of position is the one which does not signify existence or non-existence: in this way a definition is a position. For the definition of "one" is laid down in arithmetic as a principle, namely, that "one is the quantitatively indivisible." Nevertheless a definition is not called a supposition, for a supposition, strictly speaking, is a statement which signifies the true or the false. Consequently, he adds that "the definition of 'one,'" inasmuch as it signifies neither the true nor the false, "is not the same as 'to be one,'" which does signify the true or the false.

Now it might be asked how it is that definition is set down as a member of the subdivision of immediate proposition, if a definition is not a proposition signifying either existence or non-existence. One might answer that in this subdivision he was not subdividing immediate propositon but immediate principle. Or one might answer that although a definition as such is not an actual proposition, it is one virtually, because once a definition is known, it becomes clear that it is truly predicated of the subject.

Lecture 6
(72a25–b4)

KNOWLEDGE OF IMMEDIATE PRINCIPLES

a25. Now since the required
a28. for the cause of an attribute's
a33. Now a man cannot believe

a36. a man must believe in
a38. he must not only have

After showing what immediate principles are, the Philosopher now determines concerning our knowledge of them. Apropos of this he does two things. First, he shows that immediate principles are better known than the conclusion. Secondly, that the falsity of their contraries ought to be most evident (72a38).

Concerning the first he does three things. First (72a25), he states his proposition and says that because we give our assent to a thing which has been concluded and we know it scientifically precisely because we have a demonstrative syllogism (and this insofar as we know the demonstrative syllogism in a scientific way), it is necessary not only to know the first principles of the conclusion beforehand, but also to know them better than we know the conclusion.

He adds, "either all or some," because some principles require proof in order to be known; so that before they are proved, they are not better known than the conclusion. Thus the fact that an exterior angle of a triangle is equal to its two opposite interior angles is, until proved, as unknown as the fact that a triangle has three angles equal to two right angles. But there are other principles which, once they are posited, are better known than the conclusion. Or, in another way, there are some conclusions which are most evident; for example, those based on sense perception, as that the sun is eclipsed. Hence the principle through which this is proved is not better known absolutely—the principle being that the moon is between the sun and the earth—although it is better known within the reasoning process that goes from cause to effect. Or, in another way, he says this because he had said above that in the order of time certain principles are known before the conclusion, but others are known along with the conclusion at the same moment of time.

Secondly (72a28), he proves his proposition in two ways: first, with an ostensive argument, thus: That in virtue of which something is so, is itself more so; for example, if we love someone because of someone else, as a master because of his disciple, we love the disciple more. But we know conclusions and give our assent to them because of the principles. Therefore, we know the principles with more conviction and give them stronger assent than the conclusion.

23

Apropos of this reason it should be noted that a cause is always more noble than its effect. When, therefore, cause and effect have the same name, that name is said principally of the cause rather than of the effect; thus fire is primarily called hot rather than things heated by fire. But sometimes the name of the effect is not attributed to the cause. In that case, although the name the effect has does not belong to the cause, nevertheless, something more noble belongs to it. For example, although the sun does not possess heat, nevertheless, there is in it a certain power which is the principle of heat.

Then (72a33) he proves the same thing with a principle which leads to an impossibility. He reasons thus: Principles are known prior to the conclusion, as has been shown above; consequently, when the principles are known, the conclusion is not yet known. If, therefore, the principles were not more known than the conclusion, it would follow that a man would know things he does not know either as well as or better than the things he does know. But this is impossible. Therefore, it is also impossible that the principles not be better known than the conclusion.

Phrase by phrase this is explained in the following manner: "A man who knows scientifically or even one who knows in a way superior to this, if such there be," (he says this, having in mind the person who has the intuition of principles, a state he has not yet explained), "cannot give more credence to things he does not know than to things he does know. But this will be the case if one who assents to a conclusion obtained through demonstration did not foreknow," i.e., did not know the principles better. In Greek it is stated more clearly: "But no one, whether he has scientific knowledge or that form of knowledge which is better than the scientific (if there be such), can believe anything more firmly than the things he knows."

Thirdly (72a36), he clarifies what he had said, saying that his statement to the effect that it is more necessary to believe the principles (either all or some) than the conclusion should be understood as referring to a person who is to acquire a discipline through demonstration. For if the conclusion were more known through some other source, such as sense-perception, nothing would preclude the principles not being better known than the conclusion in that case.

Then (72a38) he shows that it is not only necessary to know the principles more than the demonstrative conclusion, but nothing should be more certain than the fact that the opposites of the principles are false. And this because the scientific knower must not disbelieve the principles, but assent to them most firmly. But anyone who doubts the falseness of one of two opposites cannot assent firmly to the other, because he will always fear that the opposite one might be true.

DISCUSSION OF TWO ERRORS—EXCLUSION
OF THE FIRST ONE

b5. **Some hold that, owing**   b15. **The other party agree**

b8. **The first school,**   b18. **Our own doctrine is that**

After determining about the knowledge of the principles of demonstration, the Philosopher now excludes the errors which have arisen from these determinations. Concerning this he does three things. First, he states the errors. Secondly, the reasons they erred (72b8). Thirdly, he removes the roots of these reasons (72b18).

He says therefore first (72b5), that two contrary errors have arisen from one of the truths established above. For it has been established above that the principles of demonstration must be known and must be even better known. But the first of these is sufficient for our purpose. For some, basing themselves on this first statement, have come to believe that there is no science of anything, whereas others believe that there is science, even to the extent of believing that there is science of everything through demonstration. But neither of these positions is true and neither follows necessarily from their reasons.

Then (72b8) he presents the reasons why they have fallen into these errors. And first of all he presents the reason given by those who say that there is no science, and it is this: The principles of demonstration either proceed to infinity or there is a halt somewhere. But if there is a process to infinity, nothing in that process can be taken as being first, because one cannot exhaust an infinite series and reach what is first. Consequently, it is not possible to know what is first. (They are correct in thus arguing, for the later things cannot be known unless the prior ones are known).

On the other hand, if there is a halt in the principles, then even so, the first things are still not known, if the only way to know scientifically is through demonstration. For first things do not have prior principles through which they are demonstrated. But if the first things are not known, it follows again that the later things are not known in the strict and proper sense, but only on condition that there are principles. For it is not possible for something to be known in virtue of something not known, except on condition that that unknown be a principle. So in either case, whether the principles stop or go on to infinity, it follows that there is no science of anything.

25

Secondly (72b15), he presents the reasoning of those who say that there is science of everything through demonstration, because to their there is science of everything through demonstration, because to their basic premise—the only way to know scientifically is by demonstration—they added another, namely, that one may demonstrate circularly. From these premises it followed that even if a limit is reached in the series of the principles of demonstration, the first principles are still known through demonstration, because, they said, those principles were demonstrated by previous ones. For a circular demonstration is one which is reciprocal, i.e., something which was first a principle is later a conclusion, and vice versa.

Then (72b18) he cuts away the false bases of these arguments. First, tion. Secondly, their statement that it is legitimate to demonstrate (their objection that the only way to know scientifically is by demonstra-) circularly (72b25).

He says therefore first (72b18), that not all scientific knowledge is demonstrative, i.e., obtained through demonstration, but the scientific knowledge of immediate principles is indemonstrable, i.e., not obtained by demonstration. However, it should be noted that Aristotle is here taking *science* in a wide sense to include any knowledge that is certain, and not in the sense in which science is set off against understanding, according to the dictum that science deals with conclusions and understanding [intuition] with principles.

But that it is necessary for some things to be held as certain without demonstration he proves in the following way: It is necessary that the prior things from which a demonstration proceeds be known in a scientific way. Furthermore, these must be ultimately reduced to something immediate; otherwise one would be forced to admit that there is an actual infinitude of middles between two extremes—in this case between the subject and predicate. Again, one would have to admit that no two extremes could be found between which there would not be an infinitude of middles. But as it is, the middles are such that it is possible to find two things which are immediate. But immediate principles, being prior, must be indemonstrable. Thus it is clear that it is necessary for some things to be scientifically known without demonstration.

Therefore, if someone were to ask how the science of immediate principles is possessed, the answer would be that not only are they known in a scientific manner, but knowledge of them is the source of all science. For one passes from the knowledge of principles to a demonstration of conclusion on which science, properly speaking, bears. But those immediate principles are not made known through an additional middle but through an understanding of their own terms. For as soon as it is known what a whole is and what a part is, it is known that every whole is greater than its part, because in such a proposition, as has been stated above, the predicate is included in the very notion of the subject. And therefore it is reasonable that the knowledge of these principles is the cause of the knowledge of conclusions, because always, that which exists in virtue of itself is the cause of that which exists in virtue of something else.

Lecture 8
(72b25–73a20)

THE SECOND ERROR IS EXCLUDED BY SHOWING THAT CIRCULAR DEMONSTRATION IS NOT ACCEPTABLE

b25. Now demonstration must

b33. The advocates of circular

b38. Thus by direct proof

a1. Since then—

a6. Moreover, even such

After excluding one false basis by showing that not all science depends on demonstration, the Philosopher now excludes another by showing that it is not possible to demonstrate circularly.

To understand this it should be noted that a demonstration is circular when the conclusion and one of the premises (in converted form) of a syllogism are used to prove the other premise. For example, we might form the following syllogism:

Every rational mortal animal is risible;
Every man is a rational mortal animal:
Therefore, every man is risible.

Now if the conclusion were to be used as one principle and the minor in converted form as the other, we would get:

Every man is risible;
Every rational mortal animal is a man:
Therefore, every rational mortal animal is risible—which was the major of the first syllogism.

Accordingly, he presents three arguments to show that it is not possible to demonstrate circularly. The first of these (72b25) is this: In a circular syllogism the same thing is at once a conclusion and a principle. But a principle of a demonstration is prior to and better known than the conclusion, as has been shown above. Therefore, it follows that a same thing is both prior to and subsequent to one same thing, and also more known and less known. But this is impossible. Therefore, it is impossible to demonstrate circularly.

But someone might say that a same thing can be both prior and subsequent, although not in the same way. For example, *this* might be prior in reference to us, but *that* prior absolutely. Thus singulars are prior in reference to us and subsequent absolutely: and conversely for universals. Again, induction makes something known in one way and demonstration in another way. For demonstration proceeds from things that are prior absolutely, but induction from things that are prior in reference to us.

Now if a circular demonstration were so constructed that something is first concluded from things that are absolutely prior, and then from things that are prior in reference to us, it would follow that our doctrine on scientific knowing was not well established. For we stated that to know scientifically is to know the cause of a thing. From this it followed that a demonstration which causes scientific knowledge must proceed from the absolutely prior. But if demonstration were at one time to proceed from the absolutely prior and at another time from things which are prior in reference to us, we would be forced to admit that scientific knowing is not confined to knowing the cause of a thing, but that there is another, namely, that form of knowing which proceeds from what is later. Therefore, one must either admit both or admit that the second form, namely, the demonstration which proceeds from what is better known to us is not a demonstration in the absolute sense.

The aforesaid also reveals why a dialectical syllogism can be circular. For it proceeds from things which are probable. But things are said to be probable if they are better known to the wise or to a great number of persons. Consequently, a dialectical syllogism proceeds from things that are better known to us. However, it happens that a same thing is better known to some and less known to others. Consequently, there is nothing to hinder a dialectical syllogism from being ciruclar. But a demonstration is formed from things that are absolutely prior. Therefore, as we have already stated, there cannot be circular demonstration.

Then he sets forth the second argument (72b33) and it is this: If there were circular demonstration, it would follow that a same thing is demonstrated by the same thing, as if I were to say: If it is this, it is this. In this way it is easy for anyone to demonstrate everything, for anyone, wise or ignorant, will be able to do this. Accordingly, science is not acquired through demonstration. But this is against the definition of demonstration. Therefore, there cannot be circular demonstration.

He proves the truth of the first consequence in the following way: It is obvious, first of all, that with a circular demonstration the same thing is proved by a same thing, as has been stated above, i.e., if only three terms are employed; although it makes no difference whether the reflexion be made with fewer terms or more. (By *reflexion* he means the process whereby one goes from principle to conclusion in a demonstration, and then from conclusion to principle). In such a reflexion it makes no difference, so far as the force of the argument is concerned, whether it involves several or fewer terms or even two. For an argument has the same force if one proceeds thus: "If it is A, it is B, and if it is B, it is C, and if it is C, it is D," and then by reflecting continues, "If it is D, it is C, and if it is C, it is B, and if it is B, it is A"; or if he proceeds by reflecting at the very start, saying: "If it is A, it is B, and if it is B, it is A." (Although he spoke above of three terms, he restricted himself to two terms in this example, because in the deduction he is about to make he will use a third term, which is the same as the first).

Then (72b38) he gives the form of the argument in three terms, namely: "If it is A, it is B, and if it is B, it is C; therefore, if it is A, it is of necessity C."

Then (73a1) he shows by the aforesaid form of arguing that in a circular demonstration a same thing is proved by a same thing, using only two terms. For it consists in saying, "If it is A, it is B," and then reflecting, "If it is B, it is A"—which is a circular demonstration. Now according to the above given form it follows from these two, that "if it is A, it is A."

That it does follow is obvious: for just as in the first deduction which involved three terms, C followed from B, so in the reflex deduction of two terms, A followed from B. Let us suppose, then, that the A of the second deduction, i.e., the reflex, signifies the same thing that C signified in the first, i.e., in the direct deduction which was composed of three terms. Therefore, to state in the second deduction that "if it is B, it is A" is to state the same thing as was stated in the first deduction, namely, that "if it is B, it is C." But when it was stated in the first deduction that "if it is B, it is C," it followed that "if it is A, it is C." Therefore, in the circular deduction it follows that "if it is A, it is A," since C is assumed to be the same as A. In this way, it will be easy to demonstrate all things, as has been said.

Then he presents the third argument (73a6) which is this: Those who suppose that everything can be known through demonstration on the ground that demonstration is circular, must grant that anything can be demonstrated by a circular demonstration and, as a consequence, grant that in a circular demonstration each of the premises can be concluded from the conclusion. However, the only cases in which this can be done are those in which mutual conversion is possible, i.e., in things that are convertible, as properties. But not all things are so related. Therefore, it is ridiculous to say that everything can be demonstrated on the ground that there are such things as circular demonstrations.

Now the reason is obvious why in a circular demonstration all the propositions must be convertible. For it has been shown in the book of *Prior Analytics* that if one thing is laid down, another does not follow of necessity, whether the thing laid down be one term or one proposition. For every syllogism must start with three terms and two propositions as a minimum. Therefore, in a circular demonstration three terms which are convertible must be taken, namely, A, B, C, such that A is in every B and in every C, and these, namely, B and C, must inhere in each other, so that every B is C and every C is B, and also inhere in A so that every A is B and every A is C. And so, the terms being thus related, it is possible, when using the first figure, to derive any one from any two circularly, i.e., the conclusion from two premises and each premise from the conclusion and the remaining premise, as we pointed out in the *Prior Analytics*, where we treated the syllogism formally.

The way it is done is this: take the three convertible terms, "risible," "rational mortal animal" and "man," and form the syllogism:

> Every rational mortal animal is risible;
> Every man is a rational mortal animal:
> Therefore, every man is risible.

Then from the conclusion it is possible to conclude both the major and the minor; the major thus:

> Every man is risible;
> But every rational mortal animal is a man:
> Therefore, every rational mortal animal is risible

and the minor thus:

> Every risible is a rational mortal animal;
> But every man is risible:
> Therefore, every man is a rational mortal animal.

However, it has also been proved in the *Prior Analytics* that in figures other than the first, namely, in the second and third, one cannot form a circular syllogism, i.e., one through which each of the premises can be syllogized from the conclusion; or if one is formed, it is done not by using the premises already used but by using propositions other than those which appear in the first syllogism.

That this is so is obvious. For the second figure always yields a negative conclusion. Consequently, one premise must be affirmative and the other negative. However, it is true that if both are negative, nothing can be concluded; and if both are affirmative, a negative conclusion cannot follow. Therefore, it is not possible to use the negative conclusion and the negative premise to obtain the affirmative premise as a conclusion. Hence, if this affirmative is to be proved, it must be proved through propositions other than the ones originally used. Again, in the third figure the only conclusion ever obtained is particular. However, at least one premise must be universal; furthermore, if either premise is particular, a universal cannot be concluded. Hence it cannot occur that in the third figure each of the premises can be syllogized from the conclusion and the remaining premise.

For the same reasons it is obvious that such a circular syllogism (through which each premise could be concluded) cannot be formed in the first figure except in the first mode, which is the only one that concludes to a universal affirmative. Furthermore, even in this mode the only case in which a circular syllogism could be formed such that each of the premises could be concluded, is when the three terms employed are equal, i.e., convertible. The proof is this: The premise must be concluded from the conclusion and the converse of the other premise, as has been stated. But such a conversion of each premise is impossible (for each is universal), except when the terms happen to be equal.

Lecture 9
(73a21–34)

HOW SOMETHING IS SAID TO BE
PREDICATED OF ALL

a21. Since the object of pure   a28. I call 'true in every
a25. and as a preliminary   a32. There is evidence for

After showing what a demonstrative syllogism is, the Philosopher in this section begins to show the nature and characteristics of the things that comprise a demonstration. Concerning this he does three things. First, he connects this with what has already been established. Secondly, he explains certain matters that must be understood first (73a25). Thirdly, he establishes what he had in mind, namely, to show what and of what sort are the things that constitute a syllogism (74b5) [L. 12].

He says therefore first (73a21), that since the definition of scientific knowledge given above spoke of that which cannot be otherwise, that which is scientifically known through demonstration will be necessary. Then he explains what it is to know something in a scientific way through demonstration, saying that demonstrative science is "what we possess in having a demonstration," i.e., what we acquire through demonstration. Consequently, it follows that the conclusion of a demonstration is necessary.

Now although the necessary could be syllogized from the contingent, it is not possible through a contingent middle to obtain scientific knowledge of the necessary, as will be proved later. Furthermore, because the conclusion of a demonstration is not only necessary, but, as has been said, is known through demonstration, it follows that a demonstrative syllogism proceeds from necessary things. Consequently, we must establish from what and from what sort of necessary things a demonstration proceeds.

Then (73a25) he interjects certain things that must be understood as preliminaries to the matters to be discussed. Apropos of these he does two things:

First, he states his intention (73a25), saying that before determining specifically the nature and characteristics of the things that form a demonstrative syllogism, we must indicate what is meant when we say, "of all," and "per se," i.e., in virtue of itself, and "commensurately universal." For if we are to understand the nature of the things that form a demonstration, we must know what these terms mean, because they describe things that must be observed in demonstrations. For in the propositions of a demonstration it is required that something be predicated universally—which he signifies by the term "said of all"—and "per se," i.e., in virtue of itself, and "first"—which he signifies by the words, "commensurately universal." But these three things are related by adding something to the previous one. For whatever is predicated *per se* is predicated universally [i.e., of all], but not vice versa. Again, whatever is predicated *first* is predicated *per se,* but not vice versa. This, therefore, shows why they are arranged as they are.

But why there are three and wherein they differ are explained by the fact that something is said to be predicated "of all" or universally in relation to things contained under the subject. For, as it is stated in *Prior Analytics,* something is said "of all," when there is nothing under the extension of the subject that does not receive the given predicate. But it is in relation to the subject that something is said to be predicated *per se,* because the subject is mentioned when this predicate is defined, or vice versa, as will be explained below. Finally, something is said to be predicated of another thing "first" in relation to items that are prior to the subject and embrace or include it, as the more universal includes the less. Thus to have three angles equal to two right angles is not predicated "first" of isosceles, because it is previously predicated of something prior to isosceles, namely, of triangle.

Secondly (73a28), he establishes his proposition. And his treatment is divided into three parts. First, he shows what is meant by "said of all." Secondly, what is meant by "said per se," i.e., in virtue of itself (73a34) [L. 10]. Thirdly, what is meant by "commensurately universal" (73b27) [L. 11].

Concerning the first he does two things. First (73a28), he states what it is to be "said of all." And it should be noted that the phrase, "said of all," is taken here in a sense somewhat different from the sense it has in *Prior Analytics,* where it is taken in a very general sense so as to accommodate both the dialectician and the demonstrator. Therefore, no more is mentioned in its definition than that the predicate be found in each of the things included under its subject. But that might be verified only at a given moment—which is the sense in which the dialectician sometimes uses it; or it might be verified absolutely and at all times—which is the sense to which the demonstrator must always limit himself.

Accordingly, two things are mentioned in the definition of "said of all": one is that there is nothing within the extension of the subject that the predicate does not apply to. And he indicates this when he says, "not of one to the exclusion of others"; the other is that there is no time in which the predicate does not belong. And this he indicates when he says, "not at this or that time only." And he gives the example of "man" and "animal," saying that "animal" is predicated of every man; and of anything of which it is true to say that it is a man, it is true to say that it is an animal, and whenever it is a man, it is an animal. The same is true between line and point: for a point is in every line and always in every line.

Secondly (73a32), he explains this definition, using as evidence the techniques employed in rebuttals. For a universal proposition is not rebutted unless one or other of things it states is not verified. For when we are asked whether something is said "of all" in a demonstration, we can say, "No," for two reasons, i.e., either because it is not true of each instance of the subject, or because now and then it is not true. Hence it is clear that "being said of all" signifies each of these.

Lecture 10
(73a34–b26)

HOW SOMETHING IS SAID TO BE PREDICATED *PER SE* OF A THING

a34. Essential attributes are
a38. (2) such that, while
b5. Further (a) that

b10. In another sense again
b16. So far then as concerns
b25. Thus, then, we have

After determining about "said of all," the Philosopher now determines about "said *per se*" [i.e., said in virtue of itself] and does three things. First, he shows the number of ways something is said *per se*. Secondly, how the demonstrator makes use of these ways (73b16). Thirdly, he summarizes (73b25).

In regard to the first it should be noted that this preposition *per* ["in virtue of" or "by"] denotes a causal relationship, although sometimes it also signifies a state, as when someone is said to be *per se,* i.e., by himself, when he is alone. But when it designates a relationship to a cause, sometimes the cause is formal, as when it is stated that the body lives in virtue of the soul; sometimes the relationship is to a material cause, as when it is stated that a body is colored in virtue of its surface, i.e., because the surface is the subject of color; again, it might even designate a relationship to an extrinsic cause, particularly an efficient cause, as when it is said that water is made hot in virtue of fire. But just as this preposition *per* designates a relationship to a cause, when something extrinsic is the cause of that which is attributed to the subject, so also when the subject or something pertaining to the subject is the cause of that which is attributed to the subject. This latter is what *per se,* i.e., in virtue of itself, signifies.

Therefore, the first way of saying something *per se* (73a34) is when that which is attributed to a subject pertains to its *form.* And because the form and essence of a thing are signified by its definition, the first mode of that which is *per se* is when the definition itself or something expressed in the definition is predicated of the thing defined. This is what he means when he says, "Essential attributes are such as belong to their subject as elements in its essential nature," i.e., included in the definition which indicates *what* it is, whether those elements are stated in the nominative case or in one of the oblique cases. Thus, "line" is stated in the definition of triangle. Hence "line" is in triangle *per se.* Again, in the definition of line, "point" is mentioned; hence "point" is *per se* in line. And the reason why they are mentioned in the definition is stated when he says, "for the very being or substance" [i.e., the essence, which the definition signifies] "of triangle and line is composed of these elements," namely, of lines and points. However, this does not mean that a line is formed out of points, but that "point" is involved in the very notion of line, just as "line" is involved in the very notion of triangle. And he asserts this in order to exclude things which are part of a thing's matter and not of its species: thus, "semicircle" is not mentioned in the definition of circle, or "finger" in the definition of man, as it is stated in *Metaphysics* VII.

He states further that all those items which are found universally in the definition expressing what a thing is are attributed to it *per se.*

The second mode of saying *per se* is when this preposition *per* implies a relationship of material cause, in the sense that that to which something is attributed is its proper matter and subject. For it is required, when defining an accident, to mention its proper subject in one of the oblique cases: thus when an accident is defined abstractly, we say that "aquilinity is a curvature *of* a nose," but when it is defined concretely, the subject is put in the nominative case, so that we say that "the aquiline is a curved nose." Now the reason for this is that since the being of an accident depends on its subject, its definition—which signifies its being—must mention that subject. Hence it is the second mode of saying *per se,* when the subject is mentioned in the definition of a predicate which is a proper accident of the subject.

And this is what he means when he states (73a38), "essential attributes are those such that while they belong to certain subjects," i.e., to subjects of accidents, "the subjects to which they belong are contained in the attribute's own defining formula," i.e., in the expression which describes what the accident is, i.e., in the definition of the accident. "Thus straight and curved belong to line *per se.*" For "line" is mentioned in their definition. For the same reason "odd" and "even" belong *per se* to number, because "number" is mentioned in their definition. Again, prime and compound are predicated *per se* of number, and "number" is mentioned in their definition. (For a prime number, for example, seven, is one which is exactly divisible by no other number but "1"; but a compound number, for example, nine, is one which is exactly divisible by some number greater than "1." Again, "isoplural," i.e., equilateral, and scalene, i.e., having three unequal sides, belong *per se* to triangle, and "triangle" is mentioned in their definition. Accordingly, he adds that their respective subjects belong to each of the aforesaid accidents and are mentioned in the expression which states what each is, i.e., in the definition: thus "line" belongs to some of them, and "number" to others.

In each of these subjects that have been mentioned, I say that its accident is in it *per se.* But those predicates which are neutral, i.e., of such a nature as not to be mentioned in the definition of their subjects, nor the subjects in their definition, are accidents, i.e., are predicated *per accidens:* for example, "musical" and "white" are predicated *per accidens* of animal.

Then (73b5) he sets down another mode of that which is *per se,* i.e., the sense in which it signifies something in isolation. Thus something which is a singular in the genus of substance and which is not predicated of any subject is said to be *per se.* The reason for this is that when I say, "walking" or "white," I do not signify either of them as something isolated or apart, since something else which is walking or white is understood. But this is not the case with terms which signify a "this something," i.e., with terms that signify first substance. For when I say, "Socrates" or "Plato," it is not to be supposed that there is something else, over and above what they really are, which would be their subject. Therefore, things which are thus not predicated of any subject are *per se,* but things which are predicated of a subject, as being in the subject, are accidents. However, not all things predicated of a subject, as universals of their inferiors, are accidents.

It should be noted, however, that this mode is not a mode of predicating, but a mode of existing; hence at the very start he said that they *exist per se* and not that they are *said per se.*

Then (73b10) he gives the fourth mode, according to which the preposition *per* designates a relationship of efficient cause or of any other. Consequently, he says that whatever is attributed to a thing because of itself, is said of it *per se;* but whatever is not so attributed is said *per accidens,* as when I say, "While he was walking, it lightened." For it is not the fact that he walks that causes lightning, but this is said by coincidence. But if the predicate is in the subject because of itself, it is *per se,* as when we say, "Slaughtered, it died." For it is obvious that because something was slaughtered, it died, and it is not a mere coincidence that something slaughtered should die.

Then (73b16) he shows how the demonstrator uses the aforesaid modes. But first it should be noted that, since science bears on conclusions, and understanding [intuition] bears on principles, the scientifically knowable are, properly speaking, the conclusions of a demonstration wherein proper attributes are predicated of their appropriate subjects. Now the appropriate subjects are not only placed in the definition of attributes, but they are also their causes. Hence the conclusions of demonstrations involve two modes of predicating *per se,* namely, the second and the fourth.

And this is what he means when he says that the predications "in the scientifically knowable in the strict sense," i.e., in the conclusions of demonstrations, are *per se* in the sense of something contained in the predicates, i.e., in the way that subjects are contained in the definition of accidents which are predicated of the former; or are present on account of them, i.e., in the way that predicates are in a subject by reason of the subject itself, which is the cause of the predicate.

Then he shows that such scientifically knowable things are necessary, because it is impossible for a proper accident not to be predicated of its subject. But this can occur in two ways: sometimes it is absolute, as when the accident is convertible with its subject, as "having three angles equal to two right angles" is convertible with triangle, and "risible" with man. At other times, two opposites stated disjunctively are of necessity in the subject, as "straight or oblique" in line, and "odd or even" in number. He shows that the reason for this is the fact that contrariety, privation and contradiction are in the same genus. For privation is nothing more than a negation in a determinate subject. Again, a contrary is equivalent to a negation in some genus, as in the genus of numbers, odd is the same as "not even" by way of consequence. Therefore, just as it is necessary either to affirm or deny, so it is necessary that one of two things that belong *per se,* be in its proper subject.

Then (73b25) he summarizes, and the text is clear.

Lecture 11
(73b27–74a3)

HOW SOMETHING IS SAID TO BE PREDICATED
AS *COMMENSURATELY UNIVERSAL*

b27. I term 'commensurately
b28. from which it clearly
b29. The essential attribute

b32. An attribute belongs
b34. Thus, e.g., (1) the
a1. and the demonstration

After determining about "said of all" and "said *per se*," the Philosopher here determines concerning the "universal." This treatment falls into two parts. In the first he shows what the universal is. Secondly, how error occurs in our understanding of it (74a4) [L. 12]. Concerning the first he does two things. First, he shows what the universal is. Secondly, how the demonstrator uses the universal (74a1). Concerning the first he does two things. First, he shows that the universal contains within itself the attributes of "being said of all" and of "being said *per se*." Secondly, he shows what the universal adds to them (73b33).

To understand what is being said here it should be noted that "universal" is not to be taken here in the sense that anything predicated of several is a universal, as when Porphyry treats of the five universals; rather "universal" is taken here according to a certain correspondence or commensurateness of the subject with the predicate, so that the predicate is not found outside the subject nor is the subject without the predicate.

With this in mind, it should be noted that he does three things with respect to the first point. First (73b27), he says that the universal, namely, the predicate, is both verified of all, i.e., is predicated universally of its subject, and is said *per se*, i.e., is in and belongs to the subject according to the essential nature of the subject. For many things are said universally of certain things to which they do not belong *per se* and as such. Thus, every stone is colored, but not precisely as stone, but as it has a surface.

Secondly (73b28), he draws a corollary from this and says that since the universal is something which is *per se* in a thing, and since it has been shown that whatever things are in something *per se* are in it of necessity, it is obvious that universal predicates, as they are being taken here, are necessarily present in the things of which they are predicated.

Thirdly (73b29), lest anyone suppose that "per se" and "precisely as such," both of which were mentioned in the definition of the universal, are different, he shows that they are the same. Thus, "point" is *per se* in line in the first way, and "straight" in the second way. For each is in line precisely as it is a line. In like manner, "two right angles" belongs to triangle precisely as triangle, i.e., its angles are equal to two right angles, which is *per se* in triangle.

Then (73b33) he shows what "universal" adds to the notions, "being said of all" and "being said *per se*." In regard to this he does two things:

First, he says that a predicate is "universal," when it is not only in each thing of which it is asserted, but it is demonstrated to be first or primarily in the thing which receives that predicate.

Secondly (73b34), he clarifies this with an example and says that "having three angles equal to two right angles" is not found in just any figure in general, although this could be demonstrated of some figure, because it is demonstrated of triangle, which is a figure; yet it is not found in any random figure, nor is just any figure used when it is demonstrated. For a rhombus is a figure, but it does not have three angles equal to two right angles. But an isosceles, i.e., a triangle with two equal sides, always has its three angles equal to two right angles. Nevertheless, isosceles is not the primary thing to which this belongs, for it belongs basically to triangle, and belongs to isosceles precisely as it is a triangle. Therefore, whatever is demonstrated basically to have its three angles equal to two right angles (or whatever else be thus demonstrated), the universal predicate is present in it primarily, as in triangle.

Then (74a1) he shows how a demonstrator uses the "universal," saying that demonstration is concerned *per se* with such a universal, but with other things qualifiedly and not *per se*. For a demonstrator demonstrates a proper attribute of its proper subject; and if he demonstrates it of anything else, he does so only insofar as it pertains to that subject. Thus, he proves that some property of triangle belongs to a figure and to an isosceles precisely as some figure is a triangle, and as the isosceles is a triangle. But the reason why "having three" is not in isosceles primarily is not because it is not predicated of it universally, but because it is found more frequently, i.e., in more things than in isosceles, since this is common to every triangle.

Lecture 12
(74a4–b4)

HOW ERROR OCCURS IN TAKING THE UNIVERSAL

a4. We must not fail to observe

a6. We make this mistake

a13. Case (3) may

a17. An example of (1)

a18. An instance of (2)

a25. Hence, even if one

a33. When, then, does our knowledge

a35. 'But', it will be asked

After specifying what the universal is, the Philosopher here shows how one might err in understanding the universal. In regard to this he does three things. First, he says that sometimes one might err in this matter. Secondly, he tells in how many ways (74a6). Thirdly, he gives the criterion for knowing whether the universal is being employed correctly (74a35).

He says therefore first (74a4), that in order to avoid mistakes in demonstrating, one should be aware of the fact that quite often something universal seems to be demonstrated, which is not being demonstrated.

Secondly (74a6), he indicates the ways in which this mistake can occur. And in regard to this he does two things.

First, he enumerates these ways and says that there are three possible errors in understanding a universal. The first is likely to occur when under some common genus there is nothing else to take as the thing to which the universal initially applies than this singular, to which it is incorrectly applied. For example, if man were the only animal existing, and "sensible," which is initially and *per se* in animal, were to be assigned as a primary universal to man. (It should be noted that *singular* is being used here in a wide sense for any inferior, in the way that a species might be called a singular contained under a genus). Or we might say that it is not possible to find a genus with only one species: for a genus is divided into species through opposing differences. But if one contrary is found in nature, so must the other, as the Philosopher explains in *On the Heavens* II. Therefore, if one species is found, another will be found. However, one species is divided into distinct individuals by the division of matter. But it sometimes happens that all the matter proportionate to a given species is comprehended under one individual, so that in that case there is only one individual under one species. Hence it is significant that he did say, "singular."

The second way is when it is possible to take several inferiors under something common which is verified in things that differ in species, but that common item has no name. For example, if "animality" had no name, and "sensibility," which is proper to animal, were to be assigned to the inferiors of animal (either collectively or distributively) as their primary universal.

The third way is when that of which something is demonstrated to be its primary universal is related to what is demonstrated of it, as a whole is related to a part. For example, if the power to see were assigned as a primary universal to animal: for not every animal can see. In this case the demonstration, i.e., what should have been demonstrated, is "in those things which are in part," i.e., in some but not all of the things included under the subject; furthermore, it will be a demonstration "of all," but not of all that the demonstration mentions. For the power to see can indeed be demonstrated universally of something, but not of animal universally, as of that to which it belongs primarily. And he explains why he says, "primarily," namely, because a demonstration bears on what is both universal and first.

Secondly (74a13), he gives examples of each of these ways. First, of the third way, saying that if someone were to demonstrate of two straight lines that they do not intersect, i.e., that they do not meet, it might seem that we have a demonstration of this sort, i.e., one that bears on a primary universal, on the ground that "not to meet" is true of certain straight lines, and not that this happens only because the straight lines are equal, i.e., equally distant. But if the lines should be equal, i.e., equidistant, then "not to meet" belongs to any and all of them, because it is universally true that lines which are straight and equally distant, even should they be lengthened *ad infinitum,* will not meet.

Secondly (74a17), he gives an example of the first way, saying that if there were no triangle but the isosceles which is a triangle having two equal sides, it might seem that what is true of triangle as triangle should be true of isosceles as isosceles. But this would not be so.

Thirdly (74a18), he gives an example of the second way. Now it seems that he saved this for last because he wished to spend more time on it. Concerning it he does three things. First, he gives the example. Secondly, he draws a corollary from what he has said (74a25). Thirdly, he gives a reason for the aforesaid (74a33).

Concerning the first it should be noted that a ratio is a relation of one quantity to another, as 6 is related to 3 in the ratio of 2 to 1. The comparing of one ratio to another is a proportion, which, if it is disjoint, has four terms: for example, as 4 is to 2, so 6 is to 3. But if it is joint, it has three terms, one of which is used twice: for example, as 8 is to 4, so 4 is to 2.

Now it is obvious that in a proportion two terms are antecedents and two are consequents. For example, in the proportion that 6 is to 3 as 4 is to 2, 6 and 4 are the antecedents, 3 and 2 the consequents. Again, a proportion is alternated by bringing the antecedents together and the consequents together. For example, when I say: As 4 is to 2, so 6 is to 3; therefore, as 4 is to 6, so 2 is to 3.

What he is saying, therefore, is that alternate proportion is verified in lines, numbers, solids, (i.e., bodies), and times. But just as this is established separately for each of them, namely, for numbers in arithmetic, for lines and solids in geometry, and for times in natural philosophy or astronomy, so it is possible to prove it of all of them in a single demonstration. But the reason why a separate demonstration was employed to prove alternation for each was that the one feature they had in common was unnamed. For although quantity is a feature common to all of them, quantity includes other things besides them; for example, speech and other things that are accidentally quantitative.

Or, better still, it was because alternate proportion does not belong to quantity precisely as quantity, but as compared to another quantity according to a fixed ratio. That is why at the very start he spoke of alternate proportion. But there is no general name for the aforesaid things precisely as they are proportional. Furthermore, when alternate proportion is demonstrated separately for each of them, it is not a universal that is being demonstrated. For "to be alternately proportional" is not in numbers and lines according to what each of them is, but according to something common. Besides, those who demonstrate alternate proportion of lines look upon this attribute as a universal predicate of line precisely as it is a line, or of number precisely as it is number.

Then (74a25), he draws a corollary from the above and says that for the same reason that something universal is not being demonstrated when a common unnamed attribute is proved to be a universal predicate of each species, so too when something is demonstrated this way of a common attribute which does have a name. For example, if someone uses the same demonstration for each species of triangle and proves that each has three angles equal to two right angles, or if he uses different demonstrations, say one for isosceles and another for scalene, even then he does not on that account know that a triangle has three angles equal to two right angles except in a sophistical way, i.e., *per accidens:* for he does not know it of triangle as triangle, but as equilateral or as having two equal sides or as having three unequal sides.

Furthermore, one who demonstrates in this way does not know the universal of triangle, i.e., he does not have a knowledge of triangle in a universal way (even if there happens to be no other triangle besides those of which he knew this: and this because he had not the knowledge of triangle as triangle but under the aspect of its various species). Again, strictly speaking, he did not know every triangle: for although he knew every triangle according to number (if there was none he did not know), yet according to species he did not know each one. For something is known universally according to species, when it is known according to the notion of the species, but according to number and not universally, when it is known according to the multifarious things contained under the species. And in this matter there is no difference whether we compare species to individuals or genera to species. For triangle is the genus of equilateral and isosceles.

Then (74a33) he assigns the reason for the aforesaid, first asking when does one know universally and absolutely, if one who knew in the aforesaid way did not know universally. And he answers that obviously if the essence of triangle in general and of each of its species (each taken separately or all taken together) were the same, then one would know universally and absolutely about triangle, when he knew about any one species of it separately or about all of them together. But if the essence is not the same, then it will not be the same but something different to know triangle and to know its several species. And by knowing something of the species one does not know it of triangle precisely as triangle.

Then (74a35) he gives the rule on how the universal can be properly understood, saying that whether something belongs to triangle precisely as triangle or to isosceles precisely as isosceles, and when it is that what is demonstrated is first and universal in the given subject precisely as this, i.e., precisely according to the subject—all this will be clear from what I shall say.

For whenever some item is removed from the subject and the original universal still applies to what remains, then it is not the first universal of that subject. For example, upon the removal of isosceles or of brazen there still remains the triangle which has three angles equal to two right angles; hence the possession of three angles equal to two right angles is not a first universal of isosceles or of brazen triangle. But if the item "figure" be removed, nothing which has three angles equal to two right angles remains, nor again if you remove "bounded" which is more universal than figure, since a figure is something enclosed by a bound or bounds. Nevertheless, the attribute in question [namely, having three angles equal to two right angles] does not belong first to figure or to bounded, because it does not belong to either of them universally.

To what then will it be first? Obviously to triangle, because it belongs to the others (both superiors and inferiors) precisely as they are triangles. For it belongs to figure to have three angles equal to two right angles only because a triangle is some figure, and similarly to isosceles, only because it is a triangle, and it is of triangle that "having three . . ." is demonstrated. Hence, it is to triangle that it belongs as a first universal.

Lecture 13
(74b5–75a17)

DEMONSTRATION PROCEEDS FROM
NECESSARY THINGS

b5. Demonstrative knowledge

b6. Now attributes attaching

b13. We must either state

b18. That demontration proceeds

b22. This shows how naive

b27. A further proof

b32. Or again, if a man

a1. When the conclusion

a13. To sum up, then:

Having finished his treatment of that which is said "of all" and "*per se*" and "universally," all of which we use in demonstration, the Philosopher now begins to discuss the items from which demonstration proceeds. And there are two parts. In the first he shows what demonstration of the reasoned fact [demonstration *propter quid*] proceeds from. In the second what demonstration of the fact [demonstration *quia*] proceeds from (78a22) [L. 23]. The first is divided into two parts. In the first he shows the sort of things from which a demonstration proceeds. In the second, what the principles of demonstration are (76a26) [L. 18]. The first is divided into three parts. In the first he shows that demonstration issues from necessary things. In the second that it issues from things that are *per se* (76a26) [L. 14]. In the third that it proceeds from proper principles (75a38) [L. 15]. Concerning the first he does two things. First, he shows that demonstration should proceed from necessary things. Secondly, he proves certain things he had presupposed (74b27). In regard to the first he does three things. First, he makes a connection with what went before. Secondly, he proves his proposition (74b6). Thirdly, he draws a conclusion from the aforesaid (74b22).

He says therefore first (74b5), as an inference from what has already been established, that if there be demonstrative science, i.e., if science is acquired through demonstration, it must issue from necessary principles. The necessity of this inference is clear, because that which is known scientifically cannot be otherwise than it is, as was pointed out in the definition of scientific knowing.

Then (74b6) he shows that demonstration issues from necessary things. First, with a reason. Secondly, with a sign (74b19).

With respect to the first he gives two reasons. The first (74b6) is this: Things predicated *per se* are in a thing necessarily. (And he manifests this in two of the modes of predicating *per se:* in the first mode, because the things predicated *per se* are "in that which is what," i.e., in the definition of the subject. But whatever is put in the definition of anything is predicated of it necessarily. In the second mode, because certain subjects are put in "that which is the what of things predicated of them," i.e., in the definition of their predicates. And if these are opposites, one or other of them is necessarily in the subject: thus, either "odd" or "even" is in number, as we showed above). Now it is clear that it is from principles of this kind, namely, *per se,* that a demonstrative syllogism proceeds. (And this is proved by the fact that whatever is predicated, is predicated either *per se* or *per accidens,* and that things predicated *per accidens* are not necessary). Therefore, since it is not a demonstration but rather a sophistic syllogism that issues from things that are *per accidens,* it follows that demonstration proceeds from necessary things.

Furthermore, it should be noted that, since in a demonstration a proper attribute is proved of a subject through a middle which is the definition, it is required that the first proposition (whose predicate is the proper attribute, and whose subject is the definition which contains the principles of the proper attribute) be *per se* in the fourth mode, and that the second proposition (whose subject is the subject itself and the predicate its definition) must be in the first mode. But the conclusion, in which the proper attribute is predicated of the subject, must be *per se* in the second mode.

Then (74b14) he sets forth the second reason and it is this: "Demonstration is concerned with the necessary and the demonstrated," i.e., the conclusion of the demonstration cannot be other than it is. This statement is to be taken as the principle proving our proposition that demonstration proceeds from necessary things. And from what has been said, the truth of this principle is obvious. From this principle one argues thus: a necessary conclusion cannot be scientifically known save from necessary principles; but a demonstration makes a necessary conclusion scientifically known: therefore, it must proceed from necessary principles.

Herein lies the difference between a demonstration and other syllogisms. For in the latter it is enough if one syllogizes from true principles. Nor is there any other type of syllogism in which it is required to proceed from the necessary: in a demonstration alone must this be observed. And this is proper to a demonstration, i.e., to proceed from the necessary.

Then (74b18) he proves the same thing in the following way, using a sign: Suit is brought against an argument solely on the ground that something is wanting that should have been observed in that argument. But against one who believes that he has demonstrated, we bring the charge that the things from which he proceeded are not necessarily true, whether we are convinced that they could be otherwise than stated, or whether we bring a charge of reason, i.e., for the sake of disputing. Therefore, demonstration should proceed from necessary things.

Then (74b22) he draws a conclusion from the foregoing, saying that "this," namely, the fact that a demonstration must conclude from necessary things, "shows" that they are obtuse who assumed that they rightly chose the principles of demonstration, if the proposition they chose was probable or true, as the Sophists do, i.e., those who appear wise but are not. For scientific knowing consists in nothing less than having science, namely, from demonstration. But when something is probable or improbable, it is not certain whether it is first or not first, whereas that on which a demonstration bears must be first in some genus and be true. This does not mean that a demonstrator may take anything that is first: it must be first in that genus with respect to which he is demonstrating. Thus, arithmetic does not choose what is first in regard to magnitude, but in regard to number.

It should be noted that Sophists are not taken here as they are in the book of *Sophistical Refutations*, i.e., who proceed from things that seem probable but are not, or seem to syllogize but do not. For just as some are called *Sophists*, i.e., seeming to be wise but not really so, inasmuch as they appear by their arguments to be scientific knowers but are not, so dialectical arguments, if they seem to prove demonstratively but do not, are sophistic.

Then (74b27) he proves something he had presupposed. And concerning this he does two things. First, he shows that a necessary conclusion cannot be scientifically known from non-necessary principles. Secondly, that although the necessary cannot be scientifically known from the non-necessary, it can nevertheless be syllogized (75a1).

He proves the first with two reasons, one of which (74b27) is this: If one does not have an argument which shows the cause why [i.e., *propter quid*], he does not know scientifically, even though a syllogism be had; because to know scientifically is to know the cause of a thing, as we stated above. But an argument which infers a necessary conclusion from non-necessary principles does not show the cause why.

To clarify this he gives an example, using general terms. Assume that the conclusion, "Every C is A," is necessary, and that it is demonstrated by a middle, B, which is not a necessary middle but a contingent one, so that, for example, one of the propositions, "Every B is A," and "Every C is B," or both, are contingent. Now it is obvious that through this contingent middle, namely, B, one cannot obtain scientific knowledge *propter quid* of the necessary conclusion, "Every C is A." For if the cause on which something depends is removed, the effect must be removed. But this middle, being contingent, can be withdrawn, whereas the conclusion, since it is necessary, cannot be withdrawn. It follows, therefore, that a necessary conclusion cannot be scientifically known through a contingent middle.

The second reason (74b32) is this: "If a man is without scientific knowledge now, then even though he possesses the same argument he had up to now, and he has been kept sound," i.e., has not ceased to be, "and the thing known has not changed; and if he has not forgotten, then obviously he has not known scientifically." In this passage the Philosopher mentions four ways in which a person loses the science he once had: one way is when there slips from his mind the argument through which he formerly knew scientifically. Another is through the destruction of the knower. A third is by a change occurring in the thing known: thus if, while you are sitting, I know that you are sitting, this knowledge perishes when you are not sitting. The fourth way is by forgetting. Hence if none of these ways has occurred, then, if a person does not know a thing scientifically now, he never did know it. Now one who holds a necessary conclusion in virtue of a contingent middle, no longer knows it scientifically when the middle ceases to be, for the middle no longer exists, even though he retains the same argument and the fact remains the same, and he has not forgotten anything. Therefore, even when the middle had not ceased to be, he did not know scientifically.

But that a contingent middle is liable to perish he proves by the fact that whatever is not necessary must at some time perish. And even though the middle has not perished, nevertheless, because it is not necessary, it is obvious that it is liable to perish. Now when something contingent is put forward, its result is not impossible but possible and contingent. But what followed in our case was impossible, namely, that one should have had science of something and later not have had it, all the conditions described above prevailing. And this follows from the fact that a contingent middle has perished, which, although it may not be true [that it has], is nevertheless liable to, as has been said.

Then (75a1) he shows that although a necessary conclusion cannot be scientifically known through a contingent middle, nevertheless a necessary conclusion can be syllogized from a non-necessary middle. Hence he says that nothing hinders a necessary conclusion from being obtained through a non-necessary middle, as witness the case in which something is syllogized with a dialectical syllogism, although not with a demonstrative syllogism which causes science. For the necessary happens to be syllogized from the non-necessary, just as the true happens to be syllogized from the untrue—although the converse does not occur. For when the middle is necessary, the conclusion too will be necessary; similarly, from true premises something true is concluded.

But that the necessary is always concluded from necessary premises he proves thus: "Let A be necessary of B," i.e., let this proposition, "Every B is A," be necessary, "and the latter of C," i.e., let "Every C is B" also be necessary. Now from these two necessary things follows a third necessary thing, namely, the conclusion, "Every C is A." For it has been proved in the *Prior Analytics* that "from two propositions of necessity follows a conclusion of necessity."

Then by way of consequence he shows that if the conclusion were not necessary, the middle could not be necessary. For example, suppose that this conclusion, "Every C is A," is not necessary, but that the two premises are necessary. According to our previous doctrine it follows that the conclusion is necessary—which is contrary to the supposition in our example, namely, that the conclusion not be necessary.

Then (75a13) he infers from the aforesaid the conclusion originally intended, saying that since a thing must be necessary if it is made known by way of demonstration, it is clear from the foregoing that a demonstration must rest on a necessary middle. For otherwise it would not be scientifically known that the conclusion is necessary, neither *propter quid* nor *quia*, since the necessary cannot be known through the non-necessary, as we have shown. But if someone rests on an argument based on a non-necessary middle, he will be in one of two states. For since he does not actually know in a scientific way, he will either believe that he does know in a scientific way, if he assumes a non-necessary middle as necessary, or he will not presume that he knows in a scientific way, i.e., if he believes that he does not have a necessary middle. And this is to be universally understood both of scientific knowledge *quia*, in which something is known through mediate principles, and of science *propter quid,* in which something is known through immediate principles. The difference between these two will be explained later.

Lecture 14
(75a18–37)

DEMONSTRATION BEARS UPON AND PROCEEDS FROM THINGS WHICH ARE *PER SE*

a18. Of accidents that are   a24. The solution is that
a21. A difficulty, however,   a28. Since it is just those

After showing that demonstration proceeds from necessary things, the Philosopher then shows that it is concerned with things that are *per se* and proceeds from things that are *per se.* In regard to this he does three things. First, he shows that demonstration is concerned with things that are *per se,* i.e., that the conclusions of demonstrations are *per se.* Secondly, he raises a problem (75a21). Thirdly, he shows that demonstration proceeds from things that are *per se,* i.e., that the principles of demonstrations must be *per se* (75a28).

He says therefore first (75a18) that demonstrative science cannot bear on accidents that are not *per se* in the way that *per se* was explained above, namely, that a *per se* accident is one in whose definition the subject is mentioned, as "even" or "odd" is a *per se* accident of number. But "white" is not a *per se* accident of animal, because animal is not mentioned in its definition.

That there cannot be demonstration bearing on accidents that are not *per se* he proves in the following way: An accident which is not *per se* might happen not to be present (and this is the accident under discussion). Therefore, if a demonstration were to bear on an accident which is not *per se,* it would follow that the conclusion of the demonstration would not be necessary: which is contrary to what has been established.

That an accident which is not *per se* does not inhere necessarily can be obtained from the following: If an accident inheres necessarily and always in a subject, it must have its cause in the subject—in which case the accident cannot but inhere. Now this can occur in two ways: in one way, when it is caused from the principles of the species, and such an accident is called a *per se* attribute or property; in another way, when it is caused from the principles of the individual, and this is called an inseparable accident. In either case every accident which is caused from the principles of the subject must, if it is defined, be defined in such a way as to mention the subject in its definition: for a thing is defined in terms of its proper principles. Thus it is clear that an accident which necessarily inheres in its subject must be a *per se* accident. Therefore, those that are not *per se* do not inhere of necessity.

It seems, however, that Aristotle is using the circular demonstration which he previously repudiated. For he had proved earlier that a demonstration is concerned with necessary things, because it is concerned with things which are *per se;* but now he shows that demonstration is concerned with things which are *per se,* because it is concerned with things which are necessary. The answer is that above Aristotle proved that demonstration is concerned with necessary things not only because it is concerned with things which are *per se* but also because of the definition of scientific knowing—and this was a true way to demonstrate. But the proof that demonstration is concerned with necessary things because it is concerned with things which are *per se,* is not a demonstration but an indication directed to a person who already knows that demonstration is concerned with things which are *per se.*

Then (75a21) he raises a problem in regard to which he does two things. First, he states the problem, saying that someone may perhaps object that if the conclusion which follows from contingent things or things which are *per accidens* is not necessary, why are inquiries made concerning contingent things or things which are *per accidens,* so that from such data one may reach a conclusion, since it is required of the syllogism that the conclusion follow of necessity. That inquiries touching contingent things or things which are *per accidens* do occur is evident from his next statement, namely, that it makes no difference whether one inquires into contingent things and then gives his conclusion. As if to say: A conclusion can be drawn from contingent things that have been investigated and verified, just as from necessary things. For each employs the same syllogistic form.

Secondly (75a24), he solves the difficulty and says that questions solved by contingent premises are not of such a nature that the conclusion is necessary absolutely, on the basis of the things investigated, i.e., in virtue of the contingent premises, but because it is necessary for the one who admits the premises to admit the conclusion and to admit truth in the conclusion, if the things premised are true. It is as though he were saying that although a conclusion which is necessary with absolute necessity does not follow from contingent premises, yet it follows with the necessity of consequence according to which the conclusion follows from the premises.

Then (75a28) he shows that demonstration proceeds from things which are *per se,* using the following argument: Demonstration proceeds from necessary things and bears on necessary things—and this because it is scientific, i.e., makes one know scientifically. But things which are not *per se* are not necessary, for they are *per accidens* and, being such, are not necessary, as has been stated above. On the other hand, those things bear with necessity on a genus which are *per se* and belong to it according to what it is. It follows, therefore, that demonstration cannot be from anything or of anything but what is *per se*.

He further shows that even if the premises were always both necessary and true but not *per se*, one would not know the cause why [*propter quid*] of the conclusion. This is clear in syllogisms which prove through signs, for although the conclusion be *per se*, one does not know it *per se* nor *propter quid*. For example, if someone were to prove that every element is corruptible on the ground that it is seen to grow old. This would be a proof through a sign but neither *per se* nor *propter quid*, because to know *propter quid* one must know through the cause. Therefore, the middle must be the cause of that which is concluded in the demonstration. And this is obvious from the premises: for the middle must inhere in the third causatively, i.e., *per se*, and likewise the first in the middle. Here he calls the two extremes the *first* and the *third*.

Lecture 15
(75a38–b20)

DEMONSTRATION DOES NOT SKIP FROM ONE GENUS TO AN ALIEN GENUS

a38. It follows that we cannot
a39. For there are three
b2. The axioms which are premises

b8. so that if the demonstration
b10. If this is not so,
b13. That is why it cannot
b17. Geometry again cannot

After showing that demonstration is from things that are *per se*, the Philosopher here concludes that demonstration is from principles which are proper and not from extraneous or common principles. His treatment falls into two parts. In the first he shows that demonstration proceeds from proper principles. In the second he establishes which principles are proper and which common (76a26) [L. 18]. The first is divided into two parts. In the first he shows that demonstration does not proceed from extraneous principles. In the second that it does not proceed from common principles (75b37) [L. 17]. The first is divided into two parts. In the first, from the preceding, he shows that demonstration is not from extraneous principles. In the second, also from the preceding, he shows that demonstrations do not bear on corruptible things but on eternal (75b21) [L. 16]. Concerning the first he does three things. First, he states his proposition. Secondly, he proves it (75a39). Thirdly, he concludes to what he intended (75b13).

He says therefore first (75a38) that inasmuch as demonstration is from things that are *per se*, it is plain that demonstration does not consist in descending or skipping from one genus to another, as geometry, demonstrating from its own principles, does not descend to something in arithmetic.

Then (75a39) he proves this proposition and does three things. First, he lays down the things that are necessary for a demonstration, saying that "three things are necessary in demonstrations. One is that which is demonstrated," namely, the conclusion which, as a matter of fact, contains within itself that which inheres in its genus *per se*. For through demonstration a proper attribute is concluded of its proper subject. Another is the dignities [maxims or axioms] from which demonstration proceeds. The third is the generic subject whose proper attributes and *per se* accidents demonstration reveals.

Secondly (75b3), he shows which of the three aforesaid can be common to various sciences and which cannot, saying that one of the three, namely, the dignities, from which demonstration proceeds, happens to be the same in diverse demonstrations and even in diverse sciences. But in those sciences whose respective generic subject is diverse, as in arithmetic which is concerned with numbers, and in geometry which is concerned with magnitudes, it does not occur that a demonstration which starts with the principles of one science, say, of arithmetic, descends to the subjects of another science, say to magnitudes, which pertain to geometry; unless perchance the subject of one science should be contained under the subject of the other, for example, if magnitudes should be contained under numbers. (How this occurs, namely, how the subject of one science may be contained under the subject of another, will be discussed later). For magnitudes are not contained under numbers except perhaps in the sense that magnitudes are numbered. In any case, the subjects of diverse demonstrations or sciences are diverse. For an arithmetical demonstration always has its proper genus in respect to which it demonstrates, and so do the other sciences.

Thirdly (75b8), he proves his proposition and does two things. First, he brings in the main intent after the manner of a conclusion on the ground that it can be obtained from the aforesaid, saying: Hence it is clear that it is necessary either that the genus with which the principles and conclusions deal be absolutely the same (in which case there is no descent or skipping from one genus to another); or if the demonstration is to descend from one genus to another, the two must be one thus, i.e., somehow. For otherwise it is impossible for a conclusion to be demonstrated from principles, since there is not the same genus either absolutely or in a qualified sense. However, it should be noted that a genus absolutely the same is being taken when on the part of the subject no determinate difference is admitted which is alien to the nature of that genus: for example, if someone using principles verified of triangle should proceed to demonstrate something about isosceles or about any other species of triangle. But a genus is one in a qualified sense when a difference alien to the nature of the genus is admitted of the subject, as "visual" is alien to the genus of line, and "sound" to the genus of number. Therefore, number absolutely, which is the generic subject of arithmetic, and sonant number, which is the generic subject of music, are not one genus absolutely speaking. The same goes for line absolutely, which geometry considers, and the visual line considered in optics. Hence it is clear that when matters pertaining absolutely to the line are applied to the visual line, a descent is being made to another genus— which is not the case when matters pertaining to triangle are applied to isosceles.

Secondly (75b10), he manifests the proposition in this way. In demonstration the middles and the extremes must belong to the same genus. Now the extremes are contained in the conclusion: for the major extreme in the conclusion is its predicate, and the minor its subject. But the middle is contained in the premises. It is required, therefore, that the principles and conclusion be taken with respect to the same genus. When we add to this the fact that diverse sciences are of necessity concerned with subjects generically diverse, it follows that from the principles of one science, something in another science not under it may not be concluded.

That the middles and extremes in a demonstration must be of one genus he proves thus: Suppose that a middle belongs to a genus other than that of the extremes which might be, for example, "triangle" and "have three angles equal to two right angles." Now a proper attribute concluded of triangle is in it *per se* but is not in "brazen" *per se;* or, conversely, if the proper attribute is *per se* in "brazen," say, "high-sounding" or the like, it is obviously in triangle *per accidens.*

This example makes it plain that if the subject of the conclusion and the middle are in entirely different genera, then the proper attribute is either not in the middle *per se* or else not in the subject *per se.* Consequently, it is in one of them *per accidens.* If it is in the middle *per accidens,* something will be in the premises *per accidens.* But if it is in the subject *per accidens,* something will be *per accidens* in the conclusion: and this on the part of a proper attribute. But either way something will be *per accidens* in the premises, inasmuch as the subject is subsumed under the middle, for example, triangle under brazen, or vice versa. However, it has been previously established that in a demonstration both the conclusion and the premises are *per se* and not *per accidens.* It is required, therefore, in demonstrations that the middle and the extremes be of the same genus.

Then (75b13) he infers two conclusions from the foregoing. The first conclusion is that no science demonstrates anything about the subject of another science, when this other science is more common than or entirely disparate from the first. Thus, geometry does not demonstrate that one and the same science deals with the both of two contraries: for contraries pertain to the common science, namely, to first philosophy or to dialectics. In like manner, geometry does not demonstrate that "two cubes are one cube," i.e., that the product of one cube and another cube is a cube. "Cube" here means the number which results from multiplying a number by itself twice: for example, 8 is a cube, for it is the result of multiplying 2 by itself twice, for 2 times 2 times 2 are 8. Similarly, 27 is a cube, whose root is 3, because 3 times 3 times 3 make 27. Now if 8 be multiplied by 27 the product is 216, which is a cube whose root is 6, because 6 times 6 times 6 make 216. Therefore, arithmetic, not geometry has the power to prove this. Similarly, that which pertains to one science cannot be proved by another science unless the one happens to be under the other, as optics is under geometry, and consonance or harmony, i.e., music, is under arithmetic.

The second conclusion (75b17) states that a science cannot prove just any random accident of its subject, but the accidents proper to its genus. Thus, if something belongs to lines not as lines or not according to the proper principles of lines, geometry does not demonstrate it of lines: for example, that a straight line is the most beautiful of lines, or whether a straight line is contrary or not to the curved. For these matters are outside the proper genus of line and belong to something more general. For beauty and contrary transcend the genus of line.

Lecture 16
(75b21–36)

DEMONSTRATION IS NOT OF PERISHABLE BUT OF ETERNAL MATTERS

b21. It is also clear that   b30. The same is true of
b24. The proof can only be   b32. Demonstration and science

After concluding from the above that demonstration does not conclude from extraneous principles, the Philosopher intends to conclude something else from the above, namely, that demonstration is not of destructible things. Concerning this he does two things. First, he shows that demonstration is of eternal and not of destructible things. Secondly, he shows how it is of things that occur now and then (75b32). Concerning the first he does two things. First, he shows that demonstration is not of

perishable but of eternal things. Secondly, he shows that the same is true
of definition (75b30). In regard to the first he does two things. First, he
proposes the intended conclusion. Secondly, he sets down the reason
proving it (75b24).

Therefore first (75b21), he sets down two conclusions, one of which follows from the other. The first is that the conclusion of this demonstration which we are now discussing and which we can call demonstration
in the full sense must be eternal: which, of course, follows from what has
been stated so far, namely, that the propositions of a syllogism should
be universal: which he signified by "said of all." The second conclusion
is that neither demonstration nor science is of destructible things, i.e.,
absolutely speaking, but only accidentally.

Then (75b24) he presents an argument to prove the proposed conclusions. It is this: It is not the character of a destructible non-eternal conclusion to contain what is universally so, but what is so for a time and in
certain instances. For it has been established above that "said of all"
contains two things, namely, that it is not such as to be so in one case
and not in another, or so at one time and not at another. But in destructible things we find that at one time something is so and at another
not so. Hence it is clear that "said of all" or "said universally" are not
found in destructible things. But where a conclusion is not universal, at
least one of the premises is not universal. Therefore, a destructible conclusion must have followed from premises, one of which is not universal.
Accordingly, when we add to this the fact that demonstration absolutely
must be from what is universal, it follows that a demonstration cannot
have a destructible conclusion, but must have an eternal one.

Then (75b30) he shows that definition, too, is not of destructible but
of eternal things. The reason for this is that demonstration, both as to
its principles and conclusions, is of eternal and not of destructible things.
But a definition is either a principle of a demonstration, a conclusion of
a demonstration, or a demonstration with a different ordering of its
terms. Therefore, a definition is not of destructible, but of eternal things.

For a better understanding of this passage it should be noted that it is
possible to give different definitions of the same thing, depending on the
different causes mentioned. But causes are arranged in a definite order
to one another: for the reason of one is derived from another. Thus the
reason of matter is derived from the form, for the matter must be such
as the form requires. Again, the agent is the reason for the form: for since
an agent produces something like unto itself, the mode of the form which
results from the action must be according to the mode of the agent.
Finally, it is from the end that the reason of the agent is derived, for
every agent acts because of an end. Consequently, a definition which is
formulated from the end is the reason and cause proving the other
definitions which are formulated from the other causes.

Therefore, let us lay down two definitions, one of which is formulated from the material cause, for example, that a house is a shelter composed of stones, cement and wood; the other being formulated from the final cause, namely, that a house is a shelter protecting us from the rain and heat and cold. Now the first definition can be demonstrated from the second in the following way: Every shelter protecting us from rain, heat and cold should be composed of wood, cement and stones; but a house is such a thing: therefore, ...

Thus it is clear that the definition formulated from the end is the principle of the demonstration, whereas the one formulated from the matter is the conclusion of the demonstration. However, the two can be combined in the following way to form one definition: A house is a shelter composed of the aforesaid, protecting us from rain, cold and heat. But such a definition contains all the elements of a demonstration, namely, a middle and a conclusion. Accordingly, such a definition is a demonstration differing merely in the arrangement of its terms, because the only way it differs from the demonstration is that it is not arranged in a syllogistic mode and figure.

Here we might remark that because demonstration, as well as definition, is not of destructible but of eternal things, Plato was led to posit "Ideas." For since sensible things are destructible, it appeared that there could be neither demonstration nor definition of them. As a consequence it seemed necessary to postulate certain indestructible substances concerning which demonstrations and definitions could be given. These eternal substances are what he calls "Forms" or "Ideas."

However, Aristotle opposed this opinion above, when he said that demonstration is not of destructible things except *per accidens*. For although those sensible things are destructible as individuals, nevertheless in the universal they have a certain everlasting status. Therefore, since demonstration bears on those sensible things universally and not individually, it follows that demonstration is not of destructible things except *per accidens*, but of eternal things *per se*.

Then (75b32) he shows how there can be demonstration of things that occur now and then, saying "that there are science and demonstrations of things that occur frequently, as the eclipse of the moon," which is not always. For the moon is not always being eclipsed, but only now and then. Now things that occur frequently, so far as they are such, i.e., so far as demonstrations are given concerning them, are always; but they are particular, so far as they are not always. But demonstration cannot be of particulars, as we have shown, but only of universals. Hence it is clear that these things, insofar as there is demonstration of them, are always. And as in the case of the eclipse of the moon, so in all kindred matters.

However, there are certain differences to be noted among them. For some are not always with respect to time, but they are always in respect to their cause, because it never fails that under given conditions the effect follows, as in the eclipse of the moon. For the moon never fails to be eclipsed when the earth is diametrically interposed between sun and moon. But others happen not to be always even in respect to their causes, i.e., in those cases where the causes can be impeded. For it is not always that from a human seed a man with two hands is generated, but now and then a failure occurs, owing to a defect in the efficient cause or material cause. However, in both cases the demonstration must be so set up that a universal conclusion may be inferred from universal propositions by ruling out whatever can be an exception either on the part of time alone, or also of some cause.

Lecture 17
(75b37–76a25)

DEMONSTRATION DOES NOT PROCEED FROM COMMON PRINCIPLES, BUT FROM PRINCIPLES PROPER TO THE THING DEMONSTRATED

b37. It is clear that if
b40. Such proofs are like
a8. The only exceptions

a17. It is no less evident
a19. This is so because
a23. But, as things are,

Above the Philosopher showed that demonstration does not proceed from extraneous principles; here he shows that it does not proceed from common principles. Concerning this he does two things. First, he states his proposition. Secondly, he draws a conclusion from what he has said (76a17).

Concerning the first he does two things. First (75b37), he states his intention, saying that since it is clear that it is not just through anything at random that something is demonstrated, but it is required that demonstration be from one or another of a thing's principles in such a way that what is demonstrated be in line with what the thing as such is, i.e., it is required that the principles of the demonstration belong *per se* to that which is demonstrated; if, I say, this is so, then in order that something be scientifically known, it is not enough that it be demonstrated from true and immediate principles, but it is further required that it be demonstrated from proper principles.

Secondly (75b40), he proves his proposition, namely, that it is not enough to demonstrate something from true and immediate principles, because then something could be demonstrated in the way that Bryson proved squaring, i.e., the squaring of a circle. For he showed that some square is equal to a circle, using common principles in the following way: In any matter in which it is possible to have something greater and something less than something else, one can find something equal to it. But in the genus of squares it is possible to find one which is less than a given circle, namely, one inscribed in the circle, and another which is greater, namely, one circumscribed about the circle. Therefore, one can be found which is equal to the circle.

But this proof is according to something common: for equal and greater and less transcend the genus of square and circle. Hence such characteristics demonstrate according to something common, because the middle is present in other things besides the one with which the demonstration is concerned. Therefore, such characteristics, since they belong to other things as well, do not belong to the things of which they are said as to proximate subjects. Consequently, one who knows through such characteristics does not know according to what the thing is as such, i.e., *per se*, but only *per accidens*. For if it were based on what the thing is according to itself, the demonstration would not apply to something of another genus. For we know a thing according to what it accidentally is, when we do not know it according to what it is in virtue of its own principles, i.e., according to what comes *per se* from its principles, as "having three angles equal to two right angles" belongs *per se* to triangle, i.e., according to what it is in virtue of its principles. Consequently, if the middle which one used belonged *per se* to the conclusion, it would necessarily have to be in the same proximity, i.e., proximate according to genus, to the conclusion.

Thirdly (76a9), he excludes a doubt. For it sometimes happens that the middle of a demonstration is not in the same genus as the conclusion. How this can happen he shows when he suggests that if the middle is not in the same proximate genus as the conclusion, but is present in the way that theorems in harmonics, (i.e., in music), are demonstrable by arithmetic, it is nevertheless true that such things are also demonstrated. For in a lower science there is demonstration through the principles of a higher science, as we have established, just as in the higher science there is demonstration through the principles of that higher science.

But there is this difference: on the part of the other science, namely, the lower one, there is only knowledge *quia* [i.e., knowledge of the fact], for the generic subject of the lower science is different from the generic subject of the higher science, from which the principles are borrowed. But knowledge *propter quid* [i.e., of the cause why] is proper to the higher science to which those proper attributes belong *per se*. For since it is in virtue of the middle that a proper attribute is in a subject, that science will consider the *propter quid* to which pertains the middle in which the proper attribute being demonstrated inheres *per se*. But if the subject belongs to another science, it will not pertain to that science to know *propter quid* but only *quia*. Nor will the proper attribute demonstrated of such a subject belong *per se* to it, but it will be through an alien middle. However, if the middle and the subject pertain to the same science, then it will be characteristic of that science to know *quia* and *propter quid*.

Having settled this doubt, he draws the conclusion chiefly intended, saying that in the light of the foregoing it is clear that one should not demonstrate haphazardly, i.e., in any random way, but in such a way that a demonstration is made from the principles proper to each thing. But even the principles proper to the particular sciences have something common prior to them.

Then (76a17) he draws a conclusion that follows from the aforesaid. And in regard to this he does three things. First, he draws the conclusion that if demonstrations in the particular sciences do not proceed from common principles, and if the principles of those sciences have something prior to them which is common, then it is clear that it is not the business of each science to prove its proper principles. For those prior principles through which the proper principles of the particular sciences can be proved are principles common to all; and the science which considers such common principles is proper to all, i.e., is related to things which are common to all, as those other particular sciences are related to things respectively proper to each. For example, since the subject of arithmetic is number, arithmetic considers things proper to number. In like manner, first philosophy, which considers all principles, has for its subject "being," which is common to all. Therefore, it considers the things proper to being (which are common to all) as proper to itself.

Secondly (76b19), he shows the pre-eminence of this science which considers common principles, namely, first philosophy, over the others. For that through which something is proved must always be scientifically more known or at least more known. For one whose science of something proceeds from higher causes must understand those causes even better, because his science proceeded from the absolutely prior, since it is not through something caused that he knows these causes. For when one's knowledge of causes proceeds from caused things, he does not derive his knowledge from the absolutely prior and better known, but from what is prior and better known in reference to us. But when the principles of a lower science are proved by the principles of a higher science, the process is not from caused things to causes, but conversely. Therefore, such a process must go from the absolutely prior and from the absolutely more known. Thus, those items of a higher science that are used in proving matters of a lower science must be more known. Furthermore, that by which all other things are proved and which is itself not proved by anything prior must be the most known. Consequently, a higher science will be science in a fuller sense than a lower; and the highest science, namely, first philosophy, will be science in the fullest sense.

Thirdly (76a23), he returns to the principal conclusion and says that demonstration does not cross over into another genus except, as already mentioned, when a demonstration from geometry is applied to certain subordinate sciences, as the mechanical arts, which employ measurements, or the perspective arts, such as the sciences which deal with vision, as optics which deals with the visual. The same applies to arithmetic in relation to harmonics, i.e., music.

Lecture 18
(76a26–b22)

DIFFERENCE BETWEEN PRINCIPLES AND NON-PRINCIPLES, COMMON AND PROPER PRINCIPLES

a26. It is hard to be sure	a40. Peculiar truths are,
a31. I call the basic truths	a42. Only so much of these
a32. As regards both these	b2. Also peculiar
a37. Of the basic truths	b16. Yet some sciences

After showing that demonstration does not proceed from common but from proper principles, the Philosopher, to elucidate this point, decides questions concerning proper and common principles. With respect to this he does two things.

First (76a26), he shows the need for such a determination, saying that it is difficult to discern whether we know from proper principles, which alone is truly scientific knowing, or do not know from proper principles. For many believe that they know scientifically if they possess a syllogism composed of things true and first. But this is not so; indeed, to know in a scientific manner it is required that the principles be proximate to the things to be demonstrated—here they are called "first," just as above they were called "extremes"—or proximate to the first indemonstrable principles.

Secondly (76a31), he determines concerning proper and common principles. And in regard to this he does two things. First, he determines concerning common and proper principles. Secondly, he shows how the demonstrative sciences are related to such principles (77a10) [L. 20]. Concerning the first he does two things. First, he distinguishes principles from non-principles. Secondly, he distinguishes the principles from each other (76a37).

In regard to the first he does two things. First (76a31), he shows what the principles are and says that the principles in any genus are those which, since they are true, happen not to be demonstrated, either not at all, if they are first principles, or at least not in that science in which they are accepted as principles. And he says, "the existence of which," (i.e., whose truth), "cannot be proved," to distinguish from the false which are not demonstrated in any science.

Secondly (76a32), he shows the points of agreement and of difference between principles and non-principles. For principles agree with non-principles in the fact that with respect to each, i.e., with respect both to the first, namely, the principles, and to the things that proceed from them, i.e., things assumed from the principles, one must accept the supposition of what they signify, because the *quod quid est* [that which the definition signifies] of a thing pertains properly to the science concerned with substance, i.e., to first philosophy, from which all other sciences accept this.

But they are unlike in the fact that in regard to the principles one must accept the supposition that they are, whereas in regard to things from principles one is required to demonstrate *that* they are. Thus in mathematics one accepts by supposing both what unity is (which is a principle) and what straight and triangle are (which are not principles but proper attributes): but the fact that unity is or that magnitude is, the mathematician accepts as principles; but the other things, namely, things that are from principles, he demonstrates. For he demonstrates that a triangle is equilateral, or that an angle is right, or even that this line is straight.

Then (76a37) he distinguishes principles from one another. First, the proper from the common. Secondly, the common, one from the other (76b23) [L. 19]. The first is divided into two parts. First, he divides proper and common principles. Secondly, he settles something which might be doubtful (76b16).

In regard to the first he does three things. First (76a37), he lays down a division, saying that "of the principles which we use in demonstrative sciences, some are proper to each single science but others common." Then, because this statement might seem contrary to what he established above, namely, that demonstrative sciences do not proceed from common principles, he hastens to add that "the common principles are taken in each demonstrative science according to an analogy," i.e., as proportionate to that science. And this is what he means when by way of explanation he further states that "it is useful" to accept such principles in the sciences insofar as they pertain to the genus of the subject which is investigated in that science.

Secondly (76a40), he gives examples of each, saying that proper principles are, for example, that a line or a right angle is such and such. For in the sciences the definitions, both of the subject and of the proper attribute, are held as principles. But common principles are, for example, that if equals be subtracted from equals, the remainders are equal, and other common conceptions in the mind.

Thirdly (76a42), he shows how the demonstrative sciences use the aforesaid principles. First, in regard to the common principles, he says that "it suffices to accept each of those common ones," so far as it pertains to the generic subject with which the science is concerned. For geometry does this if it takes the above-mentioned common principle not in its generality but only in regard to magnitudes, and arithmetic in regard to numbers. For the geometer will then be able to reach his conclusion by saying that if equal magnitudes be taken from equal magnitudes, the remaining magnitudes are equal, just as if he were to say that if equals are taken from equals, the remainders are equal. The same must also be said for numbers.

Secondly (76b2), he shows how the demonstrative sciences employ proper principles. And he says that proper principles are things supposed in the sciences as existing, namely, the subjects, whose proper attributes are investigated in the sciences. In this way arithmetic considers unities, and geometry considers "signs," i.e., points, and lines. For they suppose these things to be and to be this, i.e., they suppose of them *that they are* and *what they are*. But in regard to the proper attributes they suppose *what* each signifies. Thus arithmetic supposes *what* "even" is and what "odd" is and *what* a "square or cubic number" is. Similarly, geometry supposes *what* is rational in lines. (For a rational line is one about which we can reason, the line being given. For example, a rational line is any line commensurable with the given lines; but one which is incommensurable with it is called irrational and surd). In like manner, geometry supposes *what* a reflex or *what* a curved line are. However, these sciences demonstrate concerning all the above-mentioned proper attributes *that* they are, and they do so through common principles and principles demonstrated from the common principles. And what has been said of geometry and arithmetic should also be understood of astronomy.

For every demonstrative science is concerned with three things: one is the generic subject whose *per se* attributes are investigated; another is the common (axioms) dignities from which, as from basic truths, it demonstrates; the third are the proper attributes concerning which each science supposes *what* their names signify.

Then (76b16) he clarifies something about which there might be doubt. For since he had said that the sciences suppose concerning the principles *that* they are and concerning the proper attributes *what* they are, but concerning the subject both *that* it is and *what* it is, someone might believe that he should have made special mention of all these. Hence he removes this by saying that nothing hinders certain sciences from neglecting some of the aforesaid, i.e., from making express mention of them, as for example, not mentioning that it takes the existence of its generic subject for granted, if it is already obvious that it does exist. For we do not have the same evidence in all cases that they do exist, as we do in the case of number and in the case of hot and cold, the one being close to reason and the other to sense. Again, certain sciences do not suppose *what* the proper attributes signify in the sense of making express mention of them, just as they do not think it necessary always to make express mention of the common principles, because they are known. Be that as it may, the three above-mentioned items are naturally to be supposed in each science.

Lecture 19
(76b23–77a9)

HOW COMMON PRINCIPLES DIFFER
FROM ONE ANOTHER

b23. That which expresses
b27. That which is capable
b35. The definitions—

b39. Nor are the geometer's
a3. A further distinction
a5. So demonstration does not

After dividing common principles from proper principles, Aristotle now distinguishes among the common principles. His treatment falls into three parts. In the first he lays down a distinction among the common principles. In the second he shows the difference between a definition and a certain genus of common principles (76b35). In the third he excludes an error (77a5). Concerning the first he does two things. First, he distinguishes the common conceptions in the mind from postulates or suppositions. Secondly, he distinguishes among the latter (76b27).

With respect to the first (76b23) it should be noted that the common conceptions in the mind have something in common with the other principles of demonstration and something proper: something common, because both they and the others must be true in virtue of themselves. But what is proper to the former is that it is necessary not only that they be true of themselves but that they be seen to be such. For no one can think their contraries. He says, therefore, that that principle of which it is not only required that it be in virtue of itself but further required that it be seen, namely, a common conception in the mind or a dignity, is neither a postulate nor a supposition.

He proves this in the following way: A postulate and a supposition can be confirmed by a reason from without, i.e., by some argumentation; but a common conception in the mind does not bear on a reason from without (because it cannot be proved by any argument), but bears on that reason which is in the soul, because it is made known at once by the natural light of reason. That it does not bear on any reason from without is shown by the fact that a syllogism is not formed to prove such common conceptions of the mind. Furthermore, that these are not made known by an outward reason but by the inward he proves by the fact that it is possible to contest an outward reason, either truly or apparently, but it is not always possible to do so with the inward reason. This is so because nothing is so true that it cannot be denied orally. (For even this most evident principle that the same thing cannot be and not be has been orally denied by some). On the other hand, some things are so true that their opposites cannot be conceived by the intellect. Therefore, they cannot be challenged in the inward reason but only by an outward reason which is by the voice. Such are the common conceptions in the mind.

Then (76b27) he distinguishes suppositions and postulates from one another. Here, too, it should be noted that they have something in common and something in which they differ. What is common to them is that although they can be demonstrated, the demonstrator assumes them without demonstrating, chiefly because they are not demonstrable by his own science but by another, as explained above. Hence they are reckoned among the immediate principles because the demonstrator uses them without a middle, since they do not have a middle in that science.

Yet they do differ, because if such a proposition is accepted as reasonable by the pupil to whom a demonstration is being made, it is called a "Supposition." In that case it is not called a supposition absolutely, but relative to him. But if the pupil has no reason for or against the proposition, the demonstrator must request him to admit it as reasonable, and then it is called a "postulate." However, if the pupil has a contrary opinion, then it will be a "question," which must be settled between them. At any rate, what is common to all of them is that the demonstrator uses each of them without demonstrating, although they are demonstrable.

Then (76b35) he distinguishes definitions from suppositions with two reasons, the second of which begins at (77a3). In regard to the first he does two things.

First, he presents this reason: Every postulate or supposition declares something to be or not to be; but terms, i.e., definitions, do not declare that something is or is not. Terms, therefore, taken by themselves, are neither postulates nor suppositions. But when they are employed in propositions they are suppositions, as in the statement, "Man is a rational mortal animal." But terms taken by themselves are only understood; and understanding is not supposing, any more than hearing is. Rather supposition bears on things that exist such that a conclusion is made from them in regard to what they are, i.e., in virtue of the premises.

Secondly (76b39), he excludes a doubt. For there were some who said that a geometer uses a false supposition when he says that a line not one foot long is one foot long, or that a line traced in the sand is straight when it really is not. But he says that a geometer does not on this account suppose something false. For since the geometer demonstrates nothing of singulars but of universals, as explained above, and these lines are singulars, it is obvious that he is not demonstrating anything about these lines or from these lines; rather he is using them as examples of the universals (which are understood by examples) from which and about which he demonstrates.

Then (77a3) he presents the second reason which is this: Every supposition or postulate is in whole or in part, i.e., is either a universal proposition or a particular. But definitions are neither of these, because nothing is placed or predicated in them universally or particularly. Therefore, ...

Then (77a5) he shows from the foregoing that it is not necessary to posit "Ideas," as Plato did. For it was shown above that demonstrations are concerned with universals and in that sense with eternal things. Therefore, it is not necessary for the validity of demonstration that there be "Forms," i.e., "Ideas," or a "one outside the many," as Plato posited separated mathematical beings along with Ideas in order that thereby demonstrations might bear on eternal things. What is required is that there be "one in many and about many," if there is to be demonstration, because it will not be universal unless it is "one about many." And if it is not universal, there will not be a middle of demonstration and, consequently, no demonstration.

That the middle of a demonstration must be universal is plain from the fact that the middle of a demonstration must be some one same thing predicated of many not equivocally but according to the same aspect, which is a universal aspect. But if it should happen to be equivocal, a defect in reasoning would occur.

Lecture 20
(77a10–35)

RELATION BETWEEN DEMONSTRATIVE SCIENCES AND COMMON PRINCIPLES

a10. The law that it is impossible
a22. The law that every predicate

a26. In virtue of the common
a29. and in communion with them

After determining about proper and common principles, the Philosopher now shows how the demonstrative sciences behave in regard to the common and to the proper principles. His treatment falls into two parts. In the first he shows how the demonstrative sciences are related to common principles. In the second he shows how they are related to proper principles (77a36) [L. 21]. Concerning the first he does two things. First, he shows how the demonstrative sciences are related to the first of the common principles. Secondly, how they are related generally to all the common principles (77a29). Concerning the first he does two things. First, he shows how the demonstrative sciences behave relative to the principle that one should not affirm and deny the same thing. Secondly, how they behave relative to the principle that there is either true affirmation or true negation of each thing, for, as is proved in *Metaphysics* IV, these two principles are the first of all principles (77a22).

He says therefore first (77a10) that no demonstration makes use of the principle that one does not affirm and deny at one and the same time. For if a demonstration were to use it to show some conclusion, it would have to use it in such a way as to assert that the first, i.e., the major, extreme is affirmed of the middle and not denied; because if it were to admit affirmation and negation on the part of the middle, it would make no difference whether it was this way or that. And the same reasoning holds for the third, i.e., minor, extreme in relation to the middle. For example, take "animal" as the first, "man" as the middle, and "Callias" as the third. If someone wished to use this principle in a demonstration, he would have to argue in the following way:

> Every man is an animal and is not a non-animal;
> But Callias is a man:
> Therefore, Callias is an animal and is not a non-animal.

For when we say that every man is an animal, it matters not whether it is also true that a non-man is an animal, or whether it is not true. Similarly, in the conclusion it matters not, Callias being an animal, whether non-Callias is an animal or not.

Now the reason for this is that the first is not limited to being said only of the middle but can also be said of something else diverse from the middle and described by a negation of the middle (since the first is sometimes said of things other than the middle, as "animal" is said of things other than man; for it is said of horse, which is not man). Hence if the middle is taken the same and not the same, i.e., if an affirmative and a negative middle be taken, as when I say, "man" and "non-man" are animals, it contributes nothing to the conclusion. However, if the affirmation and negation are taken on the part of the major extreme, it does make a difference both as to the conclusion and as to the truth of the premises. For if man were not an animal, it would not be true that man is an animal, nor would it follow that Callias is an animal. Yet nothing more is verified by stating that man is an animal and is not a non-animal than by merely stating that man is an animal, for the same thing is conveyed by each. And thus it is clear that demonstrations do not use the principle that affirmation and negation are not simultaneously true, either on the part of the predicate or on the part of the subject.

Then (77a22) he shows how demonstrative sciences use the principle that "of anything there is either true affirmation or negation." And he says that this principle is utilized in a demonstration leading to the impossible. For in this demonstration something is proved to be true by the fact that its opposite is false. (This of course would never happen, if it were possible for the two opposites to be false).

Nevertheless such a demonstration does not always employ this principle, for sometimes that opposite which is shown to be false is not a negation but an immediate contrary. For example, if a number were shown to be even on the ground that its opposite, namely, "it is odd," is false, and this were done by leading to the impossible. Neither does it use this principle universally, i.e., in its universality, namely, under the terms "being" and "non-being," but only so far as is sufficient for a genus or so far as it is narrowed to a generic subject. And I mean the first genus involved in the demonstration. For example, in leading to the impossible in geometry the terms would be "straight" and "non-straight" in the case where it is shown that some line is straight on the ground that it is false to state that it is not straight.

Then (77a26) he shows how the sciences as a community function relative to all common principles. In regard to this he does two things. First, he says that all the sciences share alike in the common principles in the sense that they all use them as items from which they demonstrate—which is to use them as principles. But they do not use them as things about which they demonstrate something, i.e., as subjects, or as things which they demonstrate, i.e., as conclusions.

Secondly (77a29), he shows that certain sciences employ the common principles in a manner other than has been described. For dialectics is concerned with common things, and a certain other science is concerned with common things, namely, first philosophy, whose subject is *being* and which considers the things which follow upon *being* as the proper attributes of *being*. Yet it should be noted that dialectics is concerned with common things under an aspect different from logic and first philosophy. For first philosophy is concerned with common things because its consideration is focused on those common things, namely, on being and on the parts and attributes of being. But because reason occupies itself with all things that are, and logic studies the operations of reason, logic will also be concerned with matters common to all things, i.e., with reason's intentionalities which bear on all things, but not in such a way that logic has these common things as its subject—for logic considers as its subject the syllogism, enunciation, predication, and things of that type.

But although the part of logic which is demonstrative is engaged in teaching about common intentionalities, the use of a demonstrative science does not consist in proceeding from common intentionalities to show anything about the things which are the subjects of the other sciences. But dialectics does this, for it goes from common intentions and argues to things that pertain to other sciences, whether they be proper or common things, but mainly common things. Thus, it argues that hatred is in the concupiscible appetite, because love is, on the ground that contraries are concerned with a same thing. Consequently, dialectics is concerned with common things not only because it treats concerning the common intentionalities of reason, which is common to all logic, but also because it argues about common characteristics of things. But any science that argues about the common characteristics of things must argue about the common principles, because the truth of the common principles is made manifest from the knowledge of common terms, as "being" and "non-being," "whole" and "part" and the like.

It is significant that he says, "and any science which might attempt," because first philosophy does not demonstrate the common principles, since they are absolutely indemonstrable, although some have unwittingly attempted to demonstrate them, as is stated in *Metaphysics* IV. Or else, because even though they cannot, strictly speaking, be demonstrated, the first philosopher attempts to uphold them in a way that is possible, namely, by contradicting those who deny them, appealing to things that must be conceded by them, though not to things which are more known.

It should also be noted that the first philosopher demonstrates them not only in this way, but also shows something about them as about subjects: for example, that "it is impossible for the mind to think their opposites," as is clear from *Metaphysics* IV. Therefore, although both the first philosopher and the dialectician debate about these first principles, yet one does so in one way and the other in another way. For the dialectician neither proceeds from demonstrative principles nor takes only one side of a contradiction but is open to both. For each side might happen to be probable or be upheld by probable statements, which the dialectician utilizes: and that is why he asks [his questions in terms of two alternatives]. But the demonstrator does not ask [in that way], because he is not open to opposites. And this is the difference between the two, as was laid down in the treatment of the syllogism, namely, in the beginning of the *Prior Analytics*. Therefore, first philosophy in treating common principles proceeds after the manner of a demonstration and not after the manner of a dialectical disputation.

Lecture 21
(77a36–77b15)

OF THE QUESTIONS, RESPONSES AND
DISPUTATIONS PECULIAR TO EACH SCIENCE

a36. If a syllogistic question

a42. only those questions will

b2. Of these questions the

b6. There is a limit, then

b8. If, then, in controversy

After showing how demonstrative sciences function in relation to common principles, the Philosopher now shows how they employ proper principles. And his treatment falls into two parts. In the first he shows that in each science there are questions, responses and disputations peculiar to each. In the second he shows how in each science there are deceptions, peculiar to each (77b16) [L. 22]. Concerning the first he does two things. First, he shows that in each science there are its own questions. Secondly, that each science employs the responses and disputations proper to it (77b6). Concerning the first he does two things. First, he shows that in each science there are questions peculiar to each. Secondly, what these are (77a42).

He shows the first (77a36) in the following way: A syllogistic question and a proposition which takes one definite side of a contradiction are the same as to content, but they have not the same function. For the answer which one gives to the question is made to serve as a proposition in some syllogism. But in each of the sciences, the propositions from which a syllogism is formed, are peculiar to it, for it has been shown that every science proceeds from things proper to it. Therefore, in each science there are questions peculiar to it. Hence not any random question is pertinent to geometry or to medicine or to some one of the other sciences.

However, it should be noted that questioning occurs one way in demonstrative sciences and another way in dialectics. For in dialectics not only the conclusion but also the premises are open to question; but in demonstrative sciences the demonstrator takes premises as *per se* known or proved by such principles. Hence, he asks only about the conclusion. And when he has demonstrated it, he uses it as a proposition to demonstrate some other conclusion.

Then (77a42) he explains which questions are peculiar to each science. First, insofar as they are taken as propositions from which the demonstrator proceeds. Secondly, when taken as conclusions (77b2).

He says therefore first (77a42) that geometric questions are ones from which something is demonstrated pertaining to matters of geometry or

pertaining to matters demonstrated from the principles of geometry—
for example, the ones from which something is demonstrated in optical
science, i.e., perspective, which proceeds from the principles of geometry.
And what is said of geometry applies to other sciences, namely, that a
proposition or question is peculiar to a science, if it is one from which a
demonstration in that science or in a subalternate science proceeds.

Then (77b2) he analyzes geometric questions insofar as they are conclusions, saying that solutions to geometric questions must be proved by
demonstrating their truth from geometric principles and from conclusions
already demonstrated by those principles. (For sometimes the proofs of
certain geometric demonstrations are not drawn from the first principles
of geometry, but from matters concluded from those first principles).
Hence when it is a matter of questions which are always conclusions in
demonstrative sciences, the proof can be obtained in the science itself, but
the proof of the principles cannot be drawn from geometry *qua* geometry.
The same also applies to other sciences. For no science proves its own
principles, as we have explained above. And he says, "from geometry *qua*
geometry," because it may happen that a science proves its own principles,
insofar as that science assumes the principles of another science, as a
geometer proves his own principles insofar as he assumes the role of first
philosopher, i.e., of metaphysician.

Then (77b6) he shows that each has its own responses and disputations.
First, that each has its own responses. Secondly, its own disputations
(77b8).

He says therefore (77b6) that from the foregoing it is clear that each
scientific knower does not ask just any question whatever. Hence it is
also clear that he will not answer just any random question but only
those which conform to his own science on the ground that a question and
its answer pertain to the same science.

Then (77b8) because disputations are concerned with a question and its
answer, he shows that there are disputations peculiar to each science, saying that if geometer disputes with geometer precisely as geometer, i.e., in
matters pertaining to geometry, then obviously the disputation goes well
so long as the disputation not only concerns a point of geometry but proceeds from the principles of geometry. But it does not go well, if the disputation in geometry does not proceed along these lines. For if someone
disputes with a geometer in matters alien to geometry, he does not argue,
i.e., does not convince, except accidentally: for example, if the dispute
concerns music, and the geometer accidentally happens to be a musician.
Hence it is clear that one should not dispute in geometry about matters
not geometric, because it will not be possible to judge by the principles
of that science whether the dispute went favorably or unfavorably: and
the same holds for other sciences.

Lecture 22
(77b16–78a21)

EACH SCIENCE HAS ITS OWN DECEPTIONS
AND AREAS OF IGNORANCE

After showing that each science has its own questions, responses and disputations, the Philosopher shows that each science has its own deceptions and errors. And his treatment is divided into two parts. In the first he raises certain questions. In the second he solves them (77b21).

Accordingly, he poses three questions, the first of which (77b16) is this: Since there are geometric questions, as we have shown, are there not also non-geometric ones? And what is asked of geometry can be asked of every other science.

Then (77b17) he poses the second question, namely: May questions which arise from ignorance bearing on some particular science be called geometric; and likewise for questions proper to any other science? (Questions arising from ignorance bearing on some science are those which ask about matters contrary to the truths of that science).

Then (77b19) he poses the third question, namely: In each science it is possible to be deceived by a syllogism which he calls "according to ignorance." But deception through a syllogism can occur in two ways: in one way when it fails as to form, not observing the correct form and mode of a syllogism. In another way, when it fails in matter, proceeding from the false. Now there is a difference between these two ways, because one that fails in matter is still a syllogism, since everything is observed that pertains to the form of a syllogism. But one that fails in form is not even a syllogism, but a paralogism, i.e., an apparent syllogism. In dialectics, deception can occur in both these ways. Hence in *Topics* I Aristotle speaks of the *contentious,* which is a syllogism, and of the one defective in form which is not a syllogism but an apparent one. Hence the question is this: Whether or not a syllogism of ignorance which is used in the demonstrative sciences is a syllogism based on matters opposed to the science, i.e., one that proceeds from false premises, or a paralogism, namely, one that fails in form, which is not a syllogism, but an apparent one?

Then (77b21) he solves these questions. First, he solves the first. Secondly, the second (77b23). Thirdly, the third (77b27).

He says therefore first (77b21) that a completely non-geometric question is one which is formed entirely from another art, say, music. For example, if one asks in geometry whether a tone could be divided into two equal semi-tones, such a question would be entirely non-geometric, because it concerns matters which do not pertain at all to geometry.

Then (77b23) he solves the second question, saying that a question about geometry, i.e., about matters pertinent to geometry, when a person is asked about something which is against the truth of geometry (for example, if the questions concerned parallels meeting, i.e., equidistant lines coming together), would be geometric in one sense and non-geometric in another. For just as *arrythmon,* i.e., without rhythm or sound, can be taken in two senses: in one sense for that which has no sound at all, as wool, and in another sense for that which does not give a good sound, as a poorly-sounding bell, so a question is called non-geometric in two ways. In one way, because it is completely alien to geometry, as a question about music. In another way, because it mistakenly holds something in the field of geometry, namely, because it holds something contrary to geometric truth. Therefore, the question about the convergence of parallel lines is non-geometric not in the first way, since it touches on a point of geometry, but in the second way, because it is mistaken about some point of geometry. Such ignorance, namely, which consists in wrongly using the principles of geometry is contrary to the truth of geometry.

Then (77b27) he solves the third question. And he does two things. First, he shows that in demonstrative sciences there is no paralogism in language. Secondly, nor apart from language (77b34).

Now although paralogism in language occurs in any of six sophistical ways, he takes one of them, namely, the paralogism which proceeds by way of equivocation, and shows that such a paralogism cannot occur in demonstrative sciences, being easier to detect. He says, therefore, that "formal paralogism," i.e., a syllogism defective in form, as in dialectics, "does not occur in the disciplines." For in a demonstrative syllogism the middle must always be the same in two ways, i.e., the same middle must be compared to the two extremes: for the major extreme is predicated universally of the middle, and the middle is predicated universally of the minor extreme, even though when it is predicated, we do not say "every," i.e., the sign of universality is not applied to the predicate.

But in the fallacy of equivocation the middle is the same according to vocal sound but not according to reality. Consequently, it escapes notice when it is proposed orally; but if it is demonstrated to the senses, the deception cannot succeed. For example, the name "circle" is said equivocally of a figure and a poem. Therefore, in reasons, i.e., in argumentations, the ambiguity may go unnoticed, i.e., deception is possible, as for example, if one were to say: "Every circle is a figure; Homer's poem is a circle: therefore, Homer's poem is a figure." But if a circle is drawn for someone to look at, there cannot be deception. For it will be obvious that songs are not circles.

Now just as in this case the deception is prevented by presenting the middle to the senses, so in demonstrative syllogisms, deception is prevented by the fact that the middle is shown to the intellect. For when something is defined, it is as plain to the intellect as something sensibly drawn is plain to the sight. Hence he says that in demonstrative syllogisms "these," i.e., things defined, "are seen by the intellect." But in demonstrations one always proceeds from definitions. Hence, deception through equivocation has no place there, much less through any of the other fallacies of language.

Then (77b34) he shows that in demonstrative syllogisms paralogism according to fallacy outside of language cannot occur. And because a paralogism of this kind is frequently challenged by citing an objection, through which the defect in the form of syllogizing is shown: therefore: First, he shows how an objection should be presented in demonstrative matters. Secondly, he shows that in demonstrative matters there cannot be paralogism according to fallacy outside the language (77b40).

He says therefore first (77b34) that "one should not bring an objection against it," i.e., against a paralogism by citing an inductive, i.e., particular, proposition. (For an induction proceeds from particulars as a syllogism proceeds from universals). The reason for this is that in demonstrative matters no proposition is admitted unless it is verified in the greater number of cases, for if it is not verified in the greater number it will not be in all. But a demonstrative syllogism must proceed from universals. Therefore, it is obvious that in demonstrative matters an objection must be universal, because the propositions and the objections must be the same. For in dialectical and in demonstrative matters that which is taken as an objection is later used as a proposition to syllogize against the one who proposed.

Then (77b40) he shows that in demonstrative matters deception through paralogisms outside of language does not occur. And just as above he showed that there was no paralogism in language in demonstrative matters by showing it for one, namely, for the paralogism which employs the fallacy of equivocation, so now he shows that in demonstrative matters there is not paralogism outside of language by showing it of the one which relies on fallacy of consequent. For it is obvious that paralogism in demonstrative matters cannot occur according to the other fallacies outside of language: not the fallacy according to accident, because demonstration proceeds from things that are *per se;* nor according to qualified and absolute, because the statements used in demonstrations are taken universally and always, and without qualification.

Therefore, he does two things in regard to his thesis. First, he shows how paralogism according to fallacy of consequent works. Secondly, that deception does not take place in this manner in demonstrative matters (78a5).

He says therefore first (77b40) that "illogical arguments do sometimes occur," i.e., do not observe syllogistic form, "because they admit both inherences," i.e., they accept a middle predicated affirmatively of each extreme, which is the same as syllogizing in the second figure but employing two affirmative propositions, thus committing the fallacy of consequent. This is what the philosopher Caeneus did in order to show that "fire is in multiple proportion," i.e., that fire is generated in greater quantity than was the body from which it is generated, on the ground that fire, being the most rarified of bodies, is generated from other bodies through rarefaction. Hence it is required that the matter of the previous body be spread out under larger dimensions when assuming the form of fire. To prove this he used the following syllogism: "Whatever is generated in multiplied proportion is generated quickly; but fire is generated quickly: therefore, fire is generated in multiplied proportion."

Then (78a5) he shows that deception arising from this form of reasoning does not occur in demonstrative sciences. In regard to this he does two things. First, he makes it clear that this form of syllogizing does not always end in deception, saying that according to this form of arguing there are cases when one cannot syllogize from the premises, namely, when the terms are not convertible—for it does not follow, if every man is an animal, that every animal is a man. But now and then there are cases when one can syllogize, namely, when the terms are convertible. For just as it follows that if a thing is a man, it is a rational mortal animal, so conversely, if a thing is a rational mortal animal, it is a man. However, it does not seem to follow syllogistically, because the due form of a syllogism is not observed.

Secondly (78a7), he shows that it is possible to syllogize in the above-mentioned manner without deception. And he shows this in three ways, the first of which is this: According to the above-mentioned manner of syllogizing, deception occurs because the consequence which was assumed convertible is not converted. But in this situation deception would not occur, if to the extent that the conclusion is true, so are the premises true: for there will then be no deception in converting. For if it is stated of Socrates that he is a man, therefore he is an animal; no deception or falsity follows: but it does if it is argued conversely that he is an animal, therefore he is a man.

But if the premise is true and the conclusion false, then deception occurs in converting. For example, if I were to say: "If an ass is a man, it is an animal; therefore, if it is an animal, it is a man." Consequently, if it were impossible to deduce the true from the false, and it were always necessary to deduce the true from the true, then it would be easy to analyze a conclusion into its principles without deception, because there would be no falsity if either of the premises were to be inferred from the conclusion. On this supposition the conclusion and premises would be converted of necessity as to truth. For just as the conclusion is true if the premise is true, so vice versa. For suppose that A is, and granting this, suppose that the same things follow as are known by me to be true, say B. Hence since both are true, I can then also infer A from B. And so, one reason why deception through fallacy of consequent does not occur in demonstrative sciences is that it is impossible in demonstrative sciences for the true to be syllogized from the false, as we have explained above.

Then (78a10) he gives the second reason. For in cases of convertible terms, deception through fallacy of consequent does not occur, because in those cases the consequent is converted. Now the things which are used in mathematical, i.e., in demonstrative sciences, are for the most part convertible, because these sciences do not admit as a middle anything predicated *per accidens,* but only definitions which are principles of demonstration, as we have explained. And this is their point of difference from the statements in dialogues, i.e., in dialectical syllogisms, in which accidens are frequently admitted.

Then (78a13) he gives the third reason and it is this: In demonstrative sciences there are determinate principles from which one proceeds to the conclusions. Hence it is possible to return from the conclusions to the principles as from something determinate to something determinate. That demonstrations do proceed from determinate principles he shows by the fact that "demonstrations are not increased by middles," i.e., in demonstrations one does not use a series of different middle terms to demonstrate one conclusion. (This, of course, is to be understood of demonstrations *propter quid,* of which he is speaking). For of one effect there can be but one sole cause why it is.

But although demonstrations are not increased by using several middles of demonstration, nevertheless they are increased in two ways: in one way, "by assuming one after another," i.e., subsuming one middle under another, say B under A, C under B, D under C, and so on. For example, when "having three angles equal to two right angles" is proved of triangle on the ground that it is a figure having an external angle equal to the two opposite interior angles, and is then proved of isosceles on the ground that it is a triangle. Another way they are increased is laterally, as when A is proved of C and of E. For example, "Every quantified number is either finite or infinite." Let A be this predicate, i.e., "to be finite or infinite." But an odd number is a quantified number. Let B represent "quantified number," and C, "odd number." It follows therefore, that A (to be finite or infinite) is predicated of C (odd number), i.e., that an odd number is either a finite or an infinite number. And he says that it is possible along the same lines to conclude concerning even number, and this through the same middle.

The passage (78a13), which begins, "A science expands," can be introduced in another way. Since he had just said that in demonstrative matters, definitions are used for middles, and since there is one sole definition of one thing, it follows that it is not through middles that demonstrations are increased.

Lecture 23
(78a22–b13)

HOW DEMONSTRATIONS "QUIA" AND "PROPTER QUID" DIFFER IN A SAME SCIENCE. DEMONSTRATION "QUIA" THROUGH AN EFFECT

a22. Knowledge of the fact
a30. Thus you might prove
a39. The major and the middle

b3. Another example is the inference
b10. Again in cases where the cause

After determining about demonstration *propter quid*, the Philosopher here shows the difference between demonstration *quia* and demonstration *propter quid*. And he does two things about this. First, he shows how they differ in the same science. Secondly, in diverse sciences (78b33) [L. 25]. Concerning the first he does two things. First, he states the twofold difference between the two in the same science. Secondly, he clarifies this with examples (78a30).

He says therefore first (78a22) that, as said above, demonstration is a syllogism causing scientific knowledge and proceeds from the causes both first and immediate of a thing. Now this is to be understood as referring to demonstration *propter quid*. But there is a difference between knowing *that* a thing is so and *why* it is so. Therefore, since demonstration is a syllogism causing scientific knowledge, as has been said, it is necessary that a demonstration *quia* which makes one know that a thing is so should differ from the demonstration *propter quid* which makes one know why. Consequently, this difference must be considered first in the same science and later in sciences that are diverse.

In one and the same science each of the above is said to differ in regard to the two things required for demonstration in the strict sense—which causes knowledge of the why—namely, that it be from *causes* and from *immediate* causes. Hence one way that scientific knowledge *quia* differs from *propter quid* is that it is the former if the syllogism is not through immediate principles but through mediate ones. For in that case the first cause will not be employed, whereas science *propter quid* is according to the first cause; consequently, the former will not be science *propter quid*.

It differs in another way, because it is science *quia* when the syllogism, although not through middles, i.e., mediate, but through immediate things, is not through the cause but through "convertence," i.e., through effects convertible and immediate. Hence a demonstration of this kind is through the better known, namely, to us; otherwise it would not effect scientific knowledge. For we do not reach a knowledge of the unknown except through something better known. However in the case of two things equally predicable, i.e., convertible, one of which is the cause and the other the effect, there is nothing to preclude that now and then the better known will not be the cause but the effect. For sometimes the effect is better known than the cause both in respect to us and according to sense-perception, although absolutely and according to nature the cause is the better known. Consequently, through an effect better known than the cause there can be demonstration which does not engender *propter quid* knowledge but only *quia*.

Then (78a30) he clarifies these differences by examples. And this is divided into two parts. In the first he develops an example of the demonstration *quia* which is through an effect. In the second of demonstration *quia* which is through a mediate cause (78b13) [L. 24]. The first is divided into two parts. In the first he gives an example of a syllogism which is through a convertible effect. In the second of a syllogism through a non-convertible effect (78b10). The first is divided into two parts according to the two examples he gives, the second of which begins at (78b3). Concerning the first he does two things. First, he gives an example of demonstration *quia* which is through an effect. Secondly, he states when it can be converted into a demonstration *propter quid* (78a39).

He says therefore first (78a30) that demonstration *quia* is through an effect if one concludes for example that the planets are near because they do not twinkle. For non-twinkling is not the cause why the planets are near, but vice versa: for the planets do not twinkle because they are near. For the fixed stars twinkle because in gazing at them the sight is beclouded on account of the distance. Therefore, the syllogism might be formed in the following way: "Whatever does not twinkle is near; but the planets do not twinkle: therefore, they are near." Here we let C be the planets, i.e., let "planets" be the minor extreme, and let B consist in not twinkling, and A "to be near" be the major extreme. Then the proposition, "Every C is B," is true, namely, the planets do not twinkle. Also it is true that "Every B is A," i.e., every star that does not twinkle is near. However, the truth of such a proposition must be obtained through induction or through sense perception, because the effect here is better known than the cause. And so, the conclusion, "Every C is A," follows. In this way, then, it has been demonstrated that the planets, i.e., the wandering stars, are near. Consequently, this syllogism is not *propter quid* but *quia*. For it is not because they do not twinkle that planets are near but rather, because they are near, they do not twinkle.

Then (78a39) he teaches how a demonstration *quia* is changed to a demonstration *propter quid*. And he says that "it is possible to demonstrate the one through the other," i.e., to demonstrate that they do not twinkle, because they are near. Then the demonstration will be *propter quid*. Thus let C be the wanderers, i.e., let "wandering star" be the minor extreme; let B consist in being near, i.e., let "to be near," which was the major extreme above, be the middle term; and let A consist in not twinkling, i.e., let "not to twinkle," which above was the middle term, now be the major term. Therefore, B is in C, i.e., "Every planet is near"; and A is in B, i.e., "Any planet which is near does not twinkle." Wherefore, it follows that A is in C, i.e., "A planet does not twinkle." In this way we have a syllogism *propter quid,* since it rests on the first and immediate cause.

Then (78b3) he presents another example of this, saying that "in this way" (i.e., by means of a demonstration *quia*), "one demonstrates that the moon is round because of its phases," according to which it waxes and wanes every month. They argue thus: "Everything which waxes thus circularly is circular; but the moon waxes thus: therefore, it is circular." "Put in this form it is a syllogism demonstrating *quia*. But if the middle be interchanged," i.e., if "circular" be made the middle term and "waxes" the major term, "it becomes a demonstration *propter quid*." For the moon is not circular because it waxes in that way, but because it is circular it undergoes such phases. Therefore, let C be "the moon," i.e., the minor extreme; let "waxing" be A, i.e., the major extreme, and let "circular" be B, the middle term. This will be the situation in the syllogism *propter quid*.

Then (78b10) he shows that a demonstration through a non-convertible effect is *quia*. He says, therefore, that even in those syllogisms in which the middles are not converted with the extremes, and in which an effect rather than a cause is taken as the middle better known in reference to us, even in those cases the demonstration is *quia* and not *propter quid*. If the middle be such that it can be converted with the major extreme and it exceeds the minor, then obviously it is a fitting syllogism; for example, if one proves that Venus is near because it does not twinkle. On the other hand, if the minor exceeded the middle, it would not be a fitting syllogism: for one cannot conclude universally of stars that they are near because they do not twinkle. Quite the contrary is true in comparison to the major term: for if the middle is in less things than is the major term, the syllogism is fitting, as when it is proved that someone has a sensible soul on the ground that he is capable of progressive local motion. But if it is in more, than the syllogism is not fitting, for from an effect which can proceed from several causes, one of them cannot be concluded. Thus, one cannot conclude from a rapid pulse that he has a fever.

Lecture 24
(78b13–34)

HOW THERE IS DEMONSTRATION "QUIA" THROUGH THINGS NOT IMMEDIATELY CONNECTED

b13. This also occurs when

b14. For example, the question

b24. A syllogism with this kind

b27. Such causes are like

b32. Thus, then, do the syllogism

After clarifying with examples how there is demonstration *quia* through effect, the Philosopher here shows how there is demonstration *quia* through things not immediately connected. First, he amplifies his proposition. Secondly, he shows how the middles relate themselves to the conclusions in this type of demonstration (78b27). Concerning the first he does three things. First, he states his intention. Secondly, he clarifies it with examples (78b14). Thirdly, he puts it in syllogistic form (78b24).

He says therefore first (78b13) that there is demonstration *quia* and not *propter quid* not only in those matters that are proved through an effect but also "in matters in which the middle is set outside." Now a middle is said to be set outside when it is diverse from the major term, as in negative syllogisms; or a middle is said to be set outside when it is outside the genus as being something more common and not convertible with the major term. That something cannot be demonstrated *propter quid* through such a middle he proves on the ground that demonstration *propter quid* is through a cause. But the middle in question is not, properly speaking, a cause.

Then (78b14) he clarifies what he had said with an example, saying that if someone attempted to prove that a wall does not breathe because it is not an animal, he would not be demonstrating *propter quid* or giving the cause. Because if the fact of not being an animal were the cause of not breathing, it would be required that being an animal would be the cause of breathing—which is false. For there are many animals which do not breathe. For it is required, if a negation is the cause of a negation, that the affirmation be the cause of the affirmation, as the fact of not being warm and cold in due measure is the cause of someone's not getting well, and the fact of being warm and cold in due measure is the cause of someone's getting well. The converse is also true, namely, that if an affirmation is the cause of an affirmation, the negation is the cause of the negation. But this does not occur in the case at hand, because the affirmation is not the cause of an affirmation, since not every animal breathes.

77

Then (78b24) he arranges the aforesaid example in syllogistic form and says that it should be arranged in the second figure. And this is so because in the first figure there cannot be a negative conclusion such that the major would be affirmative, as our example requires. For "to breathe," which is the major extreme, must be joined with "animal," which is the middle term, according to affirmation. But "wall," which is the minor extreme, must be joined with "animal," which is the middle, according to negation. Consequently, the major will be affirmative and the minor negative. But such a thing never occurs in the first figure, but only in the second.

Let "animal," then, be A, i.e., the middle term, "breathe" be B, i.e., the major extreme, and "wall" be C, i.e., the minor extreme. It therefore follows that A is in every B, because everything that breathes is an animal; but A is in no C, because no wall is an animal. Hence it follows that B, too, is in no C, i.e., that no wall breathes. Furthermore, if the most proximate middle were used, it would be demonstration *propter quid:* for example, if it were shown that a wall does not breathe because it does not have lungs. For whatever has lungs breathes, and conversely.

Then (78b27) he shows how these middles are related to the conclusion, saying that such far-away causes are compared to what they explain as being too remote, because they go beyond the pale of the conclusion to be proved. Furthermore, a middle of this sort happens to assign what is far-fetched, as in Anacharsis' proof that there are no flutists among the Scythians because there are no vines there. For this is quite a far-fetched middle. A nearer one would be that they have no wine, and nearer still, that they do not drink wine, from which follows a merry heart which moves one to sing—if fluting is taken to mean singing. Or it might be better to say that fluting is not taken for just any singing but for the song of the grape harvesters, called "celeuma."

Then (78b32) he summarizes what he had said and declares that these are the differences between the syllogism *quia* and the syllogism *propter quid* in the same science, "and according to the position of the same," i.e., of those that have the same order. This he says to exclude what he will discuss later, namely, that one science is under another.

Lecture 25
(78b34–79a16)

HOW DEMONSTRATION "QUIA" DIFFERS FROM DEMONSTRATION "PROPTER QUID" WHEN THE FORMER PERTAINS TO ONE SCIENCE AND THE LATTER TO ANOTHER

b34. But there is another way

b35. This occurs in the case

a1. (Some of these sciences

a3. Here it is the business

a10. As optics is related

a13. Many sciences not standing

After showing how demonstration *quia* differs from demonstration *propter quid* in the same science, the Philosopher shows how they differ in sciences that are diverse. And he does two things:

First, he states his proposition, saying (78b34) that in a way other than the above the *propter quid* differs from the *quia* due to the fact that they are considered in diverse sciences, i.e., that the *propter quid* pertains to one science and the *quia* to another.

Secondly (78b34) he elucidates his proposition. First, he elucidates it in sciences one of which is under the other. Secondly, in sciences one of which is not under the other (79a13). Concerning the first he does two things. First, he shows how those sciences are related, one of which is under the other and to one of which pertains the *quia* and to the other the *propter quid*. Secondly, he shows how in these sciences the *quia* pertains to one and the *propter quid* to the other (79a3). Concerning the first he does two things. First, he shows how such sciences relate to one another as to order. Secondly, how they relate to one another as to agreement (79a1).

He says therefore first (78b35) that these sciences (i.e., to one of which pertains *quia* and to the other *propter quid*) are the ones so related that one is under the other. But this occurs in two ways: in one way, when the subject of one science is a species of the subject of the higher science, as animal is a species of natural body—consequently, the science of animals is under natural science; in another way, when the subject of the lower science is not a species of the subject of the higher science but is compared to the latter as material to formal. An example of this latter way of one science being under another is the way "specular," i.e., optics, is under geometry. For geometry is concerned with lines and other magnitudes, whereas optics is concerned with a line determined to matter, i.e., the visual line. Now the visual line is not, strictly speaking, a species of line any more than wooden triangle is a species of triangle: for wooden is not a difference in respect to triangle. In like manner mechanical engineering, i.e., the science of making machines, is related to stereometry, i.e., the science of measuring bodies. This science is said to be under the other as applying the formal to the material. For the measures of bodies absolutely are compared to the measures of wood and other material required for machines as the application of the formal to the material. In like manner, harmonics, i.e., music, is related to arithmetic: for music applies formal number, which arithmetic considers, to matter, i.e., to sounds. And the same is true of "appearance," i.e., nautical science (which considers the signs indicative of calm or storm), as compared to astronomy, which considers the motions and positions of the stars.

Then (79a1) he shows how the aforesaid sciences relate to one another in point of agreement. And he says that these sciences are almost mutually univocal. And he says, "almost," because they agree in the name of their genus and not in the name of their species. Thus, all the sciences mentioned above are called mathematical: some, indeed, because they are concerned with a subject which is abstracted from matter, as geometry and arithmetic, which are absolutely mathematical; but others are so through applying mathematical principles to material things, as astronomy is called mathematical and as nautical science is. Similarly, harmonics, i.e., music, is called mathematical and so is acoustics, i.e., practical music, which knows sounds through experience based on hearing. Or it might be said that they are univocal because they also agree in the name of their species, for we speak of nautical astronomy as astronomy and of practical music as music. But because this is not so in all but only in some, he says "almost."

Then (79a3) he shows how in these sciences the *quia* pertains to the one science and the *propter quid* to the other. In regard to this there are two points. First, he shows how those sciences which contain others under them state the *propter quid*. Secondly, how sciences which are contained under another one state the *propter quid* of some others (79a10).

One should note, therefore, with respect to the first point that in all the above-mentioned sciences, the ones which are contained under others apply mathematical principles to sensible things, while the ones which contain others under them are more mathematical. Accordingly, the Philosopher first of all says (79a3) that to know the *quia* pertains to the sensible, i.e., to the lower sciences, which make application to sensible things; but to know the *propter quid* pertains to the mathematical, i.e., to those sciences whose principles are not applied to sensible things. For these latter sciences are concerned with demonstrating matters which are accepted as causes in the lower sciences.

But because someone might suppose that whoever knows the *propter quid* also necessarily knows the *quia*, he dismisses this, saying that very frequently those who know the *propter quid* do not know the *quia*. And he gives as an example of this those who, when considering the universal often take no account of the singulars precisely because their speculation does not consider them: thus, one who knows that every mule is sterile, does not know this of the one he does not consider. In like manner, a mathematician who demonstrates *propter quid*, now and then does not know the *quia*, because he does not apply the principles of the higher sciences to matters demonstrated in the lower science.

And because he had said that it belongs to mathematics to know the *propter quid*, he proposes to indicate which genus of cause is used by mathematics. Hence he says that those sciences which receive the *propter quid* from mathematics "are something else," i.e., they differ from the mathematical according to subject, i.e., insofar as they make application to matter. Hence these latter "use forms," i.e., formal principles, which they receive from mathematics: "for the mathematical sciences concern forms." For their considerations do not bear on the subject, i.e., on matter, because although the items which geometry considers exist in matter, for example, the line, plane and so on, nevertheless geometry does not consider them precisely as they are in matter, but as abstracted. For those things that are in matter according to existence, geometry abstracts from matter according to consideration. Conversely, the sciences subalternated to it accept those things which were considered in the abstract by geometry and apply them to matter. Hence it is plain that it is according to the formal cause that geometry states the *propter quid* in those sciences.

Then (79a10) he shows that even the subalternated sciences state the *propter quid*, not of its subalternating science but of some other science. Thus, optics is subalternated to geometry, so that if we compare the one with the other, optics states the *quia* and geometry the *propter quid*. But just as optics is subalternated to geometry, so the science of the rainbow is subalternated to optics, for it applies to a determinate matter the principles which optics hands down absolutely. Hence it belongs to the naturalist who treats of the rainbow to know the *quia*, but to the expert in optics to know the *propter quid*. For the naturalist says that the cause of the rainbow is the convergence of a visual line at a cloud arranged in some relation to the sun; but the *propter quid* he takes from optics.

Then (79a13) he shows how *quia* and *propter quid* differ among sciences that are diverse but not subalternate. And he says that many sciences which are not subalternate are nevertheless related, i.e., in such a way that one states the *quia* and the other the *propter quid*. This is true of medicine and geometry. For the subject of medicine is not subsumed under the subject of geometry as the subject of optics is. Nevertheless, the principles of geometry are applicable to certain conclusions reached in medicine: for example, it belongs to the man of medicine who observes it to know *quia* that circular wounds heal rather slowly; but to know the *propter quid* belongs to the geometer, whose business it is to know that a circle is a figure without corners. Hence the edges of a circular wound are not close enough to each other to allow them to be easily joined. It should also be noted that this difference of *quia* and

propter quid between sciences that are diverse is contained under one of
the modes previously discussed, namely, when the demonstration is
made through a remote cause.

Lecture 26
(79a17–b22)

DEMONSTRATIVE SYLLOGISMS BEST MADE
IN THE FIRST FIGURE.
ON MEDIATE AND IMMEDIATE
NEGATIVE PROPOSITIONS

a17. Of all the figures
a23. Thirdly, the first is
a30. Finally, the first figure
a33. Just as an attribute

a36. It follows that if either
b5. That the genus of A
b12. If on the other hand
b21. Hence it is clear

After determining about the material of the syllogism, the Philosopher
here determines about its form, showing in which figure chiefly the
demonstrative syllogism is formed. His treatment is divided into two
parts. In the first he shows that the demonstrative syllogism is formed
first and foremost in the first figure. In the second, because it is possible
in the first figure to proceed from negatives and because a demonstration
must proceed from things immediate, he shows how a negative proposition happens to be immediate (79a33).

He shows the first with three reasons, the first of which (79a17) is this:
In whatever figure the *propter quid* syllogism is best made, that figure is
the best for causing scientific knowledge and for that reason is most suitable for demonstrations, since demonstration is a syllogism which causes
scientific knowledge. But a syllogism *propter quid* is best made in the
first figure, and this is evidenced by the fact that the mathematical sciences of arithmetic and geometry and all other sciences which demonstrate *propter quid* employ the first figure in most cases. Therefore, the
first figure is the one which first and foremost causes scientific knowledge
and is most suitable for demonstrations.

But the reason why demonstration *propter quid* is best made in the
first figure is this: in the first figure the middle term is both subjected
to the major extreme, which is the predicate of the conclusion, and
predicated of the minor extreme, which is the subject of the conclusion.
Now in demonstrations *propter quid* the middle must be the cause of
the proper attribute which is predicated of the subject in the conclusion.
Furthermore, one of the modes of "saying per se" is when the subject is
the cause of the predicate, as "being butchered, he died," as has been

explained above; and this is verified in the first figure in which the middle is subject to the major extreme, as has been said.

The second reason (79a23) is this: the *quod quid est* [i.e., the definition as signifying the essence] plays a most important role in demonstrative sciences because, as has been said, a definition is either the principle of a demonstration or the conclusion or a demonstration differing in the position of its terms. Now when it is a question of formulating a definition the first figure alone is suitable. For that is the only figure in which a universal affirmative is concluded, which alone produces science of the *quod quid est*. For the *quod quid est* is known through an affirmation. Furthermore, the definition is predicated affirmatively and universally of the defined: for it is not some man that is a two-legged animal, but every man. Therefore, the first figure is foremost in causing scientific knowledge and is best accommodated to demonstrations.

Then (79a30) he gives the third reason which is this: For purposes of demonstration the other figures need the first, but the first does not need them. Therefore, the first figure is better equipped for causing scientific knowledge than the others. That the others need the first is evidenced by the fact that if complete scientific knowledge is to be had, the mediate propositions present in demonstrations must be reduced to immediate ones. But this reduction is made in two ways, namely, by condensing middles [i.e., by inserting fresh middles, the movement proceeding from the extremes toward the middle first employed] and by expanding outwards [i.e., by going from the middle toward the remote extreme].

It is done by condensing when the middle actually employed is joined mediately to each of the extremes or only to the minor extreme. Hence when other middles are introduced between the first middle and the extremes, the middles, as it were, close in. Thus, if someone first says, "Every E is C," [minor], "Every C is A," [major], and then a middle, say D, is introduced between C and E, and a middle B between C and A. It is done by expanding when the middle is immediate to the minor extreme and mediate to the major: for then it is necessary to introduce several other middles more general than the middle first taken. Thus, if one says, "Every E is D," "Every D is A," and the later other middles more general than D are introduced [between D and A].**

Now these processes of condensing and expanding can be performed

---

** Let A be most universal, B less universal, ... and E least universal, according to the diagram on the left:

		First Case — Condensing		
———	A			
———	B	#1 $c<a \rightarrow c<B<a$	#2	$b<a \rightarrow b<a$
———	C	$e<c \rightarrow e<D<c$		$e<b \rightarrow e<D<C<b$
———	D	Second Case — Expanding		
——	E	$d<a \rightarrow d<C<B<a$		
		$e<d \rightarrow e<d$		

only in the first figure, both because the first figure is the only one which yields a universal affirmative conclusion, and because it is only in the first figure that the middle lies between both extremes. For in the second figure the middle lies outside the extremes, as being predicated of them; in the third figure [the middle] is below each of the extremes, as being subjected to them.

Then (79a33) he teaches how a negative proposition can be immediate. In regard to this he does two things.

First (79a33), he states his intention, saying that "just as it is possible for every A to be in B atomically," i.e., immediately, "so too not to be," i.e., so too it is possible for a proposition signifying that A is not in B to be immediate. Then he goes on to explain what it is to be or not to be atomically, namely, when the affirmation or negation does not have a middle through which it might be proved.

Secondly (79a36), he elucidates his proposition. In regard to this he does two things. First, he shows when a negative proposition is mediate. Secondly, when immediate (79b12). Concerning the first he does two things. First, he clarifies his proposition. Secondly, he proves something he had presupposed (79b5).

He says therefore first (79a36), that when A, i.e., the major term, or B, i.e., the minor term, is in some whole as a species in its genus, or both are under diverse genera or predicaments, it does not occur that A is not in B first, i.e., it does not occur that this proposition, "No B is A," is immediate. First, then, he manifests this when A is in some whole, say in C, and B is in no whole. For example, if A is "man," C is "substance," and B is "quantity," it is possible to form a syllogism to prove that A is in no B on the ground that C is in every A and in no B. Thus we get a syllogism in the second figure:

> Every man is a substance;
> No quantity is a substance:
> Therefore, no quantity is a man.

In like manner, if B, i.e., the minor term, is in some whole, say D, but A is not in that whole, it is possible to syllogize that A is in no B. For example if A is "substance," B "line," and D "quantity," we get a syllogism in the first figure:

> No quantity is a substance;
> Every line is a quantity;
> Therefore, no line is a substance.

In the same way, a negative conclusion could be demonstrated if either is in some whole. For example, if A is "line," C "quantity," B "whiteness," and D "quality," it is possible to form a syllogism in the first and in the second figure. In the second figure thus:

> Every line is a quantity;
> No whiteness is a quantity:

Therefore, no whiteness is a line.
And in the first figure thus:
> No quality is a line;
> Every whiteness is a quality:
> Therefore, no whiteness is a line.

We should understand, however, that a negative proposition is mediate, when both terms exist in some whole which is not the same but different for each. For if they are in the same whole, the proposition will be immediate, as "No rational being is irrational," or "No biped is a quadruped."

Then (79b5) he explains something he had presupposed, namely, "on condition that one of the extremes exist in some whole and that the other be not in the same," saying that it is "clear from the 'orderings' of the various predicaments, which are" not mutually interchangeable. In other words, because that which is in one predicament is not in another, it is plain that B happens not to be in the whole in which A is, or vice versa, because one of the terms happens to be taken from one predicament in which the other is not found. Thus, let one ordering of the predicaments be ACD, say the predicament of substance, and another ordering be BEF, say the predicament of quantity. Then if none of those in the ordering ACD be predicated of none in the ordering BEF, while A is in P as in that most general item which is the principle of the whole first ordering, it is plain that B is not in P, because then the orderings, i.e., the predicaments, would be interchanged. Similarly, if B is in some whole, say in E, it is plain that A is not in E.

Then (79b12) he indicates how a negative proposition may be immediate, saying that "if neither is in some whole," i.e., neither A nor B, and A is not in B, it is necessary that this proposition, "No B is A," be immediate. Because if a middle were taken to syllogize it, then one of them would have to be in some whole, for the syllogism would have to be made either in the first figure or in the second, since in the third figure a universal negative cannot be concluded, as is required for an immediate proposition. However, if it is made in the first, B would have to be in some whole, because B is the minor extreme, and in the first figure the minor proposition must always be affirmative. For a syllogism with the major affirmative and the minor negative cannot be formed in the first figure.

But if it be in the second figure, either may, i.e., A or B, may be in a whole, because in the second figure the first proposition may be negative in some moods and the minor in other moods. Of course it is never permitted, neither in the first nor the second, to have both propositions negative. And so it is required that when either proposition is affirmative, one of the extremes must be in some whole. Thus it is clear that a negative proposition is immediate, when neither of its terms is in some whole. This does not mean, however, that although neither is in some whole, a middle could be found to conclude it, namely, if one were to take a convertible middle, because it is necessary that such a middle be prior and better known. And this is either the genus itself or the definition, which is not without a genus.

Then (79b21) he concludes and summarizes what has been said. Here the text is sufficiently clear.

Lecture 27
(79b23–80a8)

HOW IGNORANCE OR DECEPTION BEARING ON FIRST AND IMMEDIATE THINGS CAN BE INDUCED BY SYLLOGISM AND LEAD ONE TO SUPPOSE SOMETHING TO BE WHICH IS NOT

b23. Ignorance—defined not as   b34. C may quite well
b28. The error, however, that   b40. On the other hand
b31. Now, two cases are   a6. Error of attribution

After determining about the demonstrative syllogism through which science is acquired, the Philosopher here determines concerning the syllogism through which ignorance or deception is produced in us. In regard to this he does two things. First, he shows what sort of ignorance can be induced by a syllogism. Secondly, he shows the mode in which such a syllogism proceeds (79b28).

He distinguishes therefore first (79b23) a twofold ignorance, one of which is negative and the other a positive state. There is ignorance in a negative way, when a man has no scientific knowledge at all about a thing. This ignorance consists in not attaining, as the Philosopher says in *Metaphysics* IX, and is exemplified in a peasant who knows absolutely nothing about whether a triangle has three angles equal to two right angles. But ignorance is present as a positive state, when one does have a definite opinion but it is unsound. For example, when he falsely thinks something about a thing, either because he thinks something to be which is not, or something not to be which is. And this ignorance is the same as error.

Now the first ignorance is not produced by a syllogism, but the second can be, and then it is called deception. Such ignorance or deception can concern two things: first, those things which are first and immediate principles, namely, when a person opines things opposed to the principles. And although he cannot so opine inwardly in the mind, as has been stated above, because these things do not fall under apprehension, nevertheless he can contradict them orally and according to a false imagination, as is said in *Metaphysics* IV of some who deny the principles. Secondly, it might be concerned with conclusions which are not first and immediate. Furthermore, the first of these ignorances or deceptions is opposed to the knowledge which is understanding, and the second to the knowledge which is science.

Each of these states of ignorance, whether concerned with things that are first or things not first, can befall a man in two ways: first, straightway, when independently of any process of reasoning he thinks a falsehood by affirming or denying. In another way, when he is brought to his opinion through some syllogized reason. Hence the Philosopher says in *Metaphysics* IV that some contradict the principles as though persuaded by reasons; but others, not as though persuaded by reasons, but through lack of erudition or through wilfullness which demands to have a demonstration in all matters.

Then (79b28) he shows how these ignorances are caused. First, how the ignorance produced by a syllogism is caused. Secondly, how ignorance befalls a man without syllogizing (81a38) [L. 30]. Concerning the first he does two things. First, he states how ignorance in regard to first and immediate principles is engendered by a syllogism. Secondly, how it is caused in regard to things not first and immediate (80b17) [L. 29]. Concerning the first he does two things. First, he states how the ignorance is caused whereby that which is not is believed to be. Secondly, that whereby that which is is believed not to be (80a8) [L. 28]. Regarding the first he does three things. First, he states how the aforesaid ignorance is generally caused. Secondly, he assigns its various possible forms (79b31). Thirdly, he answers a tacit question (80a6).

He says therefore first (79b28) that the deception according to false opinion which above was said to occur straightway is simple, i.e., is engendered in only one way. For it is not caused by a reason, which might vary, but by the lack of a reason which [lack] is not diversified into various modes each having its own characteristics any more than other negations are.

Yet because false reasons can be various and many, this ignorance, when it is engendered by a syllogism can occur in many ways according to the several ways in which a syllogism can be false. The common way is set forth when he says, "Let A be in no B individually" (79b29), i.e., let this proposition be immediately true, "No B is A." For two negations are stated in the place of one—for instance if we should say, "No quality is a substance"—according to the doctrine on immediate negative propositions presented above. Therefore, if someone were to conclude the opposite of this with a syllogism, taking C as a middle to show that every B is A, there will be a deception through syllogism.

Then (79b31) he shows in how many ways this can vary. And first of
all it should be noted that a false conclusion is not concluded except when
the syllogism is false. But a syllogism can be false in two ways: first, because it lacks syllogistic form, in which case it is not a syllogism but
appears to be one. In a second way, because it employs false propositions,
in which case it is a syllogism as to form, but it is a false one because of
the false propositions used. Therefore, in a dialectical disputation, which
bears on probables, use could be made of both types of false syllogism,
because such a disputation proceeds from common premises. Consequently, error can arise in it both as regards the matter employed, which
is common, and also as regards the form, which is common.

But in a demonstrative disputation, which bears on necessary things,
the type of syllogism used is the one which could be false only on account
of the matter, because as it is stated in *Topics* I, a paralogism in a given
discipline proceeds from things proper to the discipline, but not from true
things. Hence, since syllogistic form must be counted among the common
things, paralogism within a discipline—which is the matter under discussion—is not defective in form but only in matter, and furthermore
in regard to proper and not in regard to common things. And so: First,
he tells how such a syllogism might proceed from two false premises.
Secondly, how it might proceed from one or the other premise being
false (79b40). But since the first can occur in two ways, namely, the false
proposition might be contrary to the true or contradictory to it, therefore:
First, he shows how such a syllogism might proceed from two false statements that are contrary to true statements. Secondly, how a contradiction
is accepted (79b34).

First, then (79b30) he says that in a syllogism causing deception it
sometimes happens that both premises are false, and sometimes only one.
Let us take the case of two false premises, each contrary to what is true.
For example, suppose that C is so related to A and to B, that no C is A
and no B is C. Now if we take the contraries of these, namely, that every
C is A and every B is C, these two propositions will be completely false.
For example, if I should say: "Every quality is a substance; every quan-
tity is a quality: therefore, every quantity is a substance."

Then (79b34) he shows how both premises can be false and not contrary, but contradictory, to what is true. For example, if C is so related
to A and to B, that it is neither contained totally under A nor is universally in B. Thus one might take C as "perfect" or "actual being," and
proceed in the following way: "Every perfect thing is a substance; every
quantity is perfect: therefore, every quantity is a substance. Now although
both are false, they are not entirely so, for their contradictories are true,
namely, "Some perfect things are not substances," and "Some quantity is
not perfect"; but their contraries are false, namely, "No perfect thing
is a substance," and "No quantity is perfect."

But that C is not in B universally (i.e., that the statement, "Every quantity is perfect," which was the minor, is not true), i.e., that "Every B is C," is not true he proves by the fact that B cannot be contained under any whole that might be predicated universally of it. And this is so because the proposition, "No B is A," was said to be immediate, which means that A is universally not in B. But, as has been stated above, those negative propositions are immediate, neither of whose terms is under a whole.

Nevertheless, this proof does not seem sufficient, because something can be predicated universally even of that which is not under some whole as a species under a genus. For the genus and the difference are not the only things predicated universally, but a property is too. But it must be said that although the proof in question is not efficacious generally speaking, it is in this case. Because, as it is stated in *Topics* I, a paralogism within a discipline—with which we are concerned here—proceeds from items that accord with the discipline. Hence he intends to use such middles as a demonstrator uses. But the middle of a demonstration is the definition, as has been stated above. Therefore, even in the syllogism of which he is speaking, he intends to use a definition as the middle. Now a definition contains the genus and difference. Hence that which is predicated universally in this syllogism should contain that in which the subject is, as in a whole.

Again, that A is not in C universally, i.e., that the statement, "Every perfect thing is a substance," is not universally true is proved by the fact that it is not required of every universal that it be universally in all things that are: because no predicament is predicated of things contained under another predicament nor universally predicated of those items that commonly follow upon being, namely, act and potency, perfect and imperfect, prior and posterior, and the like.

Then (79b40) he shows how the aforesaid syllogism might proceed from one true and one false. And he says that in the aforesaid syllogism we might take one true, i.e., the major, which is AC, and the other false, namely, the minor, which is BC. That the minor proposition, which is BC, is always the false one he proves, as he did above, on the ground that B is in no C as in a whole. But that this proposition AC could be true, while the other is false he proves in terms. Let A be in B and in C individually, i.e., immediately, as a genus in its species; for example, as color is to whiteness and blackness. Now under these conditions it is obvious that the major will be true, namely, "Every C is A," for example, "Every whiteness is a color," and the minor false, namely, "Every blackness is whiteness": for when something is predicated "first" of several, none of the several is predicated of any other of them. For the first predication of a genus is of species which are opposite.

Here, too, a doubt arises, because from the terms used here, not a

false but a true conclusion follows. For the conclusion will be that A is
in B, it having also been assumed that it is in B individually. But it must
be answered that this example was used merely to illustrate how the
major could be true and the minor false; although it is of no use in a case
where a false conclusion is sought. Hence the Philosopher at once adds,
"It is equally the case of AC if not atomic." However, we could take
terms such that A is not in B either individually or in any way, but is
rather immediately removed from B. Neither is it necessary that it be in
C individually, because it is not necessary that a demonstrator employ
only immediate propositions: for he may use ones which are supported
by immediate propositions. We can, therefore, take other terms pertaining to the present case, for example, "intellectual substance," as the
middle, for "Every intelligence is a substance," and take as the false
minor, "Every quantity is an intelligence." Hence a false conclusion
follows.

Then (80a6) he answers a tacit question. For someone might request
that he exemplify the diversity of such a syllogism in the other figures. But
he answers that a deception, which bears on being, i.e., through which
someone opines a false affirmative proposition, can be derived only by
the first figure, because in the next figure, i.e., in the second, an affirmative syllogism cannot be formed. As for the third figure, it has no bearing
on the case, because it cannot conclude a universal, which is principally
intended in demonstration and in this syllogism.

Lecture 28
(80a8–b16)

HOW BY SYLLOGIZING IN THE FIRST OR SECOND
FIGURE A FALSE NEGATIVE IS CONCLUDED
CONTRARY TO AN IMMEDIATE AFFIRMATIVE

a8.   On the other hand,   a27. In the second figure
a11. It may occur when   a38. Or one premiss may
a14. It is also possible   b6. The case is similar
a20. Or again, C-B   b14. It is thus clear

After showing how a false affirmative conclusion contrary to an immediate negative is obtained by syllogizing, the Philosopher here shows
how by syllogizing a false negative is concluded contrary to an immediate affirmative. First, in the first figure. Secondly, in the second (80a28).
Concerning the first he does two things. First (80a8), he states his intention and says that since a universal negative may be concluded in the first

as well as in the second figure, we must first show in which moods a syllogism of ignorance is formed in the first figure and under which conditions of truth and falsity in the propositions. Secondly (80a11), he establishes his proposition. First, he shows how such a proposition is formed from two false premises in the first figure. Secondly, how it is formed from one false and one true premise (80a14).

He says therefore first (80a11) that the aforesaid syllogism can be formed from premises, both of which are false. This is clear if A is both in B and in C individually, i.e., immediately. It is thus that a genus is immediately in the proximate species into which it is first divided, as color into blackness and whiteness. For the genus is predicated *per se* of the species, because the former is placed first in the definition of the latter; and it is predicated immediately of a proximate species, because it is put in its definition immediately and not in the way that a remote genus—which is put in the definition of a defining part—is related to an ultimate species. Therefore, let the terms be "color," "whiteness" and "blackness." If, then, we assume that A is in no C, for example, if we say, "No whiteness is a color," but C is in every B, say "All blackness is whiteness," both propositions are false, as is the conclusion, "No blackness is a color."

Then (80a14) he shows how there can be one false and one true premise in the syllogism under discussion. First, he shows how the major can be true and the minor false. Secondly, how it might be the reverse (80a20).

He says therefore first (80a14) that a negative syllogism of ignorance can be formed in the first figure no matter which one of the propositions happens to be false. For it might happen that the proposition AC, which is the major, is true, and the proposition BC, which is the minor, is false. That the major proposition could be true he proves by the fact that the term A, whatever it be, need not be in all things, as color is not predicated of all beings. That the minor would be false he proves on the ground that it is not possible to assume a term of which A would be universally denied and which would also be predicated of B: for we are supposing that the proposition, "Every B is A," is true and immediate. Therefore, if something were universally predicated of B, so that "Every B is C" would be true, then A cannot be universally denied of C. Consequently, this proposition, "No C is A," which was the major, will not be true. For if every B is A, as we supposed, and every B is C, as we are now assuming, it follows in the third figure that some C is A, which contradicts the major. Therefore the proposition, "No C is A," will be false. Hence if this is true, which is the major, it is required that this be false, which is the minor, i.e., "Every B is C."

Then he proves the same thing on the ground that if both premises are true, then as has been proved above, a false conclusion cannot follow —which is out of place in a syllogism of ignorance, which ought to conclude to a false conclusion. But it was given that this is true, namely, "No C is A": if then it is also true that "Every B is C," it follows that the conclusion, "No B is A," is true, whereas it is supposed to be false, being contrary to this immediate proposition, "Every B is A."

Then (80a20) he shows how the minor can be true, the major being false. And he says that the proposition CB, namely, the minor, can be true, while the major is false. For since this proposition, "Every B is A," whose contrary is to be concluded, is immediate, it is necessary that B exist in A as a part in a whole, as "whiteness" in "color." But it is possible to take something else in which B also exists as in a whole, though not immediately—let this other thing be "quality," i.e., C. It is necessary, therefore, according to the aforesaid, that as between these two, namely, A and C, one should be under the other, i.e., color under quality. Now if someone assumes that A is in no C and says, "No quality is a color," the proposition will be false. But the minor will be true, namely, "Every whiteness is a quality." The conclusion, however, "No whiteness is a color," will be false and contrary to an immediate proposition. And so it is clear that a negative syllogism of ignorance can be formed in the first figure when either one or both of the premises are false.

Then (80a27) he shows how a negative syllogism of ignorance is formed in the second figure. First, when both are false. Secondly, when one or the other is false (80a38).

He says therefore first (80a27) that in the second figure it does not happen that both propositions are entirely false. And he calls those propositions entirely false which are contrary to true propositions. He proves this: For since we are trying to conclude a false negative contrary to an immediate affirmative, we must assume that this proposition, "Every B is A," is true and immediate, say, "Every whiteness is a color." But with terms so related it is impossible to find a middle term which would be predicated universally of one and universally removed from the other. For suppose that the term C could be universally removed from A and universally predicated of B. Then the proposition, "No A is C," will be true; consequently, its converse, "No C is A," will also be true. But every B is C. Therefore, no B is A, the contrary of which was supposed.

Similarly, it cannot be universally removed from B and universally predicated of A. For if it is true that every A is C, the converse, "Some C is A," will be true. But if it is true that no B is C, its converse, "No C is B," will be true. So, then, from these two propositions, "Some C is A" and "No C is B," there follows, "Some B is not A," which is the contradictory of what was supposed, namely, that "Every B is A." What remains, therefore, is that it is impossible to find any middle which, A and B being related in the way we have supposed, can be predicated of one and removed from the other. Yet if a syllogism is to be formed in the second figure, the middle must be predicated of one of the extremes and denied of the other. Therefore, if both are totally false, the contraries would have to be true, which is impossible as has been proved.

However, nothing prevents both from being false particularly: thus we may take some middle which is predicated particularly of A and of B, say "male," which is predicated particularly of animal and of man. Now if C is taken in every A, say "Every animal is male," and in no B, say "No man is male," each proposition will be false, not entirely but particularly. And the same holds if, conversely, the major is negative and the minor affirmative, i.e., if we should say, "No animal is male" and "Every man is male."

Then (80a38) he shows how it happens when one is false. First, in the second mode of the second figure. Secondly, in the first mode (80b6).

He says therefore first (80a38) that in this figure it occurs that either proposition may be false. This is clear from the fact that if A is supposed to be predicated *per se* and immediately of B, whatever is in every A is in every B, as whatever is predicated universally of animal is predicated universally of man. Therefore, if some middle, C, be taken which is universally predicated of A, say "Every animal is living," and universally removed from B, say "No man is living," it is evident that AC, which is the major proposition, will be true, but BC, which is the minor, will be false.

Similarly, he proves that the converse occurs when the major is false. For it cannot be that something be universally removed from B and universally predicated of A, when the terms have that position. For it has been stated that if something is in A universally, it follows that it is also in B. Consequently, if something be removed universally from B, it cannot be that it is predicated universally of A. For example, anything universally removed from "man" cannot be universally predicated of "animal." Therefore, if something is taken which is universally removed from man, say "irrational," and you state that "Every animal is irrational" and "No man is irrational," it follows that the minor proposition is true and the major false. But in these terms the major premise is not totally false. However, one can take a term in which it is totally false, for example, if we should take "inanimate" as the middle.

Then (80b6) he shows the same in the first mode of the second figure, where the major is negative. For it is clear that with the terms A and B so related, as was said, something universally removed from A cannot be in any B. Therefore, if a middle, C, be taken which is universally removed from A and universally predicated of B, the major will be true and the minor false. For example, if the terms are "inanimate," "animal" and "man."

Similarly, he shows that the minor can be true and the major false. For it is clear, according to the aforesaid, that that which is universally predicated of B cannot be universally removed from every A, because

what is universally predicated of B must be in some A at least. Therefore, if C be taken as a middle which is universally predicated of B, say,
"rational" or "living," and universally denied of A, there will be a true
minor proposition, namely, "Every man is rational" or "living." But the
major, namely, "No animal is rational," is false in part, while "No animal
is living," is false entirely.

Then summarizing (80b14) he concludes that a deceptive syllogism can
be formed in immediates, when both propositions are false or only one is
false.

Lecture 29
(80b17–81a37)

SYLLOGISM OF IGNORANCE IN REGARD
TO MEDIATE PROPOSITIONS

b17. In the case of attributes   a16. If the conclusion is
b27. Similarly if the middle   a20. This is equally true
b32. On the other hand   a25. The middle may be
a5. When the erroneous   a35. Thus we have made

After showing how a syllogism of ignorance in regard to immediate
propositions is made, the Philosopher here shows how it is made in regard
to mediate propositions. First, how a false negative proposition is concluded
which is opposed to a true affirmative. Secondly, how a false affirmative is
concluded which is opposed to a true negative (81a16). Concerning the first
he does two things. First, he shows this in the first figure. Secondly, in the
second (81a4). In regard to the first he does three things. First, he shows
how a syllogism of ignorance is constructed in mediate propositions
through a proper middle. Secondly, how one is constructed through a
middle which although not proper has a relationship to the terms, a relationship akin to that of a proper middle (80b27). Thirdly, he shows how
such a syllogism is constructed through an extraneous middle (80b32).

He says therefore first (80b17) that when a syllogism is constructed
which concludes something false in propositions which are not individual, i.e., not immediate, if the "proper middle" through which the syllogism is formed be taken, then both propositions cannot be false, but
only the major. He explains what he means by "proper middle." For
since the proposition whose contrary is to be syllogized is mediate, it is
required that the predicate be syllogized of the subject through some
middle. Therefore, the same middle can be employed to conclude the

opposite. Say that the mediate proposition is "Every triangle has three angles equal to two right angles." The middle through which the predicate is syllogized of the subject is, "A figure having an exterior angle equal to the two opposite interior angles." Now if we would prove through the same middle that no triangle has three angles equal to two right angles, it will be a syllogism of falsity through a proper middle. Hence he says that a proper middle is one through which the syllogism of contradiction is made, i.e., leading to the opposite conclusion. In the above example, A would be "triangle," B, "having three. . . ." and C, the middle, "such a figure." Now in the first figure the minor must be affirmative; therefore, that which was the minor in the true syllogism must remain unconverted and not changed into its opposite in the syllogism of falsity. Hence it must always be true. But the major proposition of the true syllogism is changed into its contrary negative; hence the major must be false. For example, we might say: "No figure having an exterior angle equal to the two opposite interior angles has three angles equal to two right angles; but the triangle is such a figure: therefore, no triangle has three angles equal to two right angles."

Then (80b27) he shows how the aforesaid syllogism is constructed through a middle which is extraneous but like the proper. And he says that it will be syllogized in like fashion if the middle is taken from another ordering. For example, if A had been demonstrated of B through C, and we were to take in the syllogism of falsity not C but D as the middle, in such a way, however, that D is also contained universally under A and predicated universally of B: say if we took for the middle, "a closed figure of three lines," because here too the minor proposition DB must remain as it was in the syllogism which concluded the true, although through a proper middle. But the major proposition will have to be changed into its contrary. And so the minor will always be true and the major always false. But as to the mode of the argument, this deception is similar to that which is formed through the proper middle.

Then (80b32) he shows how a syllogism of falsity is made through a middle which is extraneous and unlike the proper. For a middle can be taken such that it is contained universally under A but is predicated of no B. In this case both propositions will have to be false, because in order that the syllogism be formed in the first figure, it will be necessary to take propositions to the contrary, namely, a major which is negative, for example, "No D is A," and the minor affirmative, for example, "Every B is D." Clearly then both are false. Now this relationship of terms cannot be found in things convertible, say in a subject and its proper attribute which is concluded of the subject through some middle. For it is obvious that no middle can be taken such that the proper attribute would be universally predicated of it, and that middle be removed universally from the subject. But this relationship can be found when the proposition is mediate, for example, when a higher genus or the proper attribute of a higher genus is predicated of an ultimate species, as when we say, "Every man is living." For "living" can be concluded of man through the middle, "animal." Therefore, if we should take something of which "living" would be universally predicated, say "olive," but would be universally removed from man, the relationship of terms that we are seeking will result. For this will be false, "No olive is living"; and the minor, too, will be false, "Every man is an olive." Similarly, the concusion will be false, "No man is living," which is contrary to the true mediate proposition.

It also happens that the major may be true and the minor false. For example, if we take as middle something which is not contained under A, say "stone"; then the major, AB, will be true, namely, "No stone is living," because "stone" is not contained under "living," but the minor will be false, namely, "Every man is a stone." For if the minor remained true, while the first was true, then the conclusion would be true, whereas it has been said that it is to be false. However, the converse does not occur, i.e., that the minor be true when the middle is extraneous, because such a middle cannot be predicated universally of B. But in the first figure the minor taken must always be an affirmative statement.

Then (81a5) he shows how a negative syllogism of ignorance is made in the second figure. And he says that in the second figure it cannot occur that both propositions be totally false. For if we are to conclude the false proposition, "No B is A," contrary to the true, it would have been required that A be predicated universally of B. Hence nothing will be able to be found which would be universally predicated of one and universally denied of the other, as has been established above when we treated concerning the syllogism of ignorance in immediates.

But one or the other of them can be totally false. And he manifests this first in the second mood of the second figure where the major is affirmative and the minor negative. Thus, let the middle be related to the extremes so that it is predicated universally of both, as "living" is predicated universally of man and of animal. Then if we take the major affirmative, say "Every animal is living," and the minor negative, say "No man is living," the major will be true, the minor false, and the conclusion false. In like manner also, if in the first mood of the second figure we take the major negative, say "No animal is living," and the minor affirmative, say "Every man is living," the major will be false, the minor true, and the conclusion false.

Having said these things he sums up and concludes that he has stated when and through which kinds of premises deception can occur, if the deceptive syllocism is privative [negative].

Then (81a16) he shows how an affirmative syllogism of deception is formulated in mediate propositions. First, when it is formulated through a proper middle. Secondly, when it is formulated through a middle similar to a proper middle (81a20). Thirdly, when it is formulated through an extraneous middle (81a25).

He says therefore first (81a16), that if an affirmative syllogism of deception is to be formulated in mediate propositions, if a proper middle such as explained above be taken, it is impossible that both propositions be false. For since a syllogism of this kind can be formed only in the first figure, both propositions being affirmative, it is required that the minor proposition remain as it was in the true syllogism. Hence the major will have to be changed, namely, from negative to affirmative, so that it will have to be false. For example, if we desire to conclude that "Every man is a quantity," which is the contrary of the statement, "No man is a quantity," whose proper middle is "substance," we will take the false proposition, "Every substance is a quantity," and the true proposition, "Every man is a substance."

Then (81a20) he shows how a syllogism of ignorance is formed when a non-proper middle is taken which is not of the same order but from some other ordering. For example, if I say, "Every agent is a quantity; every man is an agent: therefore, every man is a quantity." For it is necessary in this case for the minor to remain, but the major will have to be changed from negative to affirmative. Hence this deception is similar to the previous deception, as was stated in the privative syllogism.

Then (81a25) he shows how an affirmative syllogism of deception is formulated through an extraneous middle. And he says that if an extraneous middle be taken such that it is contained under the major extreme, then the major will be true and the minor false. For A, the major extreme, can be predicated universally of many things that are not under one another, say "habit" of grammar and virtue. For this is mediate, "No grammar is a virtue." There we can conclude the contrary of this, namely, "All grammar is virtue," through a middle which is contained under virtue. Then the major will be true and the minor false. For example, we might say: "All temperance is a virtue; grammar is temperance: therefore, all grammar is a virtue."

But if a middle is taken which is not under the major extreme, the major will always be false, because it will be affirmative. But the minor may sometimes be false with such a major; then both will be false. For example, if we should say: "Every whiteness is a virtue; all grammar is whiteness: therefore. . . ." But sometimes it can be true. For when the terms are so related, there is nothing to hinder A from being removed from every D, and D from being in every B, as happens in these terms, namely, "animal," "science," "music." For the major extreme, "animal," is removed universally from all science; hence this proposition which is taken as the major in the syllogism of ignorance is false, namely, "Every science is an animal." But the minor, namely, "All music is science," is true. And the conclusion will be false, being contrary to the true mediate negative. It can also happen that A is in no D, and D in no B, as has been said.

Thus it is evident that when the middle is not contained under the major extreme, they may both be false or just one of them, because the major and the minor may be false. However, with the three terms so related, as we have said above, the major cannot be true.

Finally (81a35), he summarizes and concludes that it is plain from the foregoing how many ways and through which alignment of true and false propositions it is possible to construct deceptions through syllogisms, both in immediate propositions and in mediate propositions, which are proved by demonstration.

Lecture 30
(81a38–b9)

CAUSE OF SIMPLE NEGATIVE IGNORANCE

a38. It is also clear   a39. since we learn either

After the Philosopher has determined concerning ignorance through deception which is caused by a syllogism, he now determines concerning the ignorance of simple negation which is produced without a syllogism. First, he shows in which type of person this ignorance is had of necessity. Secondly, he proves his proposition (81a39).

He says therefore first (81a38) that if a person lacks any of the senses, say sight or hearing, then necessarily the science of the sensible objects proper to those senses will be lacking. Thus, if a person lacks the sense of sight, then of necessity the science of colors will be lacking in him. And so he will have ignorance of negation in regard to colors, being entirely ignorant of colors. However, this must be understood of persons who never had the sense of sight, as a person born blind. But if someone loses the sight he once had, he does not on that account necessarily lack a science of colors, because the memory of colors previously sensed remains in him.

But it is possible that ignorance of negation be had of certain things which can nevertheless be known through a sense we possess. For example, if someone with sight were always in the dark, he would *de facto* lack a science of colors, but not of necessity, because he could acquire it by sensing colors—which does not occur in one who lacks the sense of sight.

Hence he adds that it is impossible to receive it because one who lacks the power of sight cannot even acquire a knowledge of colors.

Then (81a39) he proves his proposition on the ground that there are two ways of acquiring science: one is through demonstration, and the other is through induction, as we have stated in the beginning of this book. But these two ways differ, because demonstration proceeds from universals, but induction from particulars. Therefore, if any universals from which demonstration proceeds could be known without induction, it would follow that a person could acquire science of things of which he does not have sense experience. But it is impossible that universals be known scientifically without induction. This is quite obvious in sensible things, because we receive the universal aspect in them through the experience which we have in regard to sensible things, as is explained in *Metaphysics* I. But this might be doubted in things which are abstract, as in mathematics. For although experience begins from sense, as it is stated in *Metaphysics* I, it seems that this plays no role in studying things already isolated or abstracted from sensible matter.

Therefore, to exclude this he says that even those things that are abstract happen to be made known through induction, because in each genus of abstract things are certain particulars which are not isolable from sensible matter, so far as each of them is a "this something." For although "line" is studied in isolation from its sensible matter, nevertheless "this line", which is in sensible matter, so far forth as it is individualized, cannot be so isolated, because its individuation is from this matter. Furthermore, the principles of abstracted [isolated] things, from which demonstrations regarding them are formed, are not made manifest to us except from certain particulars which we perceive by sense. Thus, from the fact that we see some single sensible whole we are led to know what a whole is and what a part, and we know that every whole is greater than its part by considering this in many. Thus the universals from which demonstration proceeds are made known to us only through induction.

Now men who lack any of the senses cannot make an induction from singulars pertaining to that sense, because sense is the sole knower of the singulars from which induction proceeds. Hence such singulars are utterly unknown, because it does not occur that anyone lacking a sense receives science of such singulars: first, because he cannot demonstrate from universals without induction through which universals are known, as has been said; secondly, because nothing can be known through induction without the sense which is concerned with the singulars from which induction prcoeeds.

It should be noted that by these words of the Philosopher two positions are excluded: the first is Plato's, who stated that we do not have science of things except through Forms participated from ideas. If this were so, universals could be made known to us without induction, and we would be able to acquire a science of things of which we have no sense. Hence Aristotle also uses this argument against Plato at the end of *Metaphysics* I. The second is the position of those who claim that in this life we can know separated substances by understanding their quiddities, which however cannot be known through sensible objects which we know and which are entirely transcended by them. Hence if they were known according to their essences, it would follow that some things would be known without induction and sense perception, which the Philosopher here denies even in regard to abstracted things.

Lecture 31
(81b10–82a20)

THREE QUESTIONS ABOUT PROCEEDING TO INFINITY IN CONFIRMING DEMONSTRATIONS

b10. Every syllogism is effected	b34. The second question is
b14. It is clear, then,	a2. A third question
b18. If our reasoning aims	a7. This is the equivalent
b24. Thus: since there are	a9. I hold that the same
b30. Suppose, then, C	a15. One cannot ask the same

After the Philosopher has determined concerning the demonstrative syllogism by showing from what and what sort of things it proceeds and in which figure demonstrations can be formed, he now inquires whether demonstrations can proceed to infinity. First, he raises the question. Secondly, he settles it (82a21) [L. 32]. Concerning the first he does two things. First, he sets down certain prefatory remarks needed for understanding the question. Secondly, he raises the question (81b30). Concerning the first he does two things. First, he prefaces something about the syllogistic form one must observe in demonstrations. Secondly, he reviews what the matter of demonstration should be (81b14).

With respect to the first (81b10) he touches on three things, the first of which is common to every syllogism, namely, that every syllogism is formed in three terms, as is indicated in *Prior Analytics* I. The second, however, pertains to an affirmative syllogism whose form is such that it concludes A to be in C, because A is in B and B in C. And this is the form of a syllogism in the first figure in which alone can be concluded a universal affirmative, the chief quest in demonstration. The third pertains to a negative syllogism which of necessity has one affirmative proposition and one negative, but differently in the first figure and in the second, as is clear from what has been shown in the *Prior Analytics*.

Then (81b14) he reviews what the matter of demonstration should be. In regard to this he does three things. First, he states what this matter is. Secondly, he shows the difference between this matter and the matter of a dialectical syllogism (81b18). Thirdly, he clarifies this difference (81b24).

He says therefore first (81b14) that since a syllogism has three terms from which are formed the two propositions which conclude the third, it is clear that these propositions, from which one proceeds in a demonstrative syllogism according to the aforesaid form, are the principles and suppositions we discussed earlier. For one who accepts such principles demonstrates through them in the syllogistic form we have mentioned, namely, that A is in C is proved through B; and if the proposition AB is mediate, another middle is used to demonstrate that A is in B. The like is done if the minor proposition, BC, is mediate.

Then (81b18), apropos of what has been said, he shows the difference between a demonstrative and a dialectical syllogism. For since the latter aims at producing opinion, the sole intent of a dialectician is to proceed from things that are most probable, and these are things that appear to the majority or to the very wise. Hence if a dialectician in syllogizing happens upon a proposition which really has a middle through which it could be proved, but it seems not to have a middle because it appears to be *per se* known on account of its probability, this is enough for the dialectician: he does not search for a middle, even though the proposition is mediate. Rather he syllogizes from it and completes the dialectical syllogism satisfactorily.

The demonstrative syllogism, on the other hand, is ordained to scientific knowledge of the truth; accordingly, it pertains to the demonstrator to proceed from truths which are really immediate. Hence if he happens upon a mediate proposition, he must prove it through its proper middle until he reaches something immediate, because he is not content with the probability of a proposition.

Then (81b24) he elucidates what he has said, asserting that his claim that the demonstrator proceeds "to the truth from things that are" is supported by the fact that it is possible to find something "which is not predicated of a thing accidentally." What this means he explains by showing how in the case of affirmative statements something is predicated accidentally.

For something is predicated accidentally in two ways: in one way, when the subject is predicated of an accident, as when we say, "The white thing is a man"; in another way, when the accident is predicated of the subject, as when we say, "The man is white." Now this way differs from the first, because when the accident is predicated of the subject, it is stated that the man is white not because something else is white but because the man himself is white. Yet it is a *per accidens* proposition, because "white" does not belong to man according to the specific nature of man.

For neither is placed in the definition of the other. But when it is stated that the white thing is a man, it is not so stated because being a man is in the whiteness, but because being a man is in the subject of whiteness, which subject happens to be white. Hence this way is further removed from *per se* predication than the first.

But there are certain things which are not predicated *per accidens* in either of these ways: these are said to be *per se*. Such are the things from which the demonstrator proceeds. But the dialectician is not so demanding; consequently, the question concerning such things as are predicated *per se* is not relevant to the dialectical syllogism but only to the demonstrative syllogism.

Then (81b30) he raises the questions he intended. Concerning this he does two things. First, he raises the questions in regard to things to which they are relevant. Secondly, he shows the cases in which they are not relevant (82a15). Concerning the first he does two things. First, he raises questions in affirmative demonstrations. Secondly, he shows that these questions also have relevance in negative demonstrations (82a9). In regard to the first he does two things. First, he raises the questions. Secondly, he shows where such questions are relevant (82a7).

In regard to the first (81b30) he raises three questions corresponding to the three terms of a syllogism. First, he raises a question concerning the major extreme, namely, whether one can go to infinity in ascending order? In this question an ultimate subject is supposed which is not predicated of any other, but other things are predicated of it. Let this subject be C, and let B be in C first and immediately, and let E be in B, as universally predicated of B; furthermore, let F be in E as universally predicated of it. The question is this: Should this ascending process come to a halt somewhere, so that something is reached which is predicated universally of other things but nothing else is predicated of it, or is that not necessary but a process to infinity occurs?

Secondly (81b34) he raises the question on the part of the minor term, namely, whether one can go to infinity in descending. In this question some first universal predicate is supposed which is predicated of other things and nothing is more universal than it so as to be predicated of it. Thus let A be such that nothing is predicated of it as a universal whole of a part, but A is predicated of H both first and immediately, and H of G, and G of B. The question then is this: Is it necessary to come to a halt in this descending process, or may it proceed to infinity?

Then he shows the difference between these two questions. For in the first one we asked: If someone begins from a most particular subject, which is in nothing else the way a universal whole is in a part but other things are in it, does an infinite ascending process occur? But in the second we are asking: If someone begins with a most universal predicate, which is predicated of other things as a universal whole of its parts but nothing is predicated of it in this way, does an infinite descending process occur?

Thirdly (82a2) he raises the third question on the part of the middle term. In this question two determinate extremes are supposed, namely, a most universal predicate and a most particular subject. The question is whether under these conditions there can be an infinity of middles. Thus, if A is the most universal predicate and C the most particular subject, and if between A and C there is the middle, B, and again between A and B another middle, and likewise between B and C; furthermore, if there are other middles of these middles between them and the extremes both in ascending and in descending order. The question then is this: May these processes go on to infinity or is that impossible?

Then (82a7) he shows what is the tenor of these questions. And he says that these questions pertain to the matter now under discussion, namely, to demonstrations. He says, therefore, that the attempt to reach true answers to these questions is the same as trying to settle the question whether demontrations proceed to infinity by ascending or descending. By ascending, i.e., so that each proposition from which a demonstration proceeds would be demonstrable by another prior proposition. This is what he means when he asks: "Is there a demonstration of everything," i.e., of every proposition? By so thinking, some have erred in regard to principles, as is stated in *Metaphysics* IV. And by descending, i.e., whether it is possible from any demonstrated proposition to proceed again to another demonstration subsequent to it. Thus, one element of the doubt is whether demonstrations proceed to infinity either by ascending or by descending. The other element is whether demonstrations are mutually limiting, so that one demonstration may be confirmed by another in an ascending process, and from one demonstration another may proceed by a descending process: and this until a limit is reached.

Then (82a9) he shows that these questions are also relevant to negative demonstrations, because a negative demonstration must employ an affirmative proposition in which the subject of the conclusion is contained under the middle and from which the predicate of the conclusion is removed. Therefore, to the extent that there is ascent and descent in affirmative, there must be ascent and descent in negative syllogisms and propositions. For example, if the conclusion of a demonstrative syllogism is, "No C is A," and the middle taken is B, from which A is removed: the first thing to be considered, therefore, is whether A is removed from B first and immediately, or whether there is another middle G to be taken, from which A would be removed before it would be removed from B. In that case it would be necessary to consider whether A would be removed from something else before G, namely, from H which is predicated universally of G. Therefore in these also the question arises whether one can proceed to infinity in removing (so that something would always remain from which it would have to be removed), or must one stop somewhere.

Then (82a15) he shows the cases in which these questions have no relevance: for in cases in which there is mutual predication and mutual conversion there is no prior and subsequent to be taken in the sense in which the prior [notion] is that with which a subsequent [notion] is not convertible, as universals are prior; because no matter whether the predicates be infinite, so that one might proceed to infinity in predicating, or whether there be infinity on both sides, i.e., on the side of the predicate as well as of the subject, all such infinites bear a like relationship to all, because any of them could be predicated of any other and be the subject of any of the convertibles. However, there can be this difference: one of them might be predicated as an accident and another as a predicament, i.e., as a substantial predicate. And this is the difference between a property and a definition: although the two are convertible with the subject, nevertheless the definition is an essential predicate and therefore naturally prior to the property, which is an accidental predicate. That is why in demonstrations we use the definition as the middle to demonstrate a proper attribute of the subject.

Lecture 32
(82a21–b34)

SOLUTION OF SOME OF THESE DOUBTS HINGES UPON SOLUTION OF OTHERS OF THESE DOUBTS

a21. Now, it is clear
a24. For suppose that A
a30. Nor is it of any effect
a37. Further, if in affirmative

b4. For a negative conclusion
b13. In the second figure
b23. The third figure shows
b28. Even supposing that the proof

After raising the questions, the Philosopher here begins to settle them. And his treatment is divided into two parts. In the first he shows that the solution of some of the doubts is reduced to the solution of others. In the second he settles the doubt as to those items in which the difficulty lies *per se* as in its source (82b34) [L. 33]. Concerning the first he does two things. First, he shows that the doubt bearing on the middles is reduced to the one which is concerned with the extremes and is solved by the solution of the latter. Secondly, he shows that the doubt bearing on negative demonstrations is reduced to the one which is concerned with affirmative demonstrations (82a37). In regard to the first he does three things.

First, he states his intended proposition. Secondly, he proves this proposition (82a24). Thirdly, he excludes a subterfuge (82a30).

He says therefore first (82a21) that it will be plain to anyone who considers the following reason that "an infinity of middles does not occur," if the predications both upwards and downwards stop at certain terms, namely, at the highest predicate and the lowest subject. And he explains what upward and downward predication consists in, saying that one proceeds upwards when there is movement to the more universal, one of whose marks it is that it be predicated; but one proceeds downwards when there is movement to the most particular, one of whose marks it is that it functions as a subject.

Then (82a24) he shows what he has proposed in the following way: Let the case be that A is the highest predicate and F the lowest subject, and that there is an infinitude of middles, each of which we shall call B. Now since A was the first predicate, it will be predicated of some middle near it, and that middle of another middle below it. Since the middles are infinite, it follows that the predication will proceed downwards to infinity—which is contrary to what we are assuming. For it was assumed that the predications do not proceed downwards to infinity. The result is the same if we start at F, which is the lowest subject, and proceed upwards to infinity before A is reached—this too would be against our assumption. Therefore, if these are impossible, namely, that one may proceed to infinity by ascending or by descending, it will be impossible for the middles to be infinite. Thus it is clear that the question of an infinity of middles is reduced to a question of the infinity of the extremes.

Then (82a30) he excludes an objection. For someone might object saying that the aforesaid proof would hold if ABF, i.e., the middle and the extremes, were so related as to be "had" to one another, i.e., so that there would be no middle between them: for this is the way the Philosopher defines "had" in *Physics* V, namely, that it is next to something without anything between. And this seemed to be supposed in the above proof, namely, that A is predicated of some middle as though "had" to it, i.e., following it immediately. But one who posits infinite middles will say that this cannot be supposed. For he will say that between any two terms that are taken there is a middle.

But the philosopher says that it makes no difference whether the infinitude be of middles that are "had" to one another, the way discrete things are (for example, in a city, house is consecutive to house, and in numbers, unity to unity), or whether something "had" cannot be found in the middles although between any two middles it is always possible to find another, as happens in continua, in which, between any two signs, i.e., between two points, another can be found between them.

That this makes no difference one way or the other to the matter at hand he manifests in the following way: Granted that between A and F there is an infinitude of middles, each of which is called B, yet no matter which of these I employ, there is either an infinitude of middles between it and A and F, or there is not an infinitude of them between it and one or the other of the extremes. For example, let us suppose that the middles are mutually "had," as happens in discrete things, and let us take a middle which is "had" to A; then it will be necessary that between that middle and F there is still an infinitude of middles; and similarly, if we assume a certain finitude of middles between that middle and A. And the same reasoning holds if the middle which is taken be joined immediately to F or is distant from it by a finitude of middles. From the fact, therefore, that from any given middle one must take an infinitude of middles to one or other of the extremes, it makes no difference whether it is joined to either extreme immediately, i.e., without a middle, or not immediately, i.e., through other middles: because even if it be joined to one extreme without a middle, it will still be necessary later to find an infinitude of middles in relation to the other. Consequently, it will always be required, if there is an infinitude of middles, to proceed to infinity in predications either by ascending or by descending, as the above proof showed.

Then (82a37) he shows that if there is no process to infinity in affirmative demonstrations, then neither in negative demonstrations: and thus the question of negative demonstrations is reduced to the question of affirmative ones. He does three things in regard to this point. First, he proposes what he intends. Secondly, he proves what he proposed (82b4). Thirdly, he excludes an objection (82b28).

He says therefore first (82a37) that it will be clear from what follows that if in the predicative, i.e., in the affirmative demonstration, a stop is made at both, i.e., upwards and downwards, it will be necessary that a stop be made in the negative demonstration.

To elucidate what he is proposing he says: Let the case be such that from the ultimate, i.e., from the lowest subject one cannot go in ascending order to infinity toward universal predicates. And he explains that "ultimate" means that which is not in any other as in a less particular, but something else is in it, and let it be F. And let the case also be that one does not go to infinity when proceeding from the first to the ultimate. And he explains that the "first" means that which is predicated of others but nothing else is predicated of it as more universal than it. Thus the "first" is understood to be the most universal, and the "ultimate" the most particular. If, therefore, on both sides there be a stop in affirmative demonstrations, he says that as a consequence, there is also a stop in negative demonstrations.

Then (82b4) he proves his proposition. First, in the first figure. Secondly, in the second (82b13). Thirdly, in the third (82b23). For a negative can be concluded in three figures.

He says therefore first (82b4) that there are three ways of demonstrating a negative proposition through which something is signified not to be. In one way in the first figure according to the mode that B is universally in C in the universal affirmative minor, but A is in no B in the universal negative major. Now since we are supposing that there is a stop in affirmatives, both upwards and downwards, it is necessary that the proposition, BC, which is affirmative, if it is not immediate but a space exists with middles between B and C, be reduced to immediates, because that space which exists between the middle term and the extreme is affirmative, in which a stop is supposed. But if we take the other space, which is between B and A, it is clear that if this proposition, "No B is A," is not immediate, it is necessary that A be removed from something else before being removed from B. Let this be D. But if this D be taken as a middle between A and B, it is necessary that it be universally predicated of B, because the minor must be affirmative. And if this too is not immediate, i.e., "No D is A," then A has to be denied of something prior to D, say E, which again will be predicated universally of D for the same reason. Therefore, since there is a stop in affirmatives when we ascend, as supposed, it follows that something is reached of which A should be denied first and immediately; otherwise one would go still further in affirmatives, as is clear from the foregoing.

Then (82b13) he proves the same thing for the negative which is concluded in the second figure. For let the case be that B, which is the middle, is predicated universally of A and denied universally of C, so that the conclusion is "No C is A." Now if the negative premise needs to be demonstrated because it is mediate, it must be demonstrated either in the first figure in the mode of demonstrating concerning which we have shown that there is a stop, if there is a stop in affirmatives; or it must be demonstrated through this mode, i.e., in the second figure, or through a third mode, i.e., in the third figure. Now it has been established that there is a stop in negatives of the first figure, if there is a stop in affirmatives. Consequently, the same will now be demonstrated as to the second figure.

Therefore, let this proposition, "No C is B," be demonstrated in such a way that D is universally predicated of B in the universal affirmative major and denied universally of C in the universal negative minor. Now if the proposition, "No C is D," is mediate, it will be required to take some other middle which will be predicated universally of D and universally removed from C. Continuing thus, it will be necessary to proceed in negative demonstrations just as we do in affirmatives, namely, B will be predicated of A and D of B, and something else of D, and so on to infinity in affirmatives. But because we are supposing an upward stop in the affirmatives, it is also necessary to come to a stop in the negatives according to this mode in which a negative is demonstrated in the second figure.

Then (82b23) he shows the same thing in the third figure. Therefore, let B be a middle of which A is universally predicated, but C is universally denied of it: the conclusion will be a particular negative, namely, C is denied of some A. Now that there is a stop in the affirmative premise, "Every B is A," is granted by our supposition. Furthermore, that there must be a stop in the negative, "No B is C," which is the major, is evident, because if it had to be demonstrated, it would be done either "through what was said above," i.e., through the first and second figure or in the way that the conclusion was concluded, namely, through the third figure, in which case this minor is not affirmed as universal but as particular. "But there is a stop in that way," i.e., if one proceeds in the first and second figure. But if one proceeds in the third figure to conclude that "Some B is not C," let a middle, E, be taken such that B is universally affirmed of it but C is particularly denied of it. "Then this happens once more in like manner," i.e., according to this, one will always proceed in the negative demonstration by accumulating affirmative predications in descending order, because B which was the first middle will be predicated of E, and E of something else, and so on to infinity. But since we are supposing that there is a stop in the descending order in affirmatives, it is clear that there will be a stop in the negatives on the part of C.

Then (82b28) he excludes an objection. For someone could say that it is necessary to stop in negative propositions when there is a stop in the affirmatives, provided that one always syllogizes according to the same figure; but if one demonstrates now in one figure and now in another, one can go to infinity. And he says that "it is obvious" that if one does not limit himself to one figure in demonstrating but uses all, proceeding now in the first figure and now in the second and third, there must still be a stop in the negatives if there is one in the affirmatives. For these various ways of demonstrating are finite, and each of them will be enlarged not to infinity but finitely by ascending or descending, as was shown. Now if finite things be taken a finite number of times, the result is finite. Hence it remains that in all the modes there must be a stop in negative demonstrations, if there is a stop in the affirmatives.

Lecture 33
(82b34–83a35)

THAT ONE DOES NOT PROCEED TO INFINITY IN ESSENTIAL PREDICATES IS SHOWN "LOGICALLY"

b34. That in fact the regress
a1. But as regards predicates
a21. It follows from this

a24. Predicates which signify
a27. White is a coincident
a33. The Forms we can dispense

After showing that if there is a stop in the extremes there must be a stop in the middles, and if there is a stop in affirmatives there must be a stop in negatives, the Philosopher now shows that there *is* a stop in affirmatives both upwards and downwards. And his treatment is divided into two parts. In the first part he shows his thesis "logically," i.e., through characteristics common to every syllogism, which are based on predicates considered commonly. In the second he shows the same thing analytically, i.e., through characteristics proper to demonstration, which are based on *per se* predicates which are proper to demonstration (84a8) [L. 35]. The first is divided into two parts. In the first he shows that one does not proceed to infinity in predicates which are predicated in *eo quod quid* [i.e., pertaining to the essence of the subject]. In the second he shows universally that one does not proceed to infinity in affirmative predicates (83a1).

He says therefore first (82b34) that since we have established that an infinite process does not occur in negatives if there is a stop in affirmatives, our present task will be to show how one speculates through logical reasons that there is a stop "in those," i.e., in affirmatives. (These reasons are called "logical," because they proceed from certain common notions that pertain to the considerations of logic).

Now this truth is clear in regard to things predicated as constituting the essence of a thing, namely, the predicates from which the *quod quid est*, i.e., the definition, is formed. For if such predicates were agreed to be infinite, the result would be that nothing can be defined, and that if something is defined, its definition cannot be known: and all because the infinite cannot be traversed. For a thing cannot be defined, or its definition known, except by reaching the ultimate through descent and the first through ascent. Therefore, if something can be defined, or if a thing's definition can be known, then in either case this consequence will follow, namely, there is no infinite process in the aforementioned predicates, but there is a stop in them.

Then (83a1) he shows universally that there is not a process to infinity in affirmative predicates. In regard to this he does two things. First, he prefaces certain things needed for establishing the thesis. Secondly, he establishes it (83a36) [L. 34]. In regard to the first he does two things. First, he distinguishes *per accidens* from *per se* predicates. Secondly, he distinguishes among the *per se* predicates (83a21).

He says therefore first (83a1) that since it has been established in regard to certain predicates that there is no infinite process in them, namely, in those which are predicated as pertaining to the essence, our task is to show that this is universally so in all affirmative predicates. And he begins his consideration with *per accidens* predicates in which there are three modes of true predication. One mode is when an accident is predicated of an accident, as when we say, "Something white is walking." The second mode is when the subject is predicated of an accident, as when we say, "Something white is wood." The third mode is when an accident is predicated of a subject, as when we say, "Wood is white," or "Man walks."

Now these modes of predicating are mutually other and diverse, because when its subject is predicated of an accident, say "Something white is wood," what is signified is that the universal predicate, "wood," is being predicated of a subject which happens to be wood, i.e., this particular wood in which there is whiteness. For when I say, "Something white is wood," the meaning is the same as "This wood which happens to be white is wood"; in other words, the sense is not that "white" is the subject of wood.

And he proves this on the ground that it is either according to its totality or according to a part that a subject comes to be that which is predicated of it as of a subject, as a man comes to be white. But neither the white nor its white part, which is really white, i.e., which pertains to the very essence of whiteness, becomes wood: for an accident is not the subject of change whereby wood comes to be from non-wood. But whatever begins to be such and such, comes to be it; therefore, if it does not come to be this, it is not it—unless it is granted that it always was this. But it was not always true to say that the white [object] is wood, because at some time the whiteness and the wood were not together. Therefore, since it is not true to say that the white [object] becomes wood, it is obvious that the white [object], properly and *per se* speaking, is not wood. Yet if it be granted that something white is wood, it is understood *per accidens,* namely, because that particular subject, which happens to be white, is wood. This, therefore, is the sense of any predication in which a subject is predicated of an accident.

But when I say, "Wood is white," predicating an accident of the subject, I do not signify, as I did in the previous mode of predication, that there is something else substantially white, such that to be wood happens to it: which, of course, is signified both in the previous mode, where a subject is predicated of an accident, and in the other mode, where an accident is predicated of an accident, as when I say, "The musician is white": for this signifies nothing but the fact that this particular man, say Socrates, who happens to be a musician, is white. But when I say, "The wood is white," I signify that the wood itself has become the subject of white, and not that something other than the wood or other than a section of the wood has become white.

Therefore, there is a difference among these three modes of predicating, because when an accident is predicated of a subject, it is not predicated in virtue of some other subject; but when the subject is predicated of an accident or an accident of an accident, the predication is made in virtue of that which is subjected to the terms acting as the subject, of which another accident is predicated accidentally in the second case, and the species of the subject is predicated essentially in the first case.

Now since in each of the above modes we use the name, "predication," and since it lies within our power to employ names as well as to restrict them, let us agree so to use our names in the following proof that only those things are said to be predicated which are said in this way, namely, not in virtue of some other subject. Consequently, whatever is said in another way, namely, by reason of another subject, as when a subject is predicated of an accident or an accident of an accident, shall not be said to be predicated—or if it is said to be predicated, it shall be said to be predicated not absolutely but *per accidens*. Furthermore, that which is after the manner of "white," let us always take on the part of the predicate, and that which is after the manner of "wood," let it be taken on the part of the subject. Therefore, in the following proof let us suppose this to be predicated which is predicated not *per accidens*, but absolutely, of that of which it is predicated. And the reason why we should use the word "predication" in this way is that we are speaking of demonstrative matters, and demonstrations use only such predications.

Then (83a21) he shows the differences among *per se* predicates. In regard to this he does two things. First, he distinguishes these predicates into diverse genera. Secondly, he shows the differences among them (83a24).

He says therefore first (83a21) that because we are saying that those things alone are being predicated which are predicated not in virtue of some other subject, and this is diversified according to the ten predicaments, it follows that whatever is thus predicated is predicated "either in *quod quid est*," i.e., after the manner of an essential predicate, or after the manner of quality or quantity or one of the other predicaments discussed in the *Categories*. And he adds, "when one is predicated of one," because if a predicate is not one but several, it cannot be said to be predicated precisely as *quid* or *quale*, but perhaps jointly as *quale quid*, as when I say "Man is a white animal." Now it was necessary to add this because if several things are predicated of one in such a way that they function as one predicate, predications will be multipliable to infinity according to the infinite modes of combining predicates one to another. Hence when there is question of a stop in things that are predicated, it is necessary to take one thing predicated of one thing.

Then (83a24) he indicates the difference among the aforesaid predicates. In regard to this he does three things. First, he proposes the difference. Secondly, he clarifies it with examples (83a27). Thirdly, he excludes an objection (83a33).

He says therefore first (83a24) that those which signify substance must signify, in respect to that of which they are predicated, "what it truly is or something that it truly is." This can be understood in two ways: in one way, as showing a distinction on the part of the predicate which might signify either the entire essence of the subject, as a definition does (and he signifies this when he says, "what it truly is"), or part of the essence, as a genus or a difference does (and he signifies this when he says, "or something that it truly is.") In another way, and better, as showing a distinction on the part of the subject, which is sometimes convertible with an essential predicate, as the definitum with the definition (and he signifies this, when he says, "what it truly is"), and sometimes is a subjective part of the predicate, as man is of animal (and he signifies this when he says, "or something that it truly is," for man is a certain animal). But those which do not signify substance but are said of some subject (which subject is not truly, i.e., essentially, that predicate nor something of it), all such predicates are accidental.

Then (83a27) he clarifies the aforesaid difference with examples, saying that when we say, "Man is white," the predicate is accidental, because man is not that which white truly is, i.e., to be white is not the essence of man "or anything of what white truly is," as was explained above. But when it is stated, "Man is an animal," perhaps man is that which animal truly is. For animal signifies the essence of man, because that which is man is essentially animal. And although predicates that do not signify substance are accidents, they are not predicated *per accidens*. For they are not predicated of some subject in virtue of some other subject; for when I say, "Man is white," "white" is not predicated of man by reason of some other subject's being white in virtue of which man is called white, as was explained above in regard to things predicated *per accidens*.

Then (83a33) he excludes an objection. For someone could say that predicates which signify the substance are not truly and essentially that which they are predicated of, nor are they something of it; and that accidents which exist in individuals as in subjects, do not correspond to any common essential predicates, because such universal predicates signify certain separated essences always subsisting by themselves, as the Platonists say.

But he answers that if Forms, i.e., Ideas, are assumed to exist, they should be happy, because according to the Platonists they have a nobler existence than the material things known to us. For the latter are particular and material, but the former universal and immaterial. For they are "premonstrations," i.e., certain exemplars, of material things (taking "premonstrations" here as above, when we spoke of something being shown beforehand in order to prove something). Therefore, since they are the premonstrations or exemplars of natural things, it is necessary that in these natural things there be found certain participations of those Forms which pertain to the essences of these natural things. Hence if such separated Forms exist, as the Platonists contend, they have nothing to do with the present matter. For we are concerned with things, the science of which is produced in us through demonstration. And these are things existing in matter and known to us and concerning which demonstrations deal. Consequently, if it be granted that "animal" is something separated, an existing premonstration, as it were, of natural animals, then when I say, "Man is an animal," in the sense that we use this preposition in demonstrating, "animal" signifies the essence of the natural thing concerning which the demonstration is made.

Lecture 34
(83a36–84a7)

LOGICAL REASONS WHY ONE DOES NOT PROCEED TO INFINITY IN PREDICATES

a36. If A is a quality of B
a37. Therefore A and B
a39. For one alternative
b1. But it has been shown
b8. Hence they will not be

b10. Nor (the other alternative)
b13. On the other hand
b24. Subject to these assumptions
b33. The argument we have given

Having set forth the distinction of predicates from one another as a necessary preliminary to demonstrating his proposition, the Philosopher now undertakes to show his proposition, namely, that there is no infinite process in predicates. And his treatment falls into two parts, according to the two ways in which he shows his proposition, the second part beginning at (83b33). Concerning the first he does two things. First, he shows that one does not proceed to infinity in predicates after the manner of circularity (see Lect. 8). Secondly, that one does not proceed to infinity in a direct line upwards or downwards (83b13). Concerning the first he does three things. First, granting what has gone before, he adds certain things required for showing his proposition. Secondly, from these and other established facts he concludes the proposition (83a37). Thirdly, he proves it (83a39).

First, therefore (83a36) he proposes two things: one of these is that since a predicate which signifies an accident signifies some genus of accident, such as quality, it cannot occur that two things be so related to one another that the first is a quality of the second and the second a quality of the first: for the nature of a quality and that of which it is the quality are diverse. The second is that universally it is not possible that a quality have some other quality inhering in it, because no accident is the subject of another accident, absolutely speaking. For to substance alone does the notion of subject properly belong.

Then (83a37) he proposes, as though concluding from these antecedents, what he intends to prove. He says, "If our preliminary rules are true, it is impossible that there be equal reciprocal predication," i.e., according to any of the above-mentioned ways. But this does not exclude the possibility of one thing's being truly predicated of another and conversely. For we say truly that man is white and that something white is a man. However, this is not done equally, i.e., according to an equal manner of predicating. And it is the same in essential predicates.

Then (83a39) he shows the proposition. First, in essential predicates. Secondly, in accidental ones (83b10). In regard to the first he does three things. First, he lays down a division of essential predicates. Secondly, he recalls something established above (83b1). Thirdly, he proves the proposition (83b8).

He says therefore first (83a39) that in order to show that they are not reciprocally predicated equally, it will be necessary to consider this in essential predicates. For that which is predicated equally will be predicated either as a substance or some other way: and if as a substance, then either as a genus or as a difference. For these are the two parts of a definition which signify the essence.

Then (83b1) he recalls what he had proved above at the beginning of the previous lecture, namely, that predicates of this kind are not infinite; because if they were to proceed to infinity, reciprocity or circularity would find no place therein. He says, therefore, that as has been shown above, an infinite process does not take place in such predicates either by ascending or by descending: for example, if "two-footed" be predicated of man, and "animal" of two-footed, something else of animal, there is no process to infinity either upwards or downwards. Thus, if "animal" were said essentially of man, and "man" of Callias, and this of someone else (supposing that there were a genus containing under it species, one of which would be Callias), it would not be possible to go on in this way to infinity. And he recalls the reason he used earlier to prove this: for every such substance which has something more universal that can be predicated of it and which can be predicated of some inferior is capable of being defined; but the most general genera of which other more universal things are not predicated, and singulars which are not predicated of any inferiors, are not capable of definition. Only the substance between these can be defined. But a substance of which an infinite number of things is predicated turns out to be indefinable, because one who would define it must go through and understand all the items which are substantially predicated of the defined, since all of them occur in the definition either as a genus or as a difference. But the infinite cannot be gone through. Therefore, it is required that neither a universal substance, which is not a supreme genus, nor a lowest subject, can have an infinitude of predicates which are predicated of it substantially. Consequently, there is no infinite process either upwards or downwards.

Then (83b8) he shows that there is no process to infinity after the manner of circularity in substantial predicates. And he says that if certain substantial predicates are predicated as genera of something, they are not predicated of one another equally, i.e., convertibly, i.e., so that one would be the genus of another and vice versa. To prove this he continues, "for the one will be what something truly is." As if to say: if something is predicated of something as a genus, that of which it is predicated is something which truly is that, i.e., something particular which receives that predication substantially. Therefore, if this be predicated of that as a genus, it will follow that something which belongs to something particularly would conversely receive the predication of it, which is tantamount to saying that a same thing is both a whole and a part in relation to the same thing—which is impossible. And the same reasoning applies to differences. Hence in *Topics* I it is stated that problems concerning a difference are reduced to problems concerning the genus.

Then (83b10) he shows that there cannot be an infinite circular process in predications in which an accident is predicated of a subject. And he says that there cannot be conversion of a quality with its subject; furthermore, none of the others which are predicated accidentally can have that sort of predication, unless the predication be made *per accidens* in the sense described above, namely, that accidents are not predicated of their subjects except *per accidens*. For quality and all these others are accidental to the subject; hence they are predicated of their substances as an accident of a subject.

Then (83b13) he shows universally that in no genus of predication is there an infinite process upwards or downwards. And he says that not only is there no infinite process in predications according to circulation, but also that in proceeding upwards or downwards the predicates will not be infinite. To prove this: First, he recalls certain things which were established above. Secondly, from these he concludes his proposition (83b24).

In regard to the first he reaffirms (83b13) that certain things can be predicated of a subject, whether they signify quality or quantity or any other genus of accident, or even items which constitute the substance of a thing, i.e., essential predicates.

Secondly, he reiterates that the latter, i.e., the substantial predicates, are finite.

Thirdly, he reaffirms that the genera of predicaments are finite, namely, quality, quantity and so on. For if someone were to say that quantity is predicated of substance, and quality of quantity, and so on to infinity, he excludes this on the ground that the genera of predicaments are finite.

Fourthly, he reaffirms that, as stated above, one thing is predicated of one thing in simple predication. And he mentions this because someone might say that one thing may well be first predicated of one thing, as "animal" of man, and this predication will be multiplied until something else can be found predicable of man, and when this is found, two things will be predicated of one, so that it will be said that man is a white animal. Thus, many more predicates might be found according to various combinations of predicates. And so by continually adding to this number, the predicates will be increased more and more, so that there will be a process to infinity in predicates, just as there is in the succession of numbers. But he excludes this by predicating one of one.

Fifthly, he repeats that we should not say that certain items are predicated absolutely "of things which are not something," i.e., of accidents, none of which is a subsistent being. For, as shown above, neither the subject nor an accident is properly predicated of an accident. For all things of this sort that are not substantial are accidents, and nothing is predicated, simply speaking, of such things. Yet they themselves are predicated: whether they be substantial predicates or accidental, they are predicated *per se* of their subjects; but if they are subjects or accidents being predicated of an accident, they are predicated in another way, i.e., *per accidens*. For it belongs to the very notion of all accidents that they be said of a subject; and since an accident is not a subject, nothing can, properly speaking, be predicated of it, because "none of such," i.e., no accidents, "are stated to be such that they are said to be that which is said," i.e., stated to be such that they themselves, rather than something else distinct from them, receives the predication of that which is predicated of them, as happens in the case of substances. For man is not called "animal" or "white" because something else is "animal" or "white," but because the very thing which is a man is animal or white; but a white thing is called "man" or "musician" because something else, namely, the subject of white is the man or musician. But the accident itself is in something distinct from it; and items which are predicated of an accident are predicated of something other than that accident, namely, of the subject of the accident: it is on this ground that they are predicated of the accident, as has been stated. (Now he mentioned this because if an accident is predicated of a subject and vice versa, and all accidents of a subject can be mutually predicated of one another, it will follow that predication could proceed to infinity, because an infinitude of things can happen to one thing).

Then (83b24) from these premises he shows his proposition, namely, that in a predication in which one thing is predicated of one thing there is no upward or downward process to infinity, because, as the fifth supposition states, all accidents are predicated of items which pertain to the substance of the thing. Furthermore, according to the second supposition, substantial predicates are not infinite; consequently, on the part of the subjects there is no infinite process downwards in these predications. Again, neither of these is infinite in the upward movement, i.e., neither the substantial nor the accidental predicates, both because the genera of accidents are finite, and because there is no infinite process upwards or downwards in any of these genera any more than there is in substantial predicates, because in each predicament the genus is predicated of a species in regard to something essential. Hence we can conclude universally that there must be some first subject of which something is predicated, thus establishing a stop in downward predication; then something else will be predicated of this, but it will come to a stop in the ascending process, so that something will be found which is not found predicated of another, either as the subsequent is predicated of its prior *per accidens,* or as the prior is predicated *per se* of its subsequent. This, therefore, is one way of demonstrating the proposition logically, and it is based on the diverse modes of predicating.

Then (83b33) he sets forth the second way of proving. And he says that when a proposition in which something is predicated of a subject is such that certain things can be predicated *per prius* of that subject, that proposition will be demonstrable: for example, this proposition, "Man is a substance," is demonstrated by the proposition, "Animal is a substance," because "substance" is predicated of animal before it is predicated of man. But if a proposition is demonstrable, there is no better way of knowing it than to know it by demonstration, just as we know indemonstrable principles better than by way of demonstration because we know them as self-evident. Besides, we cannot scientifically know such demonstrable propositions except through demonstration, because a demonstration is a syllogism productive of scientific knowledge, as we showed above. Furthermore, if a proposition is known through another one, and if we do not scientifically know the one through which it is known, or know it in the way which is better than knowing scientifically, then we do not scientifically know that proposition which is made known through it.

With these three suppositions in mind he proceeds thus: If one does know something purely through demonstration "and not from something or from supposition," it is necessary that there be a stop in the predicates which are taken as middles. (He says, "purely and not from something," to exclude demonstrations leading to the impossible, in which one proceeds against certain positions by arguing from propositions that have been agreed upon. Furthermore, he says, "or from supposition," to exclude such demonstrations as are formed in subalternate sciences, which suppose the conclusion of higher sciences, as explained above).

Therefore, one knows purely through demonstration when each one of the premised propositions, if it is demonstrable, is known through demonstration; and if it is not demonstrable, is known in virtue of itself. Under these suppositions it is necessary that there be a stop in predications, because if there is no stop but something prior can always be taken, it follows that there is demonstration of everything, as was said above. Therefore, if a conclusion is demonstrated, each of the premises must be demonstrable. But if we can have knowledge of it in no better way than by knowing it through demonstration, and if it will be necessary to demonstrate it through other propositions, and those through others again, and so on to infinity, then, since it is not possible to go through those infinites, we shall not be able to make it known through demonstration or through the method better than demonstration, since all things are demonstrable. The consequence will be that one knows nothing purely through demonstration, but only from supposition.

Finally, by way of summary he concludes the main proposition.

Lecture 35
(84a8–b2)

THAT THERE IS NOT AN INFINITE PROCESS UPWARD OR DOWNWARD IN PREDICATES IS SHOWN ANALYTICALLY

a8. but an analytical process

a10. Demonstration proves

a11. Now attributes may be

a18. In neither kind of

a23. Note, moreover, that all

a25. Attributes which are

a28. If this is so

a29. An immediately obvious

After showing logically that there is no infinite process upwards or downwards in predicates, the Philosopher now shows the same thing analytically. And his treatment falls into two parts. In the first he shows the principal proposition. In the second he infers certain corrolaries from the aforesaid (84b3) [L. 36]. Concerning the first he does two things. First, he proposes what he intends. Secondly, he proves his proposition (84a10).

He says therefore first (84a8) that the fact an infinite process upwards or downwards does not occur in the demonstrative sciences with which we are concerned can be more briefly and quickly manifested analytically than it was logically. Here we might note that analytic, i.e., demonstrative, science which is called judicative, because it resolves to self-evident principles, is a part of logic which even contains dialectics under it. However, it pertains to logic in general to consider predication universally, i.e., as containing under it predication which is *per se* and predication which is not *per se*. But predication *per se* is proper to demonstrative science. Therefore, above he proves his proposition logically, because he showed universally in every genus of predication that there is no infinite process. But here he intends to show it analytically, because he proves it only in things which are predicated *per se*. And this is a more efficient way; furthermore, it suffices for our purpose, because that is the only mode of predication we use in demonstration.

Then (84a10) he shows his proposition concerning which he does three things. First, he proposes which predication analytic, i.e., demonstrative, science employs, for it uses *per se* predication. Secondly, he recalls how many modes there are of such predication (84a11). Thirdly, he shows that there cannot be an infinite process in any mode of *per se* predication (84a18).

He says therefore first (84a10) that demonstration is concerned exclusively with items that are *per se* in things. For such are its conclusions and from such does it demonstrate, as was established above.

Then (84a11) he lays down two modes of predicating *per se*. For in the first place those things are predicated *per se* which are present in their subjects as constituting their essence, namely, when predicates are placed in the definition of a subject. Secondly, when the subjects themselves are in the essence of the predicate, i.e., when the subjects are placed in the definition of the predicate. And he gives examples of each of these ways: for "odd" is predicated *per se* of number in the second way, because "number" is placed in the definition of odd. For the odd is a number not divisible by two. Multitude or divisible, however, are predicated of number and are present in its definition; hence these are predicated *per se* of number in the first way. The other ways, which he mentioned previously, are reduced to these.

Then (84a18) he shows that there must be a stop in each of these modes of *per se* predication. In regard to this he does three things. First, he shows that there must be a stop both upwards and downwards in both of these modes of *per se* predication. Secondly, he concludes that there cannot be an infinitude of middles (84a28). Thirdly, he concludes that one cannot proceed to infinity in demonstrations (84a29). Concerning the first he does two things. First, he shows his proposition in regard to the second way of "saying *per se*," namely, when the subject is placed in the definition of the predicate. Secondly, in the first way, when the predicate is placed in the definition of the subject (84a25). In regard to the first he gives two reasons, in the first of which he proceeds in the following way.

First (84a18) he states his proposition, namely, that in neither of these modes of saying *per se* does an infinite process occur. Then he proves this of the second mode, as when "odd" is predicated of number. For if one goes further and states that something else should be predicated *per se* of "odd" according to that mode of saying *per se*, it follows that "odd" is present in its definition. But "number" is placed in the definition of odd; hence it will follow that "number" is also present in the definition of that third thing which is present *per se* in "odd." However, this cannot go on to infinity, so that an infinitude of things would be in the definition of something, as was established above. It remains, therefore, that in such *per se* predications an upward process to infinity does not occur, i.e., on the side of the predicate.

He presents the second reason (84a23) and says that no matter how far one advances in these *per se* predications of the second mode, it will be required that all the predicates taken in order be in their first subject, say in number, as predicated of it, because if "odd" is predicated *per se* of number, it will be required that whatever is predicated of odd be also predicated of number. And it is further required that "number" be in all of them, because if "number" is placed in the definition of odd, it has to be placed in the definition of all those things which are defined by "odd." And thus it follows that they are mutually in one another. Therefore, they will be convertible and none of wider extent than another: for this is the way proper attributes are related to their subjects. Hence, even though there be an infinitude of *per se* predicates in this way, it offers nothing to the purpose of one who intends to establish that there is an infinitude of predicates upwards or downwards.

Then (84a25) he proves his own point in regard to the first mode of saying *per se*, and he states that those things which are predicated in essence, i.e., as pertaining to the definition of the subject, cannot be infinite; otherwise, definition would be impossible, as we showed above. From this, therefore, he concludes that if all the items predicated in demonstrations are predicated *per se*, and if there is no infinite upward process in *per se* predicates, it is necessary that the predicates in demonstrations stop in the upward movement. And from this it also follows that they must stop in the downward movement, because no matter on which side infinity is posited, science and definition are destroyed, as is evident from what has been said above.

Then (84a28) he concludes from the foregoing that if there is a stop upwards and downwards, the middles cannot be infinite. For it has been established above that if the extremes are determinate, there cannot be an infinitude of middles.

Then (84a29) he further concludes that there is no infinite process in demonstrations. And he says that if the above statements are true, it is necessary that there be certain first principles of demonstration that are not demonstrated; consequently, there will not be demonstration of everything, as some claim, as was stated in the beginning of this book.

Then he goes on to show that his consequence follows. For if it is granted that there are certain principles of demonstrations, it is necessary that they be indemonstrable: for since every demonstration proceeds from things that are prior, as has been established above, then if the principles are demonstrated, it will follow that something would be prior to the principles, and this is contrary to the notion of a principle. And so, if not all things are demonstrable, it will follow that demonstrations do not proceed to infinity.

But all these follow from what has been established, namely, from the fact that there is no infinite process in middles, because the position that any of the foregoing statements is true, i.e., that demonstrations proceed to infinity, or that all things are demonstrable, or that there are no principles of demonstrations is tantamount to the position that no distance is immediate and indivisible, i.e., to the position that the two terms of any affirmative or negative proposition belong together only in virtue of a middle. For if any proposition is immediate, it follows that it is indemonstrable; because when something is demonstrated, it is necessary to take a term by interposing, i.e., by setting it between the subject and predicate, so that the predicate will be predicated of that term before being predicated of the subject—or removed from it. But the middle in demonstrations is not taken by assuming extraneously; for this would be to assume an extraneous middle and not a proper middle—which occurs in contentious and dialectical syllogisms. Therefore, if demonstrations were to proceed to infinity, it would follow that there is an infinitude of middles between two extremes. But this is impossible if, as has been established above, the predications stop in the upward and downward process. But as we have shown, first logically and then analytically, these predications do stop both upwards and downwards, as explained. Therefore, in virtue of this conclusion finally induced, he manifests the intent of the entire chapter and why each proposition was introduced.

Lecture 36
(84b3–85a11)

CERTAIN COROLLARIES FROM
PRECEDING LECTURES

After showing that a process to infinity does not occur in demonstrations, the Philosopher here adduces certain corollaries from what has been established. In regard to this he does two things. First, he shows that it is necessary to accept certain first propositions. Secondly, how those first things are to be used in demonstrations (84b32). Concerning the first he does two things. First, he shows that it is necessary to arrive at a first, when one thing is predicated of several. Secondly, when one thing is predicated of one (84b19). In regard to the first he does four things. First, he states the intended proposition. Secondly, he manifests the proposition (84b6). Thirdly, he proves it (84b9). Fourthly, he excludes an objection (84b15).

He says therefore first (84b3) that having demonstrated the aforesaid, namely, that there is no process to infinity in predications and demonstrations, it is clear that if something is predicated of two things, say A of C and of D, such that one of them is not predicated of the other, i.e., either not at all, as animal is predicated of man and ox, but neither of them is predicated of the other in any way; or not in all cases, as animal is predicated of man and male, neither of which is universally predicated of the other: when the terms, I repeat, are thus related, it is clear that there is no need for that predicate, which is predicated of both, to be in them in virtue of something common to both and this again in virtue of something else, and so on to infinity.

Then (84b6) he cites an example to clarify what he is proposing. For there are two species of triangle, one of which is scalene (none of whose three sides is equal to any other) and the other is isosceles (having two sides that are equal). But neither of these species is predicated of the other, and yet this proper attribute of having three angles equal to two right angles is present in both. Furthermore, this attribute is present in them in virtue of something common, namely, that each is a certain figure, namely, a triangle. However, this process does not continue forever so that something would always belong to it in virtue of something else and so on to infinity, so that "having three" would belong to triangle in virtue of something else again, and so on to infinity.

Then (84b9) he proves his proposition and says: Let the case be that B is predicated of C and of D in virtue of this common feature A. It will then be clear that B will be in C and in D in virtue of that common feature which is A. Now if A in turn is in them in virtue of something common, which again is in them in virtue of some other common item, there will be an infinite process in the middles. It follows, therefore, that between the two extremes C and B there falls an infinitude of middle terms. But this is impossible. Therefore, if a same thing is in several things, it is not necessary that it be in them always in virtue of something else *ad infinitum*, because it is necessary to reach certain "immediate distances," i.e., certain immediate predications, which he calls "distances," as explained above.

As can be seen from this proof of Aristotle's, it is not his understanding that it is not always true that when some item is predicated of several, which are not in turn predicated of one another, that item is not in the several in virtue of something common. For this is true in everything predicated as a proper attribute: for if it is in several, it is required that it be in them in virtue of something common which might even be nameless, as we explained above when we treated concerning the universal. But there is no infinite process in that which is common, as this reason introduced by the Philosopher clearly proves. However, if something be taken which is in several as a genus in its species, it will not always be necessary to find something prior in virtue of which it is in them. For example, "living" is in man and in ass in virtue of something prior, namely, in virtue of "animal," but it is not in animal and plant in virtue of something prior, because these are the first species of "living," i.e., of animate, body.

Then (84b15) he excludes an objection. For someone could say that it is always taken in virtue of something common, in the sense that something from another genus might be found common to them: for example, if we say that "to be self-movent" is in man and in ass in virtue of this common feature which is "animal" and also in virtue of some other common feature such as "having quantity" or having color or other things of this sort that can be taken *ad infinitum*.

In order to exclude this he says that it is required of the middle terms that they be taken from the same genus and "from the same atoms," i.e., indivisibles. (By "atoms" he means those extreme terms between which the middle must be taken, if that common item which is taken as a middle term is to be numbered among things which are predicated *per se*). Why the middle terms must be taken from the same genus he shows from the fact that, as stated above, a demonstration does not cross from one genus into another.

Then (84b19) he shows that it is necessary to arrive at a first among the predicables in which one thing is predicated of one. First, in affirmatives. Secondly, in negatives (84b24).

He says therefore first (84b19) that it is clear that when A is predicated of B, if there is a middle between them, we can use that middle to demonstrate that A is in B: and these are the principles of this kind of conclusion. And what things soever be taken as middles are the principles of the mediate conclusions which are concluded through them. For the "elements" or principles of demonstrations are none but immediate propositions: and I mean "either all such propositions or universal ones."

Now this can be understood in two ways: in one way so that universal proposition is taken as set off against singular. For it is not in virtue of a middle that the most special species is predicated of a singular. Hence this proposition, "Socrates is a man," is immediate, although it is not a principle of demonstration, because demonstrations are not concerned with singulars, since there is no science of such. Consequently, not every immediate proposition, but only one that is universal, is a principle of demonstration. In another way it can be understood in the sense that of all the propositions of any science, the universal propositions are the common propositions, such as "Every whole is greater than its part." Hence these are absolutely the principles of demonstrations and self-evident to all. But the proposition, "Man is an animal," or "The isosceles is a triangle," is not a principle of demonstration throughout the science but only for some particular demonstrations; hence such propositions are not self-evident to all.

Consequently, if there is a middle for a given proposition, one will demonstrate through a middle until something immediate is reached. But if there is no middle for a given proposition, it cannot be demonstrated. But this is the way to find the chief principles of demonstrations, namely, to proceed by analysis from mediates to immediates.

Then (84b24) he shows that it is necessary to arrive at a first in negatives, saying that if A is denied of B, if there is a middle to be taken from which A is removed prior to being removed from B, then this proposition, "B is not A," will be demonstrable. But if there is no such middle to be taken, that proposition will not be demonstrable but will be a principle of demonstration. And there are as many "elements," i.e., principles of demonstrations as there are terms at which a stop is reached in such a way that there is no further middle to find. For propositions formed of such terms are principles of demonstrations. Thus, if C be predicated immediately of B, and A be immediately removed from B or immediately predicated of it, B is the final term reached among the middles to be taken; hence each proposition will be immediate and a principle of demonstration.

Furthermore, it is clear from the foregoing that just as there are certain indemonstrable affirmative principles in which one thing is predicated of one thing by signifying that this is essentially that (as when a genus is predicated of a proximate species) or that this is in that (as when a proper attribute is predicated of its proper and immediate subject), so there are indemonstrable principles in negatives, namely, by denying that something is an essential predicate or a proper attribute. From this it is evident that there are certain principles of demonstration for demonstrating an affirmative conclusion (which must be concluded from all affirmative propositions), and there are certain principles of demonstration for proving a negative conclusion (to infer which requires that something negative be taken).

Then (84b32) he shows how first propositions are to be used in demonstrating. First, in affirmative demonstrations. Secondly, in negatives (85a3). In regard to the first he does three things. First, he shows how first and immediate propositions should be taken in demonstrations. Secondly, how such propositions are related to demonstrations (84b38). Thirdly, he summarizes (85a2).

He says therefore first (84b32) that when one is required to demonstrate an affirmative conclusion, for example, "Every B is A," it is first necessary to take something which is first predicated of B before A is, and of which A is also predicated, say C. Furthermore, if there is something of which A is predicated before A is predicated of C, and something ahead of that, and so on, then no proposition and no term signifying a being outside of A will be taken in the demonstration, because it will be necessary that A be predicated of it *per se* in such a way that it is contained under it and is not extraneous to it; but it will always be necessary to condense [crowd together] the middles. (Here he is speaking according to an example of men who appear crowded together when they are sitting on a bench and there is no room for anyone else to sit between any two who are seated; in like fashion, the middles in demonstrations are condensed when no middle falls between the terms taken). And this is his meaning when he says, "the middle is condensed until the spaces become indivisible," i.e., the distances between two terms are such that they cannot be divided into several such distances, but there is only one space. And this occurs when a proposition is immediate. For it is then that a proposition is one, not only actually but potentially, when it is immediate. For if it is mediate, then although it is actually one (because one thing is predicated of one thing), it is in fact several in potency, because when the middle is taken, two propositions are formed. In the same way, a line which is actually one, inasmuch as it is continuous, is several in potency, inasmuch as it is divisible at an intermediate point. Hence he says that an immediate proposition is one as a simple indivisible.

Then (84b38) he shows the relation between an immediate proposition and a demonstration. Here we should note that, as it is stated in *Meta-*

physics X, in every genus there must be one first thing which is the most simple in that genus and is the measure of all the things in that genus. And because a measure is homogeneous to the thing measured, such first indivisibles will vary according to the diversity of genera. Hence these will not be the same in all genera: but in regard to weights one indivisible, the ounce or *mina,* is taken as the minimum weight (even though it is not the absolute minimum, because every weight is further divisible into smaller weights, but it is taken as a minimum by supposition). Again, in melodies there is taken as the one principle "a tone," which consists in a proportion of an octave and a half or a "diesis," which is the difference between a tone and a semi-tone. Similarly, in diverse genera there are diverse indivisible principles.

Now the principles of a syllogism are propositions; hence it is required that the most simple proposition, which is immediate, be the unit which is the measure of syllogisms. But demonstration has, over and above a syllogism, the added feature that it causes science. Now "understanding" and science are related as the indivisible unit is related to the many. For science is effected by going from principles to conclusions, whereas "understanding" is the absolute and simple acceptance of a self-evident principle. Hence "understanding" corresponds to the immediate proposition, and science to a conclusion, which is a mediate proposition. Consequently, the indivisible unit of a demonstration regarded as a syllogism is the immediate proposition. But on the part of the science which it causes, the unit is "understanding."

Then (85a2) he sums up and concludes what was established above, namely, that the middle in affirmative syllogisms does not fall outside the extremes.

Then (85a3) he shows how to use immediate propositions in negative syllogisms. First, in the first figure. Secondly, in the second (85a7). Thirdly, in the third (85a10).

He says therefore first (85a3) that in negative syllogisms in the first figure, none of the middles taken while proceeding to immediates will fall outside the genus of the terms of an affirmative proposition; for example, if it is to be demonstrated that "No B is A," and the middle taken is C, we have the following syllogism: "No C is A; but every B is C: therefore, No B is A." Now if it should be necessary to prove that "No C is A," one will be required to take a middle of C and A, i.e., one that will be predicated of C and consequently of B; thus it will belong to the genus of the terms of the affirmative proposition. And so it will always turn out that the middles taken will not fall outside the affirmative proposition, although they will fall outside the genus of the negative predicate, i.e., outside the genus of A.

Then (85a7) he shows how it is in the second figure, saying that if one is required to demonstrate in the second figure that "No E is D," by taking C as middle, so as to form the syllogism, "Every D is C; but No E is C or Some E is not C: therefore, No E is D or Not every E is D," the middle term taken will never fall outside of E. For if it should be necessary to demonstrate that "no E is C," one will have to find a middle between E and C, because in the second figure it will always be necessary to prove a negative, since an affirmative cannot be concluded in this figure. Hence, just as in the first figure the middles are always taken on the side of the affirmative proposition, so in the second figure the middles will always be taken on the side of the negative proposition.

Then (85a10) he shows how it is in the third figure, saying that in the third figure the middles which are taken will not be outside the predicate which is denied, nor outside the subject of which it is denied. The reason for this is that the middle is the subject in both propositions, whether affirmative or negative: hence if it is necessary to take yet another middle, it will again have to act as the subject of both, whether affirming or denying. And so the middles which are taken will never be taken outside the predicate which is denied, or outside the subject of which it is denied.

Lecture 37
(85a12–b21)

WHETHER UNIVERSAL DEMONSTRATION IS STRONGER THAN PARTICULAR DEMONSTRATION

a12. Since demonstrations may
a17. Let us first examine
a20. The following considerations
a31. The universal has not

b4. We may retort
b15. If there is a single
b18. Because the universal has

After determining about the demonstrative syllogism, the Philosopher now treats of the comparison of demonstrations one to another. And because science is caused by demonstration, his treatment is divided into two parts. In the first he treats of the comparison of demonstrations. In the second of the comparison of sciences (87a31) [L. 41]. In regard to the first he does three things. First, he raises a doubt concerning the comparison of demonstrations. Secondly, he lays down the order of procedure (85a17). Thirdly, he deals with the doubts raised (85a20).

He says therefore first (85a12) that demonstration is divided in three ways: for in one way it is divided into universal and particular; in another way into categorical and privative, i.e., affirmative and negative; in a third way into that which demonstrates ostensively and that which leads to the impossible. In each division, therefore, the question arises as to which is the stronger.

Then (85a17) he shows what order should be followed, saying that the comparison of universal to particular demonstration should be treated first. And when this has been done, we shall speak of demonstrations which demonstrate something affirmatively and of those which demonstrate to the impossible, namely, whether the affirmative is stronger and whether the demonstration to the impossible is stronger.

Then (85a20) he deals with the problems he has proposed. First, of the comparison of the particular with the universal. Secondly, of the comparison of the affirmative with the negative (86a32) [L. 39]. Thirdly, of the comparison of the ostensive with that which leads to the impossible (87a1) [L. 40]. Concerning the first he does three things. First, he proposes reasons to show that the particular demonstration is more powerful than the universal. Secondly, he solves them (85b4). Thirdly, he gives reasons to the contrary (85b22) [L. 38].

In regard to the first he sets forth three reasons, remarking that in virtue of these reasons to be set down forthwith, it will perhaps seem to some that a particular demonstration is of more value than a universal one.

The first reason (85a20) is this: That demonstration is stronger through which we know best in a scientific way. And he proves it on the ground that the strength of a demonstration consists in knowing in a scientific way. For the most that a thing can do is called its strength: for the strength of a man able to carry 100 pounds is not that he can carry ten but that he can carry 100, which is the limit of his power, as it is stated in *On the Heavens* I. Now the most that a demonstration can do is to cause scientific knowledge; consequently, that is the strength of a demonstration. But a thing is more perfect to the extent that it attains the strength appropriate to it, as is clear from *Physics* VII. Hence this proposition is quite evident, namely, that the better a demonstration causes scientific knowledge, the stronger it is. (He assumes that we know a thing better when we know it according to itself than when we know it according to something else: thus we know more in regard to Coriscus when we know that Coriscus himself is a musician than when we merely know that some man is a musician). And this proposition is true, absolutely speaking, because that which is *per se* is always prior to and the cause of that which is through something else, as it is stated in *Physics* VIII.

From these facts the conclusion is gathered that a demonstration which makes one know something according to itself is stronger than one which makes one know something according to something else. But a universal demonstration demonstrates and makes one know something not according to itself, but according to something else, namely, according to the universal, as that a triangle with two equal sides, i.e., an isosceles, "has three," not because it is isosceles but because it is a triangle. A particular demonstration, on the other hand, demonstrates about a particular thing according to itself. Hence according to this it follows that a particular demonstration is stronger than a universal.

Then (85a31) he gives a second reason. It is this: The universal is not something apart from singulars, as was proved in *Metaphysics* VII. But a universal demonstration leads one to think, from the very manner of its demonstration, that the universal is "something," i.e., a certain nature in the realm of beings: for example, when it demonstrates something of triangle apart from particular triangles, and of number apart from particular numbers.

To these two propositions he adds two others: to the first one, which stated that the universal is not something apart from the singulars, he adds this proposition, namely, that a demonstration concerned with being is stronger than one concerned with non-being. But to the second proposition, which stated that a universal demonstration leads one to think that a universal is something existing as a real nature, he adds another proposition, namely, that a demonstration which does not cause error is stronger than one which leads to error.

Then he shows that one is led into error on account of a universal demonstration, because one who proceeds according to a universal demonstration demonstrates concerning some universal as of some analogue, i.e., as of something common which is referred to many things proportionally, as though there existed something common which is neither a line nor a number nor a solid, i.e., a body, nor a plane, i.e., a surface, but "something apart from these," i.e., a universal quantity; or "something owing to them," i.e., something which must be posited, if they are to have the formality of quantity.

Thus, therefore, in virtue of two middles, equivalent as it were to two arguments, he concludes to one conclusion, saying that if the universal demonstration is as described, i.e., is less an entity than the particular, and more likely to create a false opinion than the particular, it follows from these two middles that the universal ranks lower than the particular.

Then (85b4) he solves these reasons in order. First, he solves the first one, saying that the first, i.e., the ground on which the first reason rests, is no different in the universal than in the particular, because in both cases we find something which is according to itself and something according to something else. And he shows that something which is according to itself is found in the universal. For "to have three angles equal to two right angles" does not belong to isosceles according to itself, i.e., precisely as isosceles, but according as it is a triangle. Consequently, one who knows that a certain triangle, namely, the isosceles, "has three," has less knowledge of that which is *per se* than if he knew that a triangle "has three." And it must be admitted universally that if there be any characteristic which does not belong to triangle as triangle, but that characteristic is nevertheless demonstrated of it, the demonstration will not be true. But if it is in it precisely as it is a triangle, then by knowing it in a universal way of triangle precisely as of triangle, he has a more perfect knowledge.

From these facts, therefore, he concludes a conditional statement in whose antecedent three things are placed: one is that "triangle" is in more things than isosceles is; the second is that "triangle" is predicated of isosceles and of those others according to the same formality and not equivocally; the third is that "having three angles equal to two right angles" is present in every triangle. With these three suppositions, the consequent is that "the having of three" does not belong to triangle precisely as it is isosceles, but vice versa.

Now the first two were put in the antecedent on the ground that if "triangle" were not the wider term or if it were predicated equivocally of its several inferiors, it would not be compared to "isosceles" as universal to particular. But he added the third, because if "having three" did not belong to every triangle, it would not belong to isosceles precisely as triangle, but in virtue of being a certain triangle; just as the characteristic of "having three" does not belong to every figure precisely as figure, but because it is a certain figure which is a triangle.

From these statements, therefore, he concludes to the opposite of that which the objection presupposed, namely, he concludes that one who knows in the universal knows the thing *per se* and *as such* in a better way than one who knows in the particular. And from this he further concludes his chief proposition, namely, that universal demonstration is stronger than particular.

Then (85b15) he answers the second reason, saying that if the universal is predicated of several according to one formality and not equivocally, the universal, so far as its formality is concerned, i.e., so far as science and demonstration are concerned, will not be less of an entity than the particular, but more. For the incorruptible is more a being than the corruptible; but the formality of a universal is incorruptible, whereas particulars are corruptible, in that they are subject to corruption as to their individual principles, although not as to the formality of the species, which is common to all and conserved through generation. And so in regard to that which pertains to their formality, the universals are beings to a higher degree than particulars. Nevertheless, in regard to natural subsistence the particulars, which are called the first and chief substances, have more being.

Then (85b18) he answers the third reason, saying that although in propositions or demonstrations that are universal, something which is one according to itself, say "triangle," is signified, nevertheless there is no need for anyone to suppose on this account that "triangle" is some one thing apart from the many, any more than there is need in the case of things which do not signify substance but some genus of accident (when we signify them absolutely, as when we say "whiteness" or "fatherhood"), to suppose that such things exist apart from the substance. For the intellect is able to understand one of the things which are joined in reality without actually thinking of some other one; yet the intellect is not false. Thus, if something white is musical, I am able to think of the white and attribute something to it and demonstrate something of it, say, that it disperses the vision, without adverting at all to musical. However, if one were to understand that the white one is not musical, then the intellect would be false. And so when we say or understand that whiteness is a color, no mention being made of the subject, we are saying something true. But it would be false, were we to say that the whiteness which is a color is not in a subject. In like fashion, when we say that every man is an animal, we are speaking truly, even though no particular man is mentioned. But it would be false were we to say that man is "an animal existing apart from particular men." And if this is so, it follows that demonstration is not the cause of the false opinion according to which someone supposes that the universal is some thing outside the singulars, but it is rather the hearer who understands incorrectly. Hence this does not detract at all from universal demonstration.

Lecture 38
(85b22–86a32)

UNIVERSAL DEMONSTRATION IS STRONGER THAN PARTICULAR DEMONSTRATION

b22. Demonstration is syllogism

b28. Our search for the reason

a3. The more demonstration

a11. Demonstration which teaches

a14. Proof becomes more and more

a21. The clearest indication

a28. Moreover, commensurately

After answering the arguments which favored the false side, the Philosopher now introduces arguments for the true side, namely, to show that universal demonstration is the more powerful. In regard to this he sets down seven reasons, adding them to the previous solutions from which the proposition can also be concluded, as was clear from the above.

The first reason (85b22), is this: Demonstration is a syllogism showing the cause and *propter quid:* for this is the way scientific knowing takes place, as stated above. But the universal does this better than the particular. For as was shown in the first solution, something is *per se* in the universal more than in the particular. But that in which something is *per se* is the cause of this something: for the subject is the cause of the proper attribute which is in it *per se*. However, the first thing in which the proper attribute is present is the universal, as is clear from what has been stated above. Hence it is plain that, properly speaking, the cause is that which is universal. From this he concludes the proposition, namely, that universal demonstration is more valuable as better declaring the cause and *propter quid*.

Then (85b28) he gives the second reason. This reason is taken from the final causes. Here it should be pointed out that something is the end of another thing both in regard to becoming and in regard to being: in regard to becoming, as generation is for the sake of form; in regard to being, as a house is for the sake of habitation.

He says, therefore, that we search for the "reason why" something is done or why something is, until we reach the point where there is nothing further to assign, beyond the point reached, as the reason why that comes to be or is, whose reason why is sought. And when we find this we think that we know the *propter quid:* the reason being that that which is ultimate in this way, i.e., leaving nothing further to be sought, is truly the end and terminus which is being sought when we seek the *propter quid*. And he gives this example: if we should ask why someone went out, and the answer is given, "to get money," and this in order to pay a debt, and "this for this other reason," namely, lest he be guilty of injustice; and we continue in this way until there is nothing further for the sake of which as for an end—as when we arrive at the ultimate end, which is happiness—we will say that it was for this, as for an end, that he went. And it is the same in all other things that are or are done for the sake of an end: when we arrive at it, we will know the reason why he went.

Now if things are so related in the other causes as they are in the final cause, namely, that we know fully when the last one has been reached, then we will know best in the others, when we shall have arrived at the fact that "this is in this" no longer because of something further. And this happens when we shall have reached the universal.

To elucidate this he offers the following example: If we should ask concerning this particular triangle, why its exterior angles are equal to four right angles, the answer will be that this happens to this triangle because it is isosceles; and it is so for the isosceles, because it is a triangle; and it is so for a triangle, because it is such and such a rectilinear figure. If no further step can be taken, then we know in the best way. But this happens when the universal has been reached. Therefore the universal demonstration is stronger than the particular.

Then (86a3) he gives the third reason, saying that the more one proceeds toward particulars, the nearer one gets to what is infinite; because, as it is stated in *Physics* III, the infinite is appropriate to matter which is the principle of individuation. On the other hand, the more one proceeds toward the universal, the nearer he gets to what is simple and to the end itself; because the universal reason is taken on the part of the form, which is simple and which has the character of an end insofar as it terminates the infinitude of matter. Now it is obvious that infinite things as such are not scientifically knowable; rather to the extent that they are finite, to that extent are they knowable; because the principle of knowing a thing is not the matter but the form. Therefore, it is obvious that universals are scientifically more knowable than particulars. Consequently, they are also more demonstrable, because a demonstration is a syllogism that makes one know scientifically. But a demonstration of the more demonstrable is more powerful; for things which are described one in terms of the other grow apace. But demonstration is described in terms of the demonstrable. Consequently, since universals are more demonstrable, universal demonstration will be more powerful.

Then (86a11) he gives the fourth reason and it is this: Since the end of demonstration is scientific knowledge, the more things a demonstration enables one to know, the more powerful it is. And this is what he states, namely, that a demonstration, according to which a man knows one thing and something additional, is preferable to one according to which a man knows only the one. But a man who has knowledge of the universal knows also the particular, so long as he knows that the particular is contained under the universal. Thus, one who knows that every mule is sterile, knows that this animal, which he recognizes to be a mule, is sterile. But one who knows the particular does not on that account know the universal. For if I know that this mule is sterile, I do not on that account know that every mule is sterile. It remains, therefore, that universal demonstration, through which the universal is known, is stronger than particular, through which the particular is known.

Then (86a14) he gives the fifth reason, and it is this: The nearer to the first principle the middle of a demonstration is, the more powerful is the demonstration. He proves this on the ground that if a demonstration which proceeds from an immediate principle is more certain than one which does not proceed from an immediate, but from a mediate, principle, then it is necessary that to the extent that a demonstration proceeds from a middle nearer an immediate principle, the more powerful it is. But a universal demonstration proceeds from a middle nearer the principle which is an immediate proposition. And he exemplifies this with terms. For if one is required to demonstrate A, which is the most universal, of B, which is the most particular, say "substance" of man, and B and C, say "living" and "animal" be taken, such that B is more general than C, as "living" than "animal," it is obvious that B, which is the more universal, will be immediate to A; consequently, more will be known through it than through C, which is less universal. Hence it remains that universal demonstration is more powerful than particular.

But he remarks that some of the above reasons are "logical," because, namely, they proceed from common principles which are not proper to demonstration; especially the third and fourth, which take as their middle something which is common to all knowledge. However, the other three, namely, the first, second and fifth, seem to be more analytic, proceeding as they do from principles proper to demonstration.

Then (86a21) he gives the sixth reason and says that the primacy of universal demonstration over particular is evident from the very propositions from which the two demonstrations proceed. For the universal demonstration proceeds from universal propositions, whereas the particular demonstration proceeds from a particular proposition. Now the comparison between universal and particular propositions is such that one who has knowledge of the former, i.e., of the universal, somehow knows the latter, namely, in potency. For the particulars are potentially in the universal, as the parts are potentially in a whole. Thus, if one knows that every triangle has three angles equal to two right angles, he already knows it potentially of isosceles. But one who knows something in a particular way does not on that account know it universally either potentially or actually. For the universal proposition is neither potentially nor actually contained in the particular. Therefore, if that demonstration is more powerful which proceeds from stronger propositions, it follows that universal demonstration is more powerful.

It should be noted that this reason does not differ from the fourth one given above, except that in the fourth one the comparison was made between the conclusions which are known through demonstration, whereas here the comparison is between the propositions from which the demonstration proceeds.

Then (86a28) he gives the seventh reason and it is this: The universal demonstration is intelligible, i.e., is terminated in the intellect, because it finishes in a universal which is known only by the intellect. On the other hand, a particular demonstration, although it begins in the intellect is terminated in sense, because it concludes a particular which is directly known by sense, and the reason demonstrating reaches out to the particular through a certain application or reflexion. Now since intellect is more powerful than sense, it follows that universal demonstration is stronger than particular.

Finally, he concludes that this is clear in virtue of all that has been said above.

Lecture 39
(86a32–b40)

AFFIRMATIVE DEMONSTRATION IS STRONGER THAN NEGATIVE

a32. That affirmative demonstration
b10. It has been proved
b12. So we are compelled

b30. The basic truth of
b39. Affirmative demonstration is more

After showing that universal demonstration is more powerful than particular, the Philosopher here shows that affirmative demonstration is more powerful than negative. In support of this he presents five reasons.

In the first reason (86a32) he presupposes that, all else being equal, the better demonstration is the one which proceeds from fewer postulates or suppositions or propositions. How these differ is clear from what has been stated above. For propositions might even be taken to mean those *per se* known statements which are neither suppositions nor postulates, as stated above. But a supposition is not the same as a postulate: for a supposition is a proposition which is not *per se* known, but is taken by the learner as opined; a postulate, on the other hand, is a proposition which is not *per se* known and has not been opined by the learner, nothing being said about whether he has opinions to the contrary or not.

Accordingly, he shows in two ways that, other things being equal, the demonstration which employs fewer of these is better. First, because if it happens that both propositions from which one proceeds are equally known, it follows that one knows more quickly through fewer propositions than through more, because a discourse through fewer propositions comes to an end sooner than one through more. For it is more desirable or more advantageous that a man learn more quickly. Hence, it remains that a demonstration which proceeds from fewer propositions, provided they are equally known, is better.

Secondly, he proves the same proposition universally without the above supposition, namely, that all the propositions used are equally known. To prove this he assumes this supposition, namely, that the middles which are of one order are equally known, but the middles which are prior are better known. For this must be universally true. Therefore, supposing this, take one demonstration in which it is demonstrated that A is in E in virtue of three middles, B, C, D, so that a conclusion is reached from four propositions, namely, "Every B is A," "Every C is B," "Every D is C" and "Every E is D." Then let the other demonstration be one which concludes the same conclusion, namely, that A is in E, through two middles which are F and G.

135

Under these conditions, from the fact that the order of knowing is proportionate to the order of middles, since the prior known are the better known, as has been said, it is obvious that the proposition, "Every D is A" in the first demonstration must be as well known as "Every E is A" in the second, because two middles are used for obtaining each. However, it is also obvious that in the first demonstration this proposition, "Every D is A," is prior and better known than the proposition, "Every E is A," because this latter is demonstrated from something prior in the first demonstration—and from what has been established above, it is apparent that that through which something is demonstrated is more credible and more known than that which is demonstrated through it. What remains, therefore, is that this proposition, "Every E is A," so far as it is concluded by the second demonstration, is better known than the same proposition so far as it is concluded by the first demonstration which used more middles. Consequently, a demonstration which proceeds from fewer is better than one which proceeds from more.

Therefore, having proved the major proposition, Aristotle assumes that an affirmative proposition proceeds from fewer things than a negative: not indeed from fewer terms or fewer propositions materially, because every demonstration, whether affirmative or negative, demonstrates through three terms and two propositions; but a negative demonstration is said to proceed from more according to the quality of the propositions. For an affirmative demonstration takes only "being," i.e., proceeds only from affirmative propositions, whereas a negative demonstration takes "being and non-being," i.e., uses an affirmative and a negative. Therefore, the affirmative is stronger than the negative.

Then (86b10) he presents the second reason. Now this second reason is introduced to support the first, which might seem deficient on the ground that it was not subsumed under the major proposition in the way in which it was proved. Therefore, to forestall any subterfuge he adds this second reason to confirm the first. For it has been shown in *Prior Analytics* I that a syllogism cannot be formed out of two negative propositions, but one proposition at least must be affirmative and the other may be negative. This clearly shows that affirmative propositions have greater efficacy for syllogizing than do negatives. Hence it follows that an affirmative demonstration which proceeds from affirmatives only, is more powerful than the negative demonstration which proceeds from a negative and an affirmative.

Then (86b12) he presents the third reason, saying that as a consequence of the foregoing reasons, we can assert that when a demonstration is augmented, i.e., by resolving propositions into their principles, it is necessary that there be several affirmative propositions, but no more than one negative. Thus, let us take the following negative demonstration: "No B is A; Every C is B: therefore, No C is A." Then let this demonstration be augmented as to both propositions, if each is mediate, by taking a middle for each, letting the middle of the major proposition, "No B is A," be D, and the middle of the minor proposition, "Every C is B," be E. Now since this proposition, "Every C is B," is affirmative and was concluded without benefit of a negative, it is necessary that its middle, namely, E, be affirmative to each extreme. Consequently, there are two affirmative propositions, namely, "Every E is B," and "Every C is E," from which "Every C is B" is concluded. But the major proposition is negative, namely, "No B is A." Now a negative is not concluded from two negatives; but in the first figure, in which demonstration is best made, according to what has been said, that major must be negative and the minor affirmative. Consequently, this middle, D, must be affirmative to B and negative to A, as in the following demonstration: "No D is A; Every B is D; therefore No B is A."

Hence by augmenting a negative demonstration by resolving the propositions into their principles, there will be four propositions: only one of these is negative, namely, "No D is A," and the other three will be affirmative, namely, "Every B is D," "Every E is B," and "Every C is E." And the same thing will happen in all other syllogisms, because it is always required that the middle, through which the affirmative propositions are proved, be affirmative to both extremes. But the middle through which the negative proposition is proved must be negative to one of the extremes only. Thus it follows that only one proposition is negative and the others all affirmative.

From this it is clear that it is mainly through affirmatives that a negative proposition is demonstrated. Therefore, if that through which something is demonstrated is more known and more credible than that which is demonstrated through it (since a negative proposition is mainly proved by affirmatives and not vice versa), it follows that the affirmative proposition is prior and more known and more credible than the negative. Accordingly, the affirmative demonstration will be more valuable.

Then (86b30) he presents the fourth reason, saying that the principle of a demonstrative syllogism is an immediate universal proposition, in the sense that the proper principle of an affirmative syllogism is an affirmative proposition and the proper principle of a negative syllogism is a universal negative proposition. But the effect of a nobler principle is itself more noble. Therefore, as an affirmative proposition is to a negative, so is an affirmative demonstration to a negative one. But an affirmative proposition is more powerful than a negative one. (He proves this in two ways: first, because the affirmative is prior and better known, since the negative is proved by the affirmative and not vice versa. Secondly, because affirmation naturally precedes negation, as being is prior to non-being—for although in one and the same thing which passes from non-being to being, the non-being is prior in the order of time, yet in the order of nature, being is prior and, absolutely speaking, is prior even in time, because non-beings are not brought into existence except by something that is). Therefore, it is clear that affirmative demonstration is more powerful than negative.

Then (86b39) he presents the fifth reason and it is this: That upon which something depends is more principal. But negative demonstration depends on affirmative, because there cannot be a negative demonstration without an affirmative proposition, which is not proved except by an affirmative demonstration. Therefore, affirmative demonstration is more principal than negative.

Lecture 40
(87a1–30)

NEGATIVE OSTENSIVE DEMONSTRATION IS STRONGER THAN DEMONSTRATION LEADING TO THE IMPOSSIBLE

a1. Since affirmative demonstration	a13. The order of the terms
a2. We must first make certain	a17. All the same the
a7. *Reductio ad impossibile*	a19. For the destructive result

After showing that universal demonstration ranks higher than particular, and affirmative higher than negative, the Philosopher here shows, thirdly, that ostensive demonstration is more powerful than that which leads to the impossible. Concerning this he does three things. First, he proposes what he intends. Secondly, he prefaces certain matters needed for showing the proposition (87a2). Thirdly, he proves his proposition (87a17).

He says therefore first (87a1) that since we have shown that affirmative demonstration is more powerful than negative, from this it further follows that an affirmative ostensive demonstration is more powerful than one which leads to the impossible.

Then (87a2) he lays down certain things that are necessary for showing his proposition. In regard to this he does three things. First, he shows what a negative demonstration is. Secondly, he shows what a demonstration to the impossible is (87a7). Thirdly, he concludes the comparison of the one with the other (87a13).

He says therefore first (87a2) that in order to manifest the proposition it is necessary to point out the difference between them, i.e., between the negative demonstration and the one leading to the impossible. If, therefore, one assumes that A is in No B, and B is in every C, and concludes that A is in no C, it will be a negative demonstration.

Then (87a7) he elucidates what a demonstration leading to the impossible is. And he says that a demonstration leading to the impossible is as follows: Suppose we are to prove that A is not in B. Let us assume the opposite of what we wish to prove, namely, assume that every B is A; then assume that B is in C, using the proposition, "Every C is B"; from these the conclusion follows that "Every C is A," which is such that everyone knows and admits that it is impossible. From this we conclude that the first proposition, namely, "Every B is A," is false. Consequently, it will be necessary either that no B is A or at least that some B is not A.

But it must be understood that "A is not in B" follows, when it is clear that B is in C, because if it is obvious that "Every C is A" is false, but not obvious that "Every C is B" is true, it would not, just in virtue of the inference, be plain that "Every B is A" is false; for the falsity of the conclusion might have proceeded from either premise, as was stated above.

Then (87a13) he concludes the comparison of each of the aforesaid demonstrations. First, he shows wherein they agree, namely, in having a like ordering of their terms. For just as in the negative demonstration, B is taken as the middle between A and C, so too in that which leads to the impossible.

Secondly, he shows wherein they differ, because it makes a difference which negative proposition in each demonstration is better known, namely, whether it be the proposition, "No B is A," or the proposition, "No C is A": for in a demonstration leading to the impossible, the proposition "C is not A" is taken to be better known, since from the fact that A is not in C one shows that A is not in B. Consequently, the proposition, "C is not A," is taken as better known. But when that which is set down as a premise of the syllogism is taken as better known, there is a demonstrative, i.e., an ostensive, negative demonstration.

Then (87a17) he shows his proposition in the following way: The proposition, "B is not A," is naturally prior to the proposition, "C is not A." And this is proved by the fact that the premises, from which the conclusion is inferred, are naturally prior to the conclusion. But in the order of the syllogism, "C is not A" is set down as the conclusion, whereas "B is not A" is set down as that from which the conclusion is inferred. Therefore, "B is not A" is naturally prior.

Then (87a19) he removes an objection. For someone could say that even the negative "C is not A" is the one from which one concludes "B is not A" in a demonstration to the impossible. But he excludes this, saying that by the fact that the conclusion is destroyed and from its destruction something in the premises is destroyed, it does not follow that what was first the conclusion is now a principle and vice versa, absolutely and according to nature, but only in a qualified sense. For the relation of conclusion to principle is such that the principle is destroyed by the conclusion's being destroyed. But that functions as the principle from which a syllogism proceeds, which is related to the conclusion as a whole to a part; while the conclusion is to the principle, as part to whole.

For the subject of a negative conclusion is subsumed under the subject of the first proposition. But the propositions AC and AB are not so related to each other that AC is to AB as whole to part. For BA is not subsumed under CA; rather it is just the opposite. Hence it remains that although from the destruction of CA, one concludes to the destruction of BA, nevertheless CA is naturally the conclusion and BA the principle. Consequently, "B is not A" is naturally better known than "C is not A."

From this, one argues in the following way: That demonstration is the worthier which proceeds from better known and prior principles. But a negative demonstration proceeds from something better known and prior than does a demonstration leading to the impossible. For each causes one to know something in virtue of a negative proposition: but the negative demonstration proceeds to cause belief from the negative proposition, "B is not A", which is naturally prior. Demonstration to the impossible, on the other hand, proceeds to cause belief from the negative proposition, "C is not A," which is naturally posterior. What remains, therefore, is that the negative demonstration is more powerful than one which leads to the impossible. Furthermore, as was shown above, the affirmative is stronger than the negative. Therefore, an affirmative ostensive demonstration is much stronger than one which leads to the impossible.

Lecture 41
(87a31–b17)

COMPARISON OF SCIENCE TO SCIENCE FROM STANDPOINT OF CERTAINTY AND OF UNITY AND DIVERSITY

a31. The science which is
a38. A single science is one
a38. all the subjects

a41. One science differs from
b1. This is verified when
b5. One can have several

After comparing demonstrations one with another, the Philosopher here treats of the comparison of science, which is the effect of demonstration. And his treatment falls into two parts. In the first he compares science to science. In the second he compares science to other modes of knowing (88b30) [L. 44]. Concerning the first he does two things. First, he compares science to science as to certitude. Secondly, as to unity and multiplicity (87a38).

Concerning the first (87a31) he lays down three modes whereby one science is more certain than another. Laying down the first mode, he says that that science is prior and more certain than another, which, namely, makes one know the same things both *quia* and *propter quid*. However, that science is not more certain which knows only the *quia* apart from one which knows *propter quid*. But this is the relation of subalternating science to subalternate, as has been said above, namely, that the subalternate science in isolation knows *quia* without knowing *propter quid:* thus a surgeon knows *that* circular wounds are healed more slowly, but he does not know *why*. But such knowledge pertains to the geometer who considers that characteristic of a circle according to which its parts do not lie close enough to form an angle, the nearness of whose sides makes triangular wounds heal more quickly.

He lays down the second mode when he says that a science which is not concerned with a subject is more certain than one which is. Here "subject" is taken to mean sensible matter because, as the Philosopher teaches in *Physics* II, some sciences are purely mathematical, those, namely, which abstract according to reason from sensible matter, as geometry and arithmetic; but other sciences are intermediate, namely, those which apply mathematical principles to sensible matter, as optics applies the principles of geometry to the visual line, and harmony, i.e., music, applies the principles of arithmetic to sensible sounds. Hence he says here that arithmetic is both more certain and prior to music: it is prior, because music uses its principles for something non-mathematical; it is more certain, because lack of certitude arises from matter's changes. Hence the closer one gets to matter, the less certain the science.

He lays down the third mode when he says that a science which arises from fewer things is prior and more certain than one which arises from an addition, i.e., than one which results from that addition. And he gives the example that geometry is posterior to and less certain than arithmetic: for the things of geometry are the result of adding to the things which pertain to arithmetic. This is easy to see if one admits the postulates of Plato, according to which Aristotle is proceeding here, using them to prove his point (as he frequently uses the opinions of other philosophers as examples in his logical works in order to explain a point). Now Plato laid it down that "one" is the substance of each thing, because he did not distinguish between "one" which is converted with being and signifies the substance of a thing, and the "one" which is the principle of number and which arithmetic considers.

Accordingly, this "one," as receiving the added characteristic of occupying a position in a continuum, takes on the guise of a point. Hence he said that "one" is a substance not occupying a position; but a point is a substance that does have a position. Consequently, a point adds something to the notion of "one," namely, position. And just as all numbers not having position are caused from "one," so from the point, according to the Platonists, all continuous quantities are caused. For a point in motion makes a line; a line in motion makes a plane, and a plane in motion makes a body. According to this, then, continuous quantities (which are treated in geometry) are the result of additions made to numbers (which are the concern of arithmetic). Hence the Platonists laid it down that numbers are the forms of magnitudes, saying that the point's form is "one," and the line's form is "two," because it has two endpoints, while a surface's form is "three," owing to the first surface's being the triangle which is terminated by three angles; but the form of bodies is "four," on the ground that the first solid figure is the triangular pyramid, which is composed of four (non-plane) solid angles, namely, one at the apex and three at the base.

According to this it is obvious that the comparison of the certitude of sciences is here based on two things: for the first mode is taken according to the cause as it is prior to and more certain than the effect; but the other two are taken according to the form as this is more certain than matter, inasmuch as the form is the principle of knowing the matter. But, as it is stated in *Metaphysics* VII, matter is twofold: one is sensible, according to which the second mode is taken; the other is intelligible, i.e., its continuity, according to which the third mode is taken. And although this third mode was explained according to Plato's theory, yet even according to Aristotle's theory, a point results from some addition to "one": for a point is an indivisible unity in a continuum, abstracting according to reason from sensible matter; but unity abstracts from both sensible and intelligible matter.

Then (87a38) he compares sciences one to another according to unity and diversity. Concerning this he does two things. First, he shows that there is unity and diversity among sciences both according to subject and according to principles. Secondly, he treats concerning both the subjects and principles (87b19) [L. 42]. Concerning the first he does two things. First, he shows what makes for unity and diversity of sciences. Secondly, he explains something which is needed for understanding what makes for multiplicity of sciences (87b5). Concerning the first he does two things. First, he shows what makes for the unity of a science. Secondly, what makes for diversity of sciences (87a41). Concerning the first he does two things. First, he lays it down that the unity of a science is considered from the unity of its generic subject. Secondly, he describes the genus which can be the subject of a science (87a38).

He says therefore first (87a38) that a science is said to be one from the fact that it is concerned with one generic subject. The reason for this is that the process of science of any given thing is, as it were, a movement of reason. Now the unity of any motion is judged principally from its terminus, as is clear in *Physics* V. Consequently, the unity of any science must be judged from its end or terminus. But the end or terminus of a science is the genus concerning which the science treats: because in speculative sciences nothing else is sought except a knowledge of some generic subject; in practical sciences what is intended as the end is the construction of its subject. Thus, in geometry the end intended is knowledge of magnitude, which is the subject of geometry; but in the science of building that which is intended as the end is the construction of a house, which is the subject of this art. Therefore, the unity of each science must be considered in terms of the unity of its subject. But just as the unity of one generic subject is more universal than another, for example, being or substance is more common than mobile being, so one science is more general than another. Thus, metaphysics, which treats of being or substance, is more general in scope than physics, which treats of mobile body.

Then (87a38) he describes the marks of those genera concerning which there can be sciences: and he lays down two marks. The first of these is stated when he says, "All the subjects constituted out of primary entities," i.e., of those subjects of which there is one genus, there is one science. To understand this it should be noted that, as has been said, the process of science consists in a certain movement of reason passing from one thing to another. But all movement starts from some principle or beginning and is terminated at something definite; hence in the progress of a science, reason must proceed from certain first principles. Therefore, if there be anything which does not have prior principles from which reason can proceed, there cannot be science of such things, if we take science to mean the effect of demonstration, as we do here. Thus, speculative sciences are not concerned with the very essences of separated substances: for we cannot, through demonstrative sciences, know the essences in them, because the essences of such substances are intelligible of themselves to an intellect proportionate to such intelligibility, and a grasp of the essences of such substances is not obtained by any prior conceptions. The only thing that can be known through speculative sciences about these substances is whether they exist and what they are not; anything else about them is known in terms of likenesses to lower things. But in that case we are really using subsequent things as though they were prior in order to understand them, because things that are subsequent according to nature are prior and better known to us. And so it is clear that those things concerning which we have science through what is absolutely prior, are of themselves composed of prior items; but things which are known through subsequent items (but prior in reference to us), even though they be simple in themselves, are nevertheless in our knowledge of them composed of things that are first to us.

He lays down the second mark when he says, "The parts of this total subject and their *per se* properties." Here it should be noted that the subject of a science can have two types of parts: first, the parts out of which, as out of first things, it is composed, i.e., the very principles of the subject; and secondly, the subjective parts. And although what is stated here can be applied to either of these types of parts, yet it seems to be truer of the first type of parts. For in every science there are the principles of its subject, and these must be considered before all else: for example, in natural science the first consideration is about matter and form, and in grammar about the alphabet. But in every science there is also something ultimate, at which the study of that science terminates, namely, that the properties of the subject be manifested. But each of these, namely, the first parts and the properties, can be attributed to something either *per se* or not *per se*. For the *per se* principles and properties of a triangle are not the *per se* principles and properties of an isosceles triangle precisely as isosceles, but precisely as triangle. Neither are they the *per se* principles and properties of brass or white, even though the triangle happens to be of brass or be white. Hence, if there were a science which manifests the properties of triangle from the principles of the triangle, the subject of that science would not be isosceles or white or brass, but triangle—whose *per se* subjective parts would be isosceles, equilateral and scalene.

Then (87a41) he shows the reason for sciences being diverse. First, he lays down this reason. Secondly, he explains it (87b1).

It should be noted in regard to the first point that although he took the reason for the oneness of a science from the oneness of its generic subject, he does not take the reason for their diversity from the diversity of their subject, but from the diversity of principles. For he says (87a41) that one science is distinct from another when their principles are diverse, in the sense that the principles of the two sciences do not proceed from any prior principles, nor the principles of the one science from those of the other; because if both proceed from the same principles, or if one proceeds from those of another, they would not be diverse sciences.

To understand this it should be noted that a material diversity of objects does not diversity habits, but only a formal diversity. Therefore, since something scientifically knowable is the proper object of a science, the sciences will not be diversified according to a material diversity of their scientifically knowable objects, but according to their formal diversity. Now just as the formality of visible is taken from light, through which color is seen, so the formal aspect of a scientifically knowable object is taken according to the principles from which something is scientifically known. Therefore, no matter how diverse certain scientifically knowable objects may be in their nature, so long as they are known through the same principles, they pertain to one science, because they will not differ precisely as scientifically knowable. For they are scientifically knowable in virtue of their own principles.

This is made clear by an example, namely, that human voices differ a great deal according to their nature from the sounds of inanimate bodies; but because the consonance of human voices and of the sounds of inanimate bodies is considered according to the same principles, the science of music, which considers both, is one science. On the other hand, if there are things which have the same nature but are considered according to diverse principles, it is obvious that they pertain to diverse sciences. Thus, the mathematical body is never really distinct from a natural body; yet because the mathematical body is known through the principles of quantity, but a natural body through the principles of motion, the science of geometry and the science of nature are not the same. It is clear, therefore, that for sciences to be diverse it is enough that the principles be diverse, this diversity of principles being accompanied by a diversity of scientifically knowable objects.

But in order to have one science absolutely, both are required, namely, unity of subject and unity of principles. That is why above he made mention of unity of subject when he said, "whose domain is one genus," but made mention of principles when he said, "all the subjects constituted out of the primary entities of the genus."

However, it should be further noted that second principles derive their force from the first principles. Hence for diversity of sciences, diversity of first principles is required. But this will not be verified if the principles of diverse things flow from the same principles, as the principles of triangle and square are derived from the principles of figure, or the principles of one are derived from the principles of another, as the principles of isosceles depend on the principles of triangle.

Yet it should not be supposed that for the unity of a science it is enough that there be unity of first principles absolutely, but unity of first principles in some scientifically knowable genus. Now the genera of the scientifically knowable are distinguished according to the diverse modes of knowing: thus things that are defined with matter are known in one mode, and those defined without matter are known in another. Hence the natural body is one genus of the scientifically knowable, and mathematical body is another genus. Hence there are diverse first principles for each of these genera and, consequently, diverse sciences. Furthermore, each of these genera is distinguished into diverse species according to diverse modes and aspects of intelligibility.

Then (87b1) he explains the reason he laid down, saying that a sign of the fact that sciences are diversified according to their principles is obtained when one resolves a science into principles that are indemonstrable, for they must be of the same genus as the things demonstrated; because, as stated above, one does not demonstrate by proceeding from an alien genus. Now the reason why the reaching of indemonstrable principles of one genus is taken as a sign is that the facts demonstrated by them are in the same genus and are co-generic, i.e., connatural, or generically proximate to them: for these have the same principles. And so it is clear that the unity of a scientifically knowable genus, precisely as it is the scientifically knowable genus from which was taken the oneness of the science, and the unity of the principles, according to which was taken the diversity among the sciences, mutually correspond.

Then (87b5) he shows how one conclusion can be demonstrated through several principles. And this can happen in two ways: in one way, when a number of middles are laid down in the same coordination, and one of these middles is used in one demonstration and another one in another, both leading to the same conclusion. This, of course, requires that the middles be non-continuous. Thus, if the two extremes, A and B, are "to have three" and "isosceles" respectively, but the middles, D and C, are coordinate, as "triangle" and "this type of figure," A could be demonstrated of B with two demonstrations. In the first one, C could be taken as middle, and D in the other, so that in neither demonstration will there be a middle continuous with the extremes, because in one demonstration a middle continuous with one extreme and not continuous with the other would be taken, and in the other demonstration the converse would be taken.

Or this can happen in a second way, namely, when diverse middles are taken from diverse coordinations; for example, if A, which is the major extreme, were "to be altered," and B, which is the minor extreme, were "to be pleased," and the middles taken were independent, say G would be "to be at rest," and D "to be in motion." In this case the same conclusion can be reached through diverse middles that are not of one order. Thus one demonstration would be this: "Whatever is at rest is altered, because it belongs to the same thing to be at rest and to be altered; but whatever is pleased is at rest, because rest in the desired good causes pleasure: therefore, whatever is pleased is altered." The other demonstration would be: "Whatever is in motion is altered; but whatever is pleased is in motion, because pleasure is a movement of the appetitive faculty [power]: therefore, whatever is pleased is altered." (Now the statement, "Whatever is pleased is in motion," is Plato's opinion and is verified in sensible pleasures which involve movement. The other statement, "Whatever is pleased is at rest," is true according to Aristotle's opinion, as is clear from *Ethics* VII and X. And this is verified particularly in intellectual pleasures.

Then he says that just as this has been proved in the first figure, so in the other figures it is easy to see that the same conclusion can be syllogized with diverse middles. Now the Philosopher mentioned this to show that diverse middles of demonstration sometimes pertain to the same science, as when they are taken from the same coordination, and sometimes to diverse sciences, when they are taken from a different coordination. Thus, astronomy demonstrates that the earth is round, using one middle, namely, the eclipse of the sun and moon; and natural science uses another middle, namely, the motion of heavy objects tending toward the center, as it is stated in *Physics* II.

Lecture 42
(87b19–88a17)

SCIENCE IS NOT CONCERNED WITH THINGS CAUSED BY FORTUNE OR WITH THINGS LEARNED THROUGH SENSE-PERCEPTION

After assigning the basis of unity and of diversity of sciences on the part of the generic subject and on the part of the principles, the Philosopher here continues with each. First, with the subjects about which there is science. Secondly, with the principles (88a18) [L. 43].

In regard to the first it should be noted that above he laid down two marks of the genus which is the subject of the science: one of these is that it be composed of first principles, and the other is that its parts and properties be *per se*. Now one of these conditions is lacking in things that happen by fortune, because they do not come about *per se*, but *per accidens* and beyond one's intention, as is proved in *Physics* II. The other mark is lacking in things that are known through sense, which are first in our knowledge. Therefore, he shows first that science is not concerned with things which come about by fortune. Secondly, that it is not of things that are known through sense (87b28).

He says therefore first (87b19) that demonstrative science cannot be concerned with things that occur through fortune, i.e., things that come about *per accidens*. He proves this in the following way: Every demonstrative syllogism proceeds either from necessary propositions or from propositions which are true for the most part. Now from necessary propositions a necessary conclusion follows, as has been proved above; in like manner, from propositions which are true for the most part, a conclusion follows which is true for the most part, or perhaps one which is necessary, in the sense that the necessary can follow from the contingent, as the true can follow from the false. However, it never happens that from propositions which are true for the most part, a conclusion will follow which is true in few cases; because that would mean that in certain cases the propositions would be true and the conclusion false, which is impossible, as has been shown. It is necessary, therefore, that the conclusion of a demonstrative syllogism either be necessary or be true in the majority of cases. But that which is by fortune is neither necessary nor is it true in the majority of cases, but it occurs rarely, as is proved in *Physics* II. There-

147

fore, demonstrative science cannot be concerned with that which is by fortune.

It should be noted, however, that there happens to be demonstration of things which occur, as it were, for the most part, insofar as there is in them something of necessity. But the necessary, as it is stated in *Physics* II, is not the same in natural things (which are true for the most part and fail to be true in a few cases) as in the disciplines, i.e., in mathematical things, which are always true. For in the disciplines there is *a priori* necessity, whereas in natural science there is *a posteriori* (which nevertheless is prior according to nature), namely, from the end and form. Hence Aristotle teaches there that to show a *propter quid*, such as if this has to be, say that if an olive is to be generated, it is necessary that this, namely, the olive seed, pre-exist, but not that an olive is generated of necessity from a given olive seed, because generation can be hindered by some defect. Hence if a demonstration is formed from that which is prior in generation, it does not conclude with necessity, unless perhaps we take as necessary the fact that an olive seed is frequently generative of an olive, because it does this according to a property of its nature, unless it is impeded.

Then (87b28) he shows that science is not concerned with things that are known according to sense. About this he does two things. First, he shows that science does not consist in sensing. Secondly, how sense is ordained to science (88a13). Concerning the first he does two things. First, he shows that science is not through sense. Secondly, he ranks science above sense (88a5). Concerning the first he does two things. First, he shows the truth. Secondly, he shows the errors of certain ones (87b34).

He says therefore first (87b28) that just as science is not of things which are by fortune, so neither does it consist in knowledge which is through sense. And he proves this in the following way: It is obvious that sense knows the qualities of a thing and not its substance. For the *per se* object of sense is not the substance and the essence, but some sensible quality, such as hot, cold, white, black, and so on. But qualities of this sort affect singular substances existing in a definite place and time: hence it is necessary that this which is sensed be a "this something," i.e., a singular substance, and that it be somewhere now, i.e., in a definite time and place. From this it is clear that that which is universal cannot fall under sense. For that which is universal is not restricted to the here and now, because then it would not be universal. For we call that a universal which is always and everywhere.

However, this is not to be understood according to the way of an affirmation, as though it pertained to the very notion of a universal or of that which is universal, namly, that it be always and everywhere. For if to exist always and everywhere pertained to the very notion of that which is universal, say to the notion of man or animal, it would then

be required that each individual man and animal be always and everywhere, because the notion of man and of animal is found in each of its
singulars. Or if this were required by the very notion of the universal, as
it is required of a genus that it contain species under it, it would follow
that nothing would be universal, if it were not found everywhere and
always. According to this, "olive" would not be universal, because it is
not found in all lands. Hence, the statement under consideration must
be understood after the manner of a negation or abstraction, i.e., that the
universal abstracts from every definite time and place. Hence of itself,
just as it is found in each thing in one place or time, so it is apt to be
found in all. Thus, therefore, it is clear that the universal does not fall
under sense. Consequently, because demonstrations are mainly universal, as has been shown above, it is obvious that science acquired by
demonstration does not consist in knowledge obtained through sense.

Then (87b34) he excludes the errors of those who believed that science
consists in sense-perception. And this notion seems to belong to those who
did not believe that understanding differs from sense and, consequently,
that there is no knowledge except sense-knowledge, as it is stated in *On
the Soul* III and *Metaphysics* IV. So, to exclude this he says that even
if we could perceive through sense that a triangle has three angles equal
to two right angles, it would still be necessary to learn this by demonstration if one is to have science; for it could not be scientifically known
through sense, because sense bears on singulars, whereas science consists in knowing the universal, as has been shown.

But because he had given the example of something that cannot be
perceived through sense, he makes his point clearer with an example
taken from things that can be sensed, namely, from an eclipse of the
moon which is caused by the opposition of the earth, which is interposed
between the sun and moon, so that the brightness of the sun cannot
reach the moon because of the earth's shadow; and the moon is eclipsed
when it enters the shadow. Let us suppose, then, that someone were on
the moon and with his senses could perceive the shadow caused by the
interposition of the earth. This person, then, would sensibly perceive
that the moon is darkened by the shadow of the earth, but this would
not mean that he would therefore know totally the cause of the eclipse.
For the *per se* cause of an eclipse is that which universally causes an
eclipse. But the universal is not known through sense; rather, we receive universal knowledge from many individually observed cases in
which the same thing is found to happen. And so it is through the universal cause that we demonstrate something in the universal way that
constitutes science.

Then (88a5) he shows that science is nobler than sense. For it is clear
that knowledge through the cause is more noble; but the *per se* cause
is the universal cause, as has been said. Therefore, knowledge through

the universal cause, such as science is, is more honorable. But because it is impossible to apprehend such a universal cause through sense, it follows that science, which shows the universal cause, is not only more honorable than any sense knowledge, but more honorable than any other intellectual knowledge, provided it concern things which have a cause: for to know something through the universal cause is more noble than any other way of knowing that which has a cause, without knowing the cause.

However, the case is otherwise in regard to first things, which do not have a cause. For these are understood in virtue of themselves; and such knowledge of these things is more certain than any science, because it is from such knowledge that science acquires its certitude.

Finally, he concludes to his chief point, namely, that it is impossible through sense to know something demonstrable, unless perhaps one takes "sense" in an equivocal meaning, calling demonstrative science "sense" on the ground that demonstrative science concerns the determinately one just as sense does: on which account sure calculations are called science.

Then (88a11) he shows how sense is ordained to science. For some problematic doubts are caused by the shortcomings of sense. For there would be no need to investigate certain matters, if we were to see them; not because science consists in seeing, but because from things seen by way of experiment the universal is obtained, concerning which there is science. For example, if we should see a porous pane of glass and observed how the light passes through the openings in the glass, we would have the scientific answer as to why the glass is transparent. (He uses this example because it is the opinion of those who supposed that light is a body and that certain bodies are transparent because of openings called pores. But because they cannot be perceived by sight, since they are so small, we wonder why glass is transparent. A similar example can be given of certain things that have a latent sensible cause).

Finally, because he had said that science of such things is not obtained by seeing, he shows that this is true. For in seeing we know isolated singulars; but to know scientifically we must know them all at once in the universal, if we are to know that such and such is the fact in all cases. For we see each individual glass singly, but we receive science that it is thus for all glass.

Lecture 43
(88a18–b29)

PRINCIPLES OF ALL SYLLOGISMS
ARE NOT THE SAME

a18. All syllogisms cannot
a20. for though a true inference
a26. Then again, (2)
a31. Not even all these
a37. Nor can any of the common
b4. Again, it is not true

b8. and lastly some of the
b10. If, on the other hand,
b15. Nor again can the contention
b20. but if it be
b22. If, however, it is not
b25. But that this cannot be

After his treatment concerning that about which there is science, the Philosopher continues here with the principles of sciences and shows that the principles of all syllogisms are not the same. First, he shows this logically, i.e., through reasons common to all syllogisms. Secondly, he shows it analytically, i.e., through reasons that are peculiar to demonstration (88b10). Concerning the first he does three things. First, he proves his proposition by showing the difference between false syllogisms and true ones. Secondly, by the difference between some false syllogisms and other false ones (88a26). Thirdly, by the difference between some true syllogisms and other true ones (88a31). Concerning the first he does two things. First, he proves his proposition. Secondly, he excludes an objection (88a20).

He says therefore first (88a18) that if we first speculate this matter in a logical way, it is clear that the principles of all syllogisms cannot be the same, inasmuch as some syllogisms are false, i.e., conclude false statements, and some are true, i.e., conclude to the truth. Now the principles of false and of true syllogisms are diverse: for the principles of true syllogisms are true, but the principles of false syllogisms are false. Therefore the principles of all syllogisms are not the same.

Then (88a20) he excludes an objection. For someone might say that there are false principles even in true syllogisms, because it is possible to syllogize the true from the false. But he excludes this, saying that although it happens that the true is syllogized from the false, this occurs only once in the first syllogism, in which the true is concluded from the false. But if one is forced to adduce other syllogisms to support the propositions in the premises, then those syllogisms would have to proceed from what is false, because from what is true the false cannot be concluded. Consequently, it is only in the first syllogism that the true is concluded from the false.

151

Then he gives an example of this: Let the proposition, "Every C is A," be true, and take for each of these extremes a false middle, B, so that A is not in B nor B in C. Now if other middles be taken to prove these propositions, all the propositions of the false syllogism will be false, because every false conclusion is concluded from the false, but a true conclusion can be concluded from the true. Hence, when the propositions from which the true is concluded are true, one need not reach anything false. Thus, therefore, since some propositions are true and some false, it follows that the principles of true syllogisms are not the same as the principles of false syllogisms.

Then (88a26) he shows that not even the principles of false syllogisms are the same. For it occurs that some false conclusions are contrary to one another and incompatible with other false conclusions. Thus, the conclusion, "Justice is injustice," is incompatible with the conclusion, "Justice is fear," since both are false. For just as fear differs generically from justice, so from injustice. In like fashion, the two conclusions, "Man is a horse," and "Man is a cow," are contrary and incompatible. Again, these two propositions are incompatible, "Something equal is greater," and "Something equal is less." For it is necessary to arrive at such conclusions from principles, from which, when they are laid down, other things follow. Therefore, since they are contrary and incompatible, so too were the principles from which they were concluded.

Then (88a31) he shows that not even in the case of true syllogisms are the principles the same. And he gives four reasons, the first of which is based on the differences among proper principles. Hence he says that "not even all these," i.e., true conclusions, "are inferred from the same basic truths." For the principles of diverse genera are themselves diverse: thus the principles of magnitudes are points, and of numbers unities; and these are not exactly the same, for numbers do not have position, but points do.

Furthermore, if all principles of syllogisms were in agreement, they would have to meet at some same middle either by ascending upwards to the major term or by descending downwards toward the minor term: because in a syllogism it is necessary that the terms be assumed either within or without. They are assumed within, when a multiplicity of syllogisms is used to prove the propositions presented. For then it is necessary to take middles that are between the predicates of the propositions and their subjects. Thus, if we form the syllogism, "Every B is A, Every C is B, therefore, Every C is A"; if it is necessary to prove "Every B is A," we must take a middle between B and A, say D. Again, if it is necessary to prove the minor, we must take another middle between C and B, say E. In this process the terms assumed are always within.

However, they are assumed from without, when the major term is taken as middle by ascending, or the minor by descending: thus, if A is concluded of C through B, and C is then concluded of B through A, and so on; similarly, by descending, if we conclude B of E through C.

Therefore, in syllogisms sharing principles in common, it is necessary either that the middle of one syllogism be taken above the propositions of another syllogism or that the extremes of one be taken above or below the extremes of the other syllogism. But this cannot occur in things whose principles are diverse, because points cannot be taken as middles or extremes in syllogisms in which something about number is concluded, nor unities in syllogisms in which something about magnitudes is concluded. What remains, therefore, is that the principles of all syllogisms cannot be the same.

The second reason is presented at (88a37) and it is based on common principles. He says that there cannot be certain common principles from which alone are syllogized all conclusions, as this common principle, "Of each thing there is affirmation or negation," which is universally true in every genus. Nevertheless, it is impossible that all things be syllogized exclusively from such common principles, because the genera of beings are diverse. Thus, the principles which pertain only to quantities are diverse from those which pertain exclusively to qualities. Such principles must be co-assumed with common principles, if one is to reach a conclusion in each matter. For example, if one wishes in quantities to syllogize from the aforesaid common principle, it is necessary to admit that since it is false that a point is a line, it must be true that a point is not a line; in like manner, in qualities, it is necessary to co-assume something peculiar to quality. Hence what remains is that it is impossible that the principles of all syllogisms be the same.

Then (88b4) he gives the third reason which is based on a comparison of premises with conclusions. And he says that the principles are not much fewer than the conclusions. They are as a matter of fact fewer, because although two principles are needed to infer one conclusion, i.e., two propositions are required, because one conclusion is not concluded immediately except from two premises, nevertheless you can use one proposition to infer a number of conclusions, insofar as many things can be taken under the subject or under the predicate. However, the principles are not much fewer than the conclusions, because most of the facts which are co-assumed with the principles to obtain other conclusions are themselves conclusions. (Here propositions are being called "principles"). But propositions are formed of terms either added or interposed, i.e., propositions in syllogisms are multiplied either by assuming terms extrinsically (either above the major term and below the minor, as has been explained above), or by accepting terms which are in the middle.

To this must be added the fact that conclusions are infinite. For anything can be concluded of anything else either affirmatively or negatively. And lest this seem to conflict with the earlier statement that predications do not proceed to infinity, he adds that the terms are finite: and this is why it was stated above that a stop must be made in predications. Nevertheless, an infinitude of conclusions can be derived from a finite number of terms according to diverse combinations, if we take "conclusions" in a general sense, as including those that are *per se* and those that are *per accidens*. For we are now speaking of syllogisms in general. Therefore, if the conclusions are infinite and the principles are not much fewer than the conclusions, it follows that principles of syllogisms are also infinite. Therefore, the principles of all syllogisms are not the same.

Then (88b8) he gives the fourth reason and it is based on the difference between the necessary and the contingent. And he says that some of the principles which we use in the syllogism are contingent and some necessary, as is clear from *Prior Analytics* I, where he taught how to syllogize from necessary and from contingent premises. However, the necessary and the contingent are not the same. Therefore, the principles of all syllogisms are not the same.

What he concludes from these last two reasons is that in view of what has been established, and because conclusions are infinite, it is impossible that the principles of all syllogisms either be the same or even be finite.

Then (88b10) he shows the same thing analytically, namely, through reasons proper to the principles by which sciences demonstrate. And he gives three reasons. Concerning the first of these he says that if someone does not say that the principles of all syllogisms are the same, but says something somewhat different, namely, that some are principles of geometry and some of logic—which are called the principles of syllogisms or reasonings—and some are principles of medicine, and so on for the principles of all sciences, so that in this sense the principles of all demonstrations are the same, this does not support his claim that principles are the same: because from the facts that are given, nothing follows except that each science has its own principles.

The contention that the principles of one science are the same as those of another—which would be required if the principles of all scientific syllogisms were the same—is impossible and ridiculous, because according to this it would follow that everything in the sciences would be the same and hence that all the sciences would be the same. For things that are the same as a same thing are the same. But the principles of each science are somehow the same as the conclusions, because they belong to the same genus: for one may not demonstrate by passing from one genus into another, as has been shown above. Therefore, if the principles are the same, it will follow that everything in the sciences would be the same.

Then (88b15) he gives the second reason and it is this: If a person who contends that the principles of all are the same, intended to say that anything is demonstrated from anything, then he is saying something foolish, because this is possible neither in "evident mathematicals nor in analysis." (By "evident mathematicals," i.e., evident considerations or disciplines he means those cases in which a conclusion is drawn immediately from evident premises; but by "analysis" he means those cases where the assumed propositions are not evident but must be analyzed into others which are more evident). And that this is impossible he proves on the ground that in each of these two cases the principles of the demonstrative syllogism are immediate propositions, which are either immediately assumed in evident mathematicals or doctrines, or are reached by analysis. But we see that a different conclusion is demonstrated, when a different immediate proposition is co-assumed. Consequently, it cannot be that anything is demonstrated from just anything.

Then (88b20) he excludes a certain objection. For someone could say that there are two genera of immediate propositions: for some are first immediate propositions and some secondary, taking the order of immediate propositions according to the order of the terms. For those immediate propositions which consist of first and common terms, as "being" and "non-being," "equal" and "unequal," "whole" and "part," are first and immediate propositions, as "It does not occur that the same thing both is and is not," and "Two things which are equal to the same thing are equal," and so on. But the immediate propositions that are concerned with later and less common terms are secondary in relation to the first, as that "a triangle is a figure," or that "man is an animal." Therefore, someone might say that secondary propositions are co-assumed for demonstrating diverse conclusions, but that the first immediate propositions are the same in all demonstrations.

To exclude this he says that if anyone should assert that those first immediate propositions are the ones from which all things are demonstrated, he ought to consider that in each genus there must yet be one principle or one immediate proposition which is first in that genus, even though it is not absolutely first; and that from one which is absolutely first, together with a co-assumed principle proper to a particular genus, one should demonstrate in that genus. Consequently, not all things can be demonstrated from common principles alone, but it is necessary to accept proper principles which are diverse for diverse genera.

Then (88b22), having excluded the injudicious interpretation of the position against which he is disputing, he concludes to his point. And he says that if it is not admitted that anything is demonstrated from just anything—as we must, in view of the foregoing—it follows, that one conclusion is not derived from some principle in such a way that a different conclusion can be derived from it; otherwise just anything is demonstrated from just anything. Hence it is necessary that the principles of diverse sciences be diverse. If it is required that the principles of each science be of the same genus as everything demonstrated from them, it will be required that from these principles be demonstrated these conclusions, and "those from those," i.e., from diverse principles, demonstration being made in diverse sciences which treat of diverse genera.

Then (88b25) he presents the third reason which states that it is clear from another angle that this does not occur, namely, that the principles of all the sciences are the same; because it has been shown above that the principles of diverse genera are themselves generically diverse. Hence since diverse sciences are concerned with diverse genera, it follows that the principles of diverse sciences are diverse.

But because the common principles which all sciences use are in some way the same, he distinguishes among the principles and says that principles are twofold: some of the first principles from which one demonstrates are as the first dignities; for example, "Being and non-being are not the same." Again, there are other principles, namely, those with which the sciences are concerned, namely, the subjects of the sciences, because we use the definitions of the subjects as principles in demonstrations. Therefore, the members of the first group of principles from which we demonstrate are common to all the sciences; but the principles with which the sciences are concerned are proper to each science, as number to arithmetic, and magnitude to geometry. But the common principles must be applied to these proper principles, if there is to be demonstration. And because one does not demonstrate only from common principles, it cannot be said that the principles of all demonstrative syllogisms are the same, which is what he intended to prove.

Lecture 44
(88b30–89b20)

SCIENCE COMPARED WITH OTHER
MODES OF KNOWING

b30. Scientific knowledge

b31. in that scientific knowledge

b33. So though there are

a5. This view also fits

a7. Besides, when a man

a11. In what sense, then,

a16. so that, since the

a23. The object of opinion

b6. Further consideration of modes

b10. Quick wit is a faculty

After comparing sciences with one another from the viewpoints of certitude, of unity and of diversity, the Philosopher here compares science to everything else that pertains to knowledge. And his treatment falls into two parts. In the first he treats of the comparison of science to opinion, which bears on the true and false. In the second, of the comparison of science to those habits of knowledge which are concerned exclusively with the true (89b6). The first part is divided into two parts. In the first he determines the truth. In the second he excludes a doubt (89a11). Concerning the first he does three things. First, he lays down the difference between science and opinion. Secondly, he shows what pertains to science (88b31). Thirdly, what pertains to opinion (88b33).

He says therefore first (88b30) that science differs from opinion; in like manner the scientifically knowable, which is the object of science, differs from the opinable, which is the object of opinion.

Then (88b31) he shows what pertains to science, setting down two things which pertain to it. One of these is that it is of the universal, for science is not concerned with singulars which fall under sense. (He explained this above). The other is that science is obtained in virtue of necessary things. And he explains that the necessary is that which cannot be otherwise. This, too, was explained above, namely, that demonstration proceeds from necessary things.

Then (88b33) he shows what pertains to opinion, namely, that it is concerned with things that could be otherwise, either universally or particularly. This he proves in three ways. First, by way of a division, saying that in addition to necessary truths, which cannot be otherwise, there are non-necessary truths, which could be otherwise. Now from what has been said above, it is clear that science is not concerned with the latter, because it would follow that contingent things would be such as could not be otherwise. For science is concerned with such things, as has been said. Similarly, it cannot be said that understanding is concerned with them. "Understanding" is taken here not as a faculty [power] of the soul, but as being the principle of science, i.e., as the habit of first principles, from which demonstration proceeds in causing science.

Hence in explaining what that understanding is which is the principle of science he adds, "Nor of indemonstrable knowledge" (88b37), i.e., not of facts that could be otherwise. As if to say: understanding is nothing more than a science of the indemonstrable. For just as science implies certainty of knowledge acquired through demonstration, so understanding implies certitude of knowledge without demonstration; not because of a shortcoming in some demonstration, but because that about which this certainty is had, is indemonstrable and *per se* known. Therefore, to explain this he adds that demonstrative science is nothing else than the certain intuition of an immediate proposition. But that understanding is science of the indemonstrable is clear from the fact that he says that it is the principle of science. For since science is concerned with the necessary, and the necessary is not concluded except from the necessary, as has been proved above, it is required that understanding, which is the principle of science, not be concerned with contingent things.

Having shown, therefore, that neither science nor understanding is concerned with contingent things, he sets down a division and says that understanding and science and opinion happen to be true as "that does which is stated by them," i.e., which is verbally stated by understanding and science and true opinion. For the true is found both in the intellect's act of composing and dividing and in the outward expression of this act insofar as it signifies the inward truth of the opinion or science or understanding. Therefore, if every truth belongs either to understanding or science or opinion, and there are some contingent truths, and they belong neither to science nor understanding, what is left is that opinion is concerned with them, whether they be actually true or actually false, provided that they could be other than they are.

In order to elucidate what opinion is, he adds that opinion is the acceptance, i.e., the grasping, of a proposition that is immediate and not necessary. And this can be understood in two ways: in one way, so that the immediate proposition in itself is indeed necessary, but it is accepted by opinion as non-necessary; in another way, so that it is in itself contingent. For an immediate proposition is one that cannot be proved through a middle, whether it be a necessary proposition or not. For it has been shown above that there is no process to infinity in predications, neither on the part of the middles nor on the part of the extremes. And this was shown not only analytically in demonstrations, but also logically in general as to syllogisms.

Therefore, if there be a contingent proposition which is mediate, it must be reduced to others that are immediate. However, it is not reduced to necessary immediate propositions, because necessary things are not the proper principles of contingent things, nor can contingent things be concluded from necessary things. Hence what remains is that some contingent propositions are immediate and some mediate. Thus, "The man does not run," is mediate, for it can be proved through this middle, "The man is not in motion," which is also contingent, albeit immediate. The acceptance of such immediate contingent propositions is opinion. Yet this does not mean that the accepting of a mediate contingent proposition is not opinion. For opinion is related to contingent things, as science and understanding to necessary things.

Secondly (89a5), he proves the same point by means of that which is commonly observed, saying that what has been said, mainly, that opinion is concerned with the contingent is confessed, i.e., in agreement with things that are observed. For opinion seems to denote something weak and uncertain and to be of such a nature that weakness and uncertainty are in it.

Thirdly (89a7), he proves the same point by experiment. For no one, when he thinks that it is impossible for a thing to be otherwise, supposes that he is forming an opinion; rather he considers himself to know scientifically. But when he thinks that something is such and such and that there is nothing to prevent its being otherwise, then it is that he considers himself to have opinions. This would indicate that opinion concerns such things, i.e., contingent things, but science necessary things.

Then (89a11) he raises a doubt concerning the aforesaid. First, he raises the doubts. Secondly, he solves them (89a16).

Concerning the first (89a11), he presents two doubts, one of which is concerned with the opinable and the scientifically knowable. If opinion is concerned with the contingent and science with the necessary, and the contingent is not the same as the necessary, a doubt remains as to how a man can opine and scientifically know the same thing.

The second doubt concerns science and opinion, namely, why opinion is not science; supposing, of course, that one claims that there can be opinion about every known thing. For in regard to everything known a man can opine that it could be otherwise (except perhaps in the case of first principles *per se* known, whose contraries cannot be conceived, and concerning which there is not science but understanding). But in regard to all mediate truths of which there is demonstration and science, someone can suppose that it is possible that they could be otherwise. Consequently, they can fall under opinion. For opinion is not concerned exclusively with things contingent in their very nature, because then a man could not have opinion about everything he knows. Rather opinion is concerned with that which is accepted as possible to be otherwise, whether it is that or not. Therefore, on this supposition, it remains that science and opinion are the same, because both the scientific knower and the man of opinion acquire science and opinion through middles until they reach things which are immediate, as is clear from the foregoing. Hence if someone proceeds through middles to immediate propositions he has science. Now this is what the man of opinion does, because just as it is possible to have an opinion that something is so, it is also possible to have an opinion why something is so. But when I say, "why," a middle is implied. Hence it is clear that opinion can proceed to immediates through a middle, whether opinion be of things that are contingent in their very nature, or of things accepted as contingent.

Then (89a16) he solves the aforesaid doubts. First, he solves the second one which is concerned with the identity of science and opinion. Secondly, he solves the first one which is concerned with the identity of the scientifically knowable and the opinable (89a23).

He says therefore first (89a16) that if someone proceeds through middles to immediates in such a way that the middles are not considered capable of being otherwise, but are considered to behave as definitions which are the middles through which demonstrations proceed, there will not be opinion but science. But if someone proceeds to the immediates through certain true middles which, nevertheless, are either not verified of the things of which they are said *per se* (as definitions which are predicated essentially or signify the species of a thing), or he does not take them as being in these things *per se*, then he will have opinion and will not truly know the *quia* and the *propter quid* at once, even if he proceeds as far as the immediates: for then he will be forming an opinion through the immediates and will not know scientifically. But if he does not proceed through immediates but through mediates, then he will not be forming an opinion bearing on the *propter quid* but only the *quia*. For even scientific knowledge, when it is not *propter quid* and immediate, is not *propter quid* science but *quia*.

Then (89a23) he solves the first doubt which concerns the identity of the scientifically known and the object of opinion. Here it should be noted first of all that it is not unfitting that what is scientifically known by one person be a matter of opinion for another, because what one takes as impossible to be otherwise than stated and as scientifically known, another might take as possible to be otherwise and as a matter for opinion. But to say that the same man has opinion and scientific knowledge of the same thing at the same time, is not entirely true, but only in a way. For just as there can be true and false opinion about the same thing somehow but not absolutely, so also in regard to opinion and scientific knowledge. For if someone were to say that there could be a completely true and completely false opinion about the same thing, as some do say (for example, those who said that whatever seems to be true to a person is true, as it is stated in *Metaphysics* IV), then a person who would say such a thing would be forced to admit certain absurdities and the many other things pointed out in *Metaphysics* IV which follow from stating that the same thing is true and false. In particular this absurdity would follow, namely, that no opinion is false and that what he opined to be false he did not opine. Hence it cannot be said that there is true and false opinion of the same thing absolutely.

But because "same" is said in many ways, it happens that somehow there is true and false opinion about a same thing, and somehow not. For if "a same thing about which there are opinions" means the same real extramental subject, then there can be true and false opinion about a same thing. But if "same" refers to the proposition that is opined, then it is impossible. For example, to opine that the diagonal is commensurable with the side of a square is to opine with a false opinion; and it is absurd to say that this statement can be opined as a true opinion. But if we take diagonal as the enunciable subject, then there can be true and false opinion of a same thing. For in regard to a diagonal, one opines truly that it is really incommensurable, and another opines falsely that it is commensurable. Thus, it is clear that although that concerning which there is science and opinion be the same in subject, it is not the same in notion. For the diagonal which is said to be commensurable and not to be commensurable is the same in subject, because the subject of each statement is the same. Nevertheless, it is clear that there is a mental distinction between diagonal insofar as it is taken as commensurable and insofar as it is taken as incommensurable. Consequently, there can be true and false opinion about the same subject, but not of the same subject according to notion.

The same is true of science and opinion. For it is science when someone knows this to be an animal in such a way that it cannot not be an animal; but it is opinion when someone knows it to be an animal in such a way that it might not be an animal. For example, if there is science concerning the fact that man is truly that which is an animal in such a way that it is impossible for it to be otherwise, there will be opinion concerning the fact that man is not truly that which is an animal, and as a result could be otherwise. For it is clear that the subject both known and opined is the same, namely, man; but in notion it is not the same. Thus, therefore, from the foregoing it is obvious that it is impossible to know scientifically and to opine the same thing at the same time, because a man would at one and the same time have a conjecture that could be otherwise and that could not be otherwise. But this could occur in the case of two men, namely, that one have science about a thing and another have opinion about the same thing, as has been stated. But this does not occur in the same person for the reason given.

Then (89b6) he compares science to certain habits that are concerned with truth. First, to those habits which deal with principles and conclusions. Secondly, to the habit which is specifically concerned with the middle (89b10).

He says therefore first (89b6) that in regard to those forms of knowledge that are other than opinion, the question of how they are distinguished into reason and understanding and science and art and prudence and wisdom, pertains somehow to the considerations of first philosophy or even of natural philosophy and somehow to the considerations of moral philosophy which is called ethics.

To understand this it should be noted that in *Ethics* VI, Aristotle lays down five things which are always concerned with the truth, namely, art, science, wisdom, prudence and understanding, adding two that are concerned with the true and false, namely, suspician and opinion. Now the first five are concerned solely with the true, because they imply rectitude of reason. But three of them, namely, wisdom, science and understanding imply reason's rectitude in regard to necessary truths: science in regard to conclusions, understanding in regard to principles, and wisdom in regard to the highest causes, which are the divine causes. But the other two, namely, art and prudence, imply the rectitude of reason in regard to contingent things: prudence in regard to things to be done, i.e., in regard to acts which remain within the one acting, such as to love, hate, choose, and similar acts that pertain to moral activity, of which prudence is the director. Art, however, implies the rectitude of reason in regard to things to be made, i.e., things that are done to external matter; for example, cutting and other activities in which art directs.

To this list he adds "reason," which pertains to bringing principles to their conclusions. Now to treat of wisdom, namely, what it is and how it works, and to treat of science and understanding and art, pertain somehow to first philosophy. Prudence, on the other hand, pertains to moral consideration; understanding and reason, insofar as they name certain powers, pertain to natural consideration, as is clear in *On the Soul*.

Then (89b10) he makes mention of the habit which is specifically concerned with the middle. And he says that quick wit is a certain accurate and facile conjecturing of the middle (the reason) why something occurs; and this when one does not have much time to inspect or deliberate, as when a person, seeing that the moon has all its brightness whenever it is turned toward the sun, immediately understands why this is, namely, because it is illumined by the sun. Similarly, in the case of human acts: if a person sees a poor man arguing with a rich man, he knows that the rich man took something from him, and the argument is about its return. Or if he should see persons formerly enemies now made friends, he knows that the reason is because both have a common enemy.

Secondly, he shows in two ways that to know the middle is to know the "why": first, with the following reason, namely, because such a quick witted person, seeing all the middle causes, knows all the ultimate ones into which they are all finally analyzed, and through which the "why" is known. Secondly, he manifests this with an example presented in a syllogism. Thus, let us suppose the moon to be C, i.e., the minor extreme, and "to be bright because of its opposition to the sun," to be A, the major extreme; but "to be illumined by the sun," to be B, i.e., the middle. For C is B, i.e., "The moon has light from the sun," and A is in B, because "that which has light from the sun is bright when turned toward the sun." Thus it is proved that A is in C through B.

Hence it is clear that quick wit is the faculty of quickly apprehending the middle, and is present in persons as a natural gift or is acquired by training. But he presented various examples of quick wit to show that in all the aforesaid habits, namely, prudence, wisdom, and so on, there can be quick wit.

BOOK II

Lecture 1
(89b21-90a35)

EACH OF THE FOUR QUESTIONS WHICH PERTAIN TO SCIENCE IS ONE WAY OR ANOTHER A QUESTION OF THE MIDDLE

After determining about the demonstrative syllogism in the first book, the Philosopher intends in this [second] book to treat concerning its principles. But there are two principles of the demonstrative syllogism, namely, its middle and the first indemonstrable propositions. Therefore this book is divided into two parts. In the first he determines concerning the knowledge of the middle in demonstrations. In the second concerning the knowledge of the first propositions (99b18) [L. 20]. For since it has been established in the first book that every doctrine and every discipline takes its start from pre-existing knowledge, and since in demonstrations the knowledge of the conclusion is acquired through some middle and through the first indemonstrable propositions, we are left with the task of investigating how these come to be known.

But the first part is divided into two parts. In the first he inquires what is a middle in demonstrations. In the second part he inquires how that middle is made known to us (90a36) [L. 2]. But because the middle in demonstrations is employed in order to make known something about which there might have been doubt or question, therefore in regard to the first he does two things. First, he lays down the number of questions. Secondly, from these questions he pursues his investigation by showing how the questions pertain to the middle of demonstrations (89b38). Regarding the first he does three things. First, he enumerates the questions. Secondly, he explains complex questions (89b26). Thirdly, simple questions (89b32).

He says therefore first (89b21) that the number of questions is equal to the number of things that are scientifically known. The reason for this is that science is knowledge acquired through demonstration. But things

163

which we previously did not know are those of which we must seek knowledge by demonstration: for it is in regard to things which we do not know that we form questions. Hence it follows that the things we inquire about are equal in number to the things we know through science. But there are four things that we ask, namely, *quia* [i.e., is it a fact *that*], *propter quid* [i.e., why, or what is the cause or reason], *si est* [if it is, i.e., whether it is], *quid est* [what is it]. To these four can be reduced whatever is scientifically inquirable or knowable.

However in *Topics* I he divides questions or problems into four kinds in a different way, but all of them are included under one of the questions listed here, namely, the one called *quia*. For in the *Topics* he is concerned only with questions to be disputed dialectically.

Then (89b26) he clarifies the questions he laid down; and first of all the complex ones. To understand this it should be noted that science bears only on the true, and the true is not signified except by an enunciation; therefore, only the enunciation can be scientifically knowable and so inquirable. But, as it is stated in *On Interpretation* II, the enunciation is formed in two ways: in one way from a name and a verb without an appositive, as when it is stated that *man is;* in another way when some third item is set adjacent, as when it is stated that *man is white.*

Therefore the questions we form can be reduced either to the first type of enunciation so that we get, as it were, a simple question; or to the second type, and then the question will be, as it were, complex or *put in number,* because, namely, the question concerns the putting together of two items.

According to this latter type a twofold question can be formed: one of them is whether this is true which is stated. This question he expounds first, saying that when we ask concerning some thing whether that thing is this or that, so that in effect we are somehow putting it in number, namely, by taking two things one of which is predicate and the other subject, as when we ask if the sun is failing because of an eclipse or not, and is man an animal or not, then we are said to ask *quia:* not in the sense that the word "quia" functions as a question mark, but because we are asking in order to find out *quia* [i.e., *that*] it is so. An indication of this is that when we have discovered it through demonstration, we cease our questioning; and if we had known it at the very beginning, we would not have asked whether it is so. But inquiry does not cease until that is obtained which was asked. And so, since the question in which we ask whether this is this ceases once we have certified that it is so, it is clear what a question of this kind asks.

Then (89b28) he clarifies the next question which also puts in number, saying that when we know *that* it is so, we ask *propter quid* [i.e., why] it is so. For example, when we know that the sun is failing through an eclipse and that the earth is moved during an earthquake, we ask *why* the sun is failing or *why* the earth is being moved. Therefore we ask it in this way, namely, by putting in number.

Then (89b32) he clarifies the other two questions which do not put in number but are simple. And he says that we ask certain things in a manner different from the aforesaid questions, namely, by not putting in number; as when we ask whether or not there be centaurs, for in this case the question we ask concerning the centaur is simply whether it exists and not whether the centaur be this, say white, or not. And just as when we knew *that* this is this, we then asked *why*, so once we know of something simply *that* it is, we ask *what* it is, for example, what is God or what is man. These then and so many are the things we ask; and when we have found the answer, we are said to know scientifically.

Then (89b38) he shows how the aforesaid questions are related to the middle. Concerning this he does three things. First, he states what he intends. Secondly, he explains what he had said (90a2). Thirdly, he proves his proposition (90a5).

In regard to the first it should be noted that two of the aforesaid questions put in number and two do not. From the first member of each of these groups, he forms another grouping composed of the question *that* it is and the question *if* it is. And he says that when we ask *that* this is this, or when we simply ask concerning something, *if* it is, we are not asking anything else than whether or not a middle is to be found of that which we ask; and this is something not conveyed by the form of the question. For when I ask whether the sun is eclipsed or whether man exists, it is not obvious from the form of the question that I am asking whether there is some middle by which it might be demonstrated that the sun is eclipsed or that man exists; but if the sun is eclipsed or man does exist, the consequence is that some middle can be found to demonstrate the things which are inquired. For no one forms a question concerning immediate things which, although they are true, do not have a middle, since things of this sort, being evident, do not fall under a question. Thus, therefore, one who asks whether this is this or whether this absolutely is, as a consequence is asking whether there is a middle of this sort. For in the question *if* it is or *that* it is, one is asking whether that which is a middle exists, because that which is the middle is the reason of that concerning which one asks whether this is this or simply whether it is, as will be explained below. Nevertheless the question is not being asked under the aspect of middle.

Now it happens that having found the answer to what is asked by these two questions, one knows either *that* it is or *if* it is: one of which consists in knowing the existence absolutely; but the other in part, as when we know that man is white, because to be white does not signify the existence of man in his entirety but signifies him to be something. This is why when a man is becoming white, we do not say that he is coming to be absolutely, but in a qualified sense. But when it is asserted that man is, his existence is signified absolutely, so that when a man comes to be, he is said to become absolutely.

Therefore, when we know *that* it is and ask *why* it is, or when we know *if* it is and ask *what* it is, we are asking what is the middle. And as in the other cases, so here, this is gathered not from the form of the question but by way of concomitance. For one who seeks the cause *why* the sun is eclipsed is not seeking it as a middle which demonstrates, but he is seeking that which is a middle, because it is by way of consequence that once he has it, he can demonstrate. And the same applies to the question *what* is it.

Then (90a2) he manifests what he had said, namely, that *that it is* and *if it is* differ as *in part* and *absolutely* differ. For when we inquire whether the moon is waning or waxing, it is a question in part, since in a question of this type we are asking if the moon is something, namely, is it waning or has it waxed or not. But when we ask whether the moon exists or whether it is night, the question bears on existence absolutely.

Then (90a5) he proves his point, namely, that the aforesaid questions pertain to the middle. First, he proves it with a reason. Secondly, with a sign (90a24).

He concludes therefore first (90a5) from the explanation given above that in all the aforesaid questions one is either asking *whether* there is a middle, namely, in the question *that* it is and in the question *if* it is, or *what* the middle is, namely, in the question *why* and in the question *what* is it.

And he proves that the question *why* inquires what the middle is. For it is obvious that a cause is the middle in a demonstration which enables one to know scientifically, because to know scientifically is to know the cause of a thing. But it is precisely the cause that is being sought in all the above questions. That this is so he manifests first in regard to the question *that*. For when it is asked whether the moon is waning, then according to the manner explained above, what is being asked is whether or not something is the cause of this waning. Then he shows this for the question *why*. For once we know *that* something is the cause of the moon's waning, we ask *what* the cause is; and this is to inquire *why*.

The same applies to the other two questions, as he shows in the following way. For he says that whether we assert not that something is this or that (for example, when I say that man is white or is a grammarian), but that the substance itself exists absolutely; or do not assert that something exists absolutely, but that some thing is something by putting in number (whether that something be a thing predicated *per se* or a thing predicated *per accidens*); no matter in which of these ways we take the thing to be, its cause is the middle for demonstrating it.

Then he explains what he means by a substance to exist absolutely when we inquire concerning the moon or the earth or a triangle or any other subject whether it is and then take some middle to demonstrate this. I say that a thing is something when we inquire concerning eclipse in regard to the moon, or equality or inequality in regard to triangle, or whether it is in the middle of the universe or not in regard to the earth. And he asserts that as far as the present point is concerned it makes no difference which way a thing is taken to be, because in all these cases *what it is* is the same as *why*.

He manifests this first of all in regard to the waning of the moon. For if one asks *what* is the eclipse of the moon, the answer is that it is the absence of light in the moon because of the earth's being set between it and the sun. And this same answer is given when it is inquired *why* the moon is eclipsed. For we say that the moon is eclipsed because there is a lack of light due to the earth's opposition.

Then he manifests the same idea with another example. For if one asks *what* is a chord, the answer is given that it is a numerical ratio according to high and low notes. Again, if one asks *why* a high note and a low note are concordant, the answer is given that it is because the high note and the low note have a numerical ratio. And so the question *what* is it and the question *why* reduce to the same thing subjectively, although they differ in formality. Hence because the question *why* leads us to inquire *what* the middle is, as has been shown, what is left is that when one asks *what is it,* the middle is likewise inquired.

Then he shows the same thing in regard to the question *that*. For, as has been said, concordance is a numerical ratio between high and low notes. When, therefore, one asks whether a high and low note concord, he is inquiring whether there is some numerical ratio of the high and low note; and this is the middle for demonstrating that a high and a low note concord. Consequently in the question *that,* one inquires whether there is a middle. But once we have found *that* there is a numerical ratio of the high and low note, we then ask *what* that ratio is: and this is to ask *what* or *why*.

Here Aristotle seems to say that the definition of a proper attribute is the middle in demonstration. However it must be remarked that the definition of the proper attribute cannot be completed without the definition of the subject. For it is obvious that the principles which the definition of the subject contains are the principles of the proper attribute. Hence a demonstration will not reach the first cause unless one takes as the middle of demonstration the definition of the subject. And so the proper attribute must be concluded of the subject by means of the definition of the proper attribute; furthermore, the definition of the proper attribute must be concluded of the subject through the definition of the subject. This is why it was laid down at the very beginning that one must know beforehand the *what is it* not only of the proper attribute but of the subject also; which would not be required unless the definition of the proper attribute were concluded of the subject through the definition of the subject.

This is clear from the following example: If we wish to demonstrate of triangle that it has three angles equal to two right angles, we first take as middle the fact that it is a figure having an exterior angle equal to its two opposite interior angles—which is, as it were, the definition of a proper attribute. But this in turn must be demonstrated by the definition of the subject, so that we would say: "Every closed figure of three straight lines has an exterior angle equal to its two opposite interior angles; but the triangle is such a figure. Therefore . . ." And the same is true if we were to demonstrate that a high note concords with a low note: for we would state the definition of the attribute which in this case consists in their having a numerical ratio; but then to demonstrate this attribute we would have to take the definition of high note and of low note. For a low note is one which is apt to act on the sense for a long time, whereas a high note is one which does so for a short time: but between the long and the short there is a numerical ratio. Therefore, there is a numerical ratio between a high note and a low note. And if the high note and the low note were defined some other way, it would make no difference. For in any case something pertaining to quantity would have to appear in their definition, so that it would be necessary to conclude that there is a numerical ratio between them.

Then (90a24) he manifests his point by means of a sensible sign. And he says that those cases in which the middle is perceptible by sense clearly show that every question is a question concerning a middle, because, namely, when the middle is known through the senses, no room is left for a question. For we ask one of the aforesaid questions in matters pertaining to sense, when the middle does not appear: thus, we ask whether or not there is an eclipse of the moon because we do not sensibly perceive the middle which is the cause making the moon to be eclipsed. But if we were to situate ourselves in a place above the moon, we would see how the moon became eclipsed by entering the earth's shadow. Then we would no longer ask *if* it is or *why* it is, but both would at once be obvious to us.

But because someone could object that sense-perception bears on singulars—whereas it is universals that are being asked about, just as it is universals that are scientifically known—and consequently, it does not seem that the matter under question can be made known through sense; therefore, as though in answer to this objection he adds that it is precisely because we do sense the particular (namely, that this body of the moon enters this shadow of the earth), that we happen at once to know the universal. For our sense would observe the fact that the light of the sun is now blocked by the earth's opposition; and through this it would be clear to us that the moon is now eclipsed. And because we would conjecture that the eclipse of the moon always occurs in this way, the sense knowledge of the singular would immediately become a universal in our science.

And so from this example he concludes that knowing the *quod quid* [*Quod quid* refers to any or all of the items that constitute the essential nature of a thing.] and the *why* are the same. For from the fact that we observe the earth situated between the sun and moon, we would know scientifically both *what* an eclipse of the moon is and *why* the moon is eclipsed. And one of these, namely, the knowledge *what* it is, is reduced to the science by which we know that something simply is, and not that something is in some thing. But the *why* is reduced to our knowledge of things that are in some thing, as when we say that three angles are equal to or greater than or less than two right angles.

Finally, he summarizes and concludes the main point, namely, that it is clear from the foregoing that in all questions there is question of the middle.

Lecture 2
(90a36–91a3)

WHETHER THE DEFINITION WHICH SIGNIFIES
THE *QUOD QUID* OF A THING
CAN BE DEMONSTRATED

a36. Let us now state	b19. What then? Can
b1. beginning what we	b23. Moreover, the basic
b3. It might, I mean,	b28. But if the definable
b7. And again, not even	b33. Moreover, every demonstration
b14. Induction too will	b38. Again, to prove essential
b16. Again, if to define	

After showing that every question is in some sense a question of the middle, which is the *quod quid* and the *propter quid,* the Philosopher now begins to make manifest how the middle becomes known to us. And it is divided into two parts. In the first part he shows how the *quod quid* and *propter quid* are related to demonstration. In the second part he shows how the *quod quid* and *propter quid* should be investigated (96a22) [L. 13]. The first part is divided into two parts. In the first he manifests how the *quid est* is related to demonstration. In the second he manifests how the *propter quid* which signifies a cause is related to demonstration

(94a20) [L. 9]. In regard to the first he does two things. First, he states his proposal. Secondly, he pursues his proposal (90b1).

He says therefore first (90a36) that since every question for whose solution a demonstration is adduced is a question of the middle which is *quid* and *propter quid,* our first task is to declare how the *quod quid* is made known to us, namely, is it through demonstration or division or some other way. Furthermore, we must point out how to reduce to the *quod quid* those items of a thing that are apparent. And because a definition is a statement which signifies the *quod quid,* it is necessary also to know what a definition is and why certain things are definable. Consequently we shall proceed in these matters in the following way. First, by raising difficulties. Secondly, by establishing the truth (93a1) [L. 7]. Then (90b1) he pursues his proposal in the order stated. First, he proceeds dialectically by raising difficulties. Secondly, by determining the truth (93a1) [L. 7]. In regard to the first he does two things. First, he proceeds by disputing about the definition which signifies *quod quid.* Secondly, about the *quod quid* which is signified by the definition (91a12) [L. 3]. Concerning the first he does three things. First, he inquires disputatively whether there is definition of all things of which there is demonstration. Secondly, whether conversely there is demonstration of all things of which there is definition (91b19). Thirdly, whether there can be definition and demonstration of the same thing (90b27). In regard to the first he does two things. First, he states his intention. Secondly, he pursues his proposal (90b1).

He says therefore first (90b1) that when a number of items are planned for discussion, one should take his start from the item which is most fruitful in settling the "had," i.e., the subsequent, problems. This would mean that in our case we should begin with the fact that someone might wonder whether the same thing and according to the same aspect could be known through definition and demonstration.

Then (90b4) he proves that there is not definition of all things of which there is demonstration. This he does in four ways, the first of which is the following: a definition is indicative of the *quod quid;* but anything which pertains to the *quod quid* is predicated both affirmatively and universally: therefore, a definition contains or signifies only those things which are predicated affirmatively and universally. But not all syllogisms demonstrate affirmative universal conclusions: in fact some are negative, as for example, all those in the second figure; and some are particular, as for example, all those in the third figure. Therefore, there is not definition of all things of which there is demonstration.

Secondly (90b7), he shows the same thing when he says that there cannot even be definition of all things which are concluded through affirmative syllogisms—which occurs only in the first figure, as when it is demonstratively syllogized that every triangle has three angles equal to two right angles. Now the reason for this statement, namely, that there cannot be definition of all things thus syllogized, is that to know something demonstratively is nothing else than to have a demonstration. From this it follows that if the science of all these things is had only through demonstration, there is not definition of them. For things which have a definition are made known through their definition. Otherwise it would follow that a person who does not have a demonstration of these things would have scientific knowledge of them, for the simple reason that nothing hinders a person who knows the definition from not having at the same time the demonstration—although the definition is a principle of the demonstration. For not everyone who knows the principles knows how to deduce the conclusion by demonstrating.

Thirdly (90b14), he shows the same thing through an induction from which a conviction can arise sufficient for admitting the above-mentioned conclusion. He says, therefore, that demonstration is concerned with things which are *per se* in something, as is clear from what has been established in the first book. But a definition never gives anyone a knowledge of those items which are *per se* in a thing, much less of those which are in it *per accidens*—not that there cannot be definitions of accidents which are in a thing *per se* or *per accidens;* but because no one has ever given the definition of that which is to be in a thing *per se* or *per accidens,* which the syllogism concludes.

Fourthly (90b16), he shows the same thing with a reason, namely, that the definition makes the substance known: first of all, because substance is defined in a primary way, whereas accident is defined secondarily by means of a definition which adds something alien, as is stated in *Metaphysics* VII; and secondly, because an accident is not defined save insofar as it is signified after the manner of a substance by employing a noun. But the things upon which demonstrations bear are not substances nor things signified after the manner of substances, but things signified after the manner of accidents, namely, after the manner of something inhering in some thing. Hence he concludes that it is not possible that there be a definition of everything of which there is demonstration.

Then (90b19) he inquires whether conversely there is demonstration of everything of which there is a definition. And he shows that there is not for two reasons, the first of which has already been touched upon above. For it seems that of one thing, precisely as it is one, there is one science, i.e., one way of knowing it. Hence if that which is demonstrable is truly known scientifically in virtue of the fact that a demonstration is had of it, then something impossible follows, if it can also be scientifically known through a definition: for the one having the definition would be knowing something demonstrable without having the demonstration—which seems absurd. And this reason was the second of the four previously presented.

Then (90b23) he gives the second reason. For definitions are principles of demonstrations, as was established in Book I; but the principles are not demonstrable—otherwise it would follow that there are principles of principles and that demonstrations would proceed to infinity, which is impossible, as we have shown in the first book. Hence it follows that definitions are not demonstrable, being as they are first principles in demonstrations. Consequently, there is not demonstration of all things of which there is definition.

Then (90b28) he inquires whether it is possible for there to be definition and demonstration of the same thing in some cases even though not of all. And with three reasons he shows that there is not. The first of these reasons is that a definition is manifestive of the *quod quid* and of the substance, i.e., of the essence, of a thing. Demonstrations, on the other hand, do not manifest this but suppose it: thus in mathematical demonstrations it is supposed from arithmetic what *unity* is and what *odd* is; and the same applies in other demonstrations. Therefore, there is not demonstration and definition of the same thing.

Then (90b33) he presents the second reason and it is this: In the conclusion of a demonstration something is predicated of something either affirmatively or negatively; but in a definition nothing is predicated of anything: thus in the definition that man is a two-footed animal, neither animal is predicated of two-footed nor two-footed of animal. Likewise in the definition that a circle or a triangle is a plane figure, neither plane is predicated of figure nor figure of plane. For if the parts of a definition were to be joined to one another, the resulting predication would have to be understood in a manner which suits a definition, namely, in *quod quid*. But this we do not observe. For the genus is not predicated *quod quid* of the difference, nor the difference of the genus. Therefore, there is not definition and demonstration of a same thing.

Then (90b38) he gives the third reason and says that it is one thing to manifest the *quod quid* and another the *quia,* as is clear from the difference between the questions listed above; but the definition shows the *quid* of something, whereas a demonstration shows either affirmatively or negatively that something is or is not so of something. But we see that for different things different demonstrations are required, unless those two different things are related as whole and part: for in that case there would be one and the same demonstration concerning both. Thus, the demonstration that a triangle has three angles equal to two right angles applies also to isosceles, which is related to triangle as part to whole. But that is not the case in these two things, namely, in the *quia* and in the *quid;* for neither is a part of the other.

Therefore, it has been established that there is not demonstration of everything of which there is definition, nor conversely. Furthermore, it has been possible from this to conclude that these are not of the same thing, and that definition and demonstration are neither the same nor is one in the other as a subjective part in its whole—otherwise it would be necessary that even those things of which they are be related after the manner of whole and part in such a way, namely, that everything definable would be demonstrable, or vice versa—which was disproved above.

Finally, he summarizes and concludes that so far we have proceeded by opposing.

Lecture 3
(91a12–b11)

WHETHER THE *QUOD QUID* SIGNIFIED BY THE DEFINITION CAN BE DEMONSTRATED BY TAKING CONVERTIBLE TERMS

After inquiring disputatively whether the definition signifying *quod quid* can be demonstrated, the Philosopher continues to inquire disputatively and asks whether the *quod quid* itself, which is signified by a definition, can be proved demonstratively. First, he states what he intends. Secondly, he pursues his proposal (91a14).

First, therefore (91a12), he raises the question: Can there be a syllogism or demonstration of that which is the *quod quid*, namely, in such a way as to conclude that this is the *quod quid* of this; or can this not be done, as the immediately preceding reason supposed?

Now it was necessary to undertake this disputation on the heels of the previous one, because in a definition one must be sure not only that what it signifies is the *quod quid*, but also that it be formulated in such a way as to be suitable for manifesting the *quod quid*, i.e., in such a way as to be composed of prior and better known items and possess the other characteristics which mark a definition. It is significant that he says, "whether there be syllogism or demonstration," for some of the reasons which follow conclude that there is not demonstration of the *quod quid*, and others that there is no syllogism at all of it.

Then (91a14) he proceeds disputatively to show that there is not syllogism or demonstration of the *quod quid*. First, he excludes certain special ways by which it might seem possible to demonstrate the *quod quid.* Secondly, he presents common reasons for this (92b3) [L. 6]. Concerning the first he does three things. First, he shows that *quod quid* cannot be demonstrated by using convertible terms. Secondly, that it cannot be demonstrated by division (91b12) [L. 4]. Thirdly, that it cannot be demonstrated by accepting that which is required for *quod quid* (92a6) [L. 5]. In regard to the first he does three things. First, he prefaces certain notions required for showing the proposal. Secondly, he induces a reason (91a17). Thirdly, he discloses the inconvenience which follows (91a32).

With respect to the first (91a14) he presupposes two things: the first of these pertains to the syllogism, namely, that every syllogism proves something about something by means of some middle, as is clear from the above. The other pertains to what is to be proved by the syllogism, namely, the *quod quid,* for which two conditions are required. The first of these is that the *quod quid* be proper, for each thing has its own proper essence or quiddity. But because not everything which is proper to something pertains to its essence, a second condition is required, namely, that it be predicated in *quid.* Furthermore, a third condition must follow on these two, namely, that the *quod quid* be convertible with that of which it is.

Then (91a17) he lays down a reason in support of his proposal. Regarding this he does three things. First, he states what sort of syllogism would be required for concluding a *quod quid,* if this were possible. Secondly, he concludes to the inconvenience that follows from this (91a25). Thirdly, he uses terms to exemplify this (91a28). Concerning the first he does three things. First, he shows what is required for a syllogism concluding the *quod quid* so far as it is something proper. Secondly, what is required so far as it is predicated in *quid* (91a18). Thirdly, he shows that without these characteristics such a syllogism would not be possible (91a21).

He says therefore first (91a18) that if A which is to be proved of C as its *quod quid* is propter to C (which is required of the *quod quid,* as has been said), it will be necessary that the first, namely, A, be proper to the middle which is B; for if A exceeded [i.e., were more universal than] B, which is predicated universally of C, it would follow that A exceeds C even more. In like manner, it is clear that B will have to be proper to C: for if B were to exceed C, it would follow that A, which is predicated universally of B, exceeds C; consequently, it would not be proper to it, as was supposed. What remains, therefore, is that if there is to be a syllogism concluding *quod quid,* the terms will have to be so related that all are mutually convertible.

Then (91a18) he shows what the syllogism in question must have, if the condition is to be fulfilled that what it concludes be predicated in *quod quid.* And he says that such a syllogism must be so formulated that the major extreme, which is A, be predicated in *quod quid* of the middle, which is B; in like manner, B will have to be predicated in *quod quid* of the minor extreme, which is C. In this way it can be concluded that A is predicated of C in *quod quid.*

Then (91a21) he shows that the aforesaid way of syllogizing is required. And he asserts that if one does not so take the terms by "thus duplicating," i.e., observing the two conditions laid down above, i.e., taking the *quod quid* on the side of both, it does not follow of necessity that A would be predicated of C in *quod quid.* Indeed, if the aforesaid conditions are observed on the part of one only, it is not sufficient for the purpose intended. For even if A were predicated of B in *quod quid,* it would not on that account follow that it must be predicated in *quod quid* of everything of which B might happen to be predicated in some random way. Consequently, it follows that the *quod quid* must be taken on the side of both in such a way, namely, that not only must A be the *quod quid* of B, but also that B must be the *quod quid* of C, as being predicated convertibly and in *quod quid.*

Then (91a25) he leads to the inconvenience: for if, as has been indicated, not only is there found on the side of both something which is predicated in *quod quid*—as a genus predicated of a species—but it is further found on the side of both that this something is the *quod quid erat esse*—which a definition signifies—it follows that the *quod quid erat esse* was already in the middle term, i.e., that the middle term is the *quod quid erat esse* of the minor extreme. Consequently, we would have been supposing the very thing we had set out to prove, namely, the quiddity of C. [*Quod quid erat esse* refers to the essential nature of a being.]

Then (91a28) he clarifies what he has just said, using terms. Thus, if we wish to show what man is, let C, i.e., the minor extreme, be "man," and A, the major extreme, be the "*quod quid* of man," say "two-footed animal," or something similar to this. Therefore, if this is what we intend to prove by the syllogism, it is necessary to find the definition of some middle, namely, B, such that A will be predicated of every B. Furthermore, to this middle will pertain some other middle definition which, namely, was the definition of the minor extreme. Hence it will follow that this middle will also be the *quod quid* of man. Consequently, one who syllogizes in this way would be supposing what he was required to prove, namely, that B is the *quod quid erat esse* of man.

Then (91a32) he shows how this inconvenience follows from the premises. To this end he does three things. First, he indicates the method by which this may be fittingly done. And he says that what has been said should be considered in two propositions which are first and which have terms that belong to each other immediately. For it would be possible to prove our point either with several propositions (which would lead to several syllogisms), or with only two propositions, but taking them as mediate. But because in the final analysis we must always arrive at two immediate propositions, then for the sake of brevity and dispatch let us assume such propositions from the very start. Thus we shall be able to manifest our point quite easily.

Secondly (91a35), he states what he intends and says, concluding from the foregoing, that those who would demonstrate through convertible terms the *quod quid* of some thing (say, what is a soul, or what is man, or anything else of this sort), necessarily commit the fault of begging the question. And he cites as an example Plato's definition of soul. For since the soul is alive and is the body's cause of being alive, it follows that it differs from the body in the fact that the body lives in virtue of some cause other than itself, but the soul lives in virtue of itself. But Plato posited that number is the substance of all things: for he failed to distinguish between *one*, which is converted with being and refers to the substance of that of which it is predicated, and *one* which is the principle of number. As a consequence, it followed that the soul as to its substance is a number, just as any other thing containing many things in itself.

Likewise Plato posited that to live is one of the ways of being moved. For the living are distinguished from the non-living on two scores, namely, sense and movement, as it is stated in *On the Soul* I. Furthermore, he asserted that sensing or knowing is one way of being moved. Thus, therefore, he said that the soul is a self-moving number in addition to saying that the soul is its own cause of being alive. Consequently, if anyone desired to prove *what* a soul is, namely, that it is something which is its own cause of being alive, and assumed as middle that the soul is a number which moves itself, it would be necessary to beg this, namely, that the soul is a self-moving number, such that this is identical with the soul as being its *quod quid*. Otherwise, it would not follow, if something is the *quod quid* of self-moving number, that it is the *quod quid* of the soul itself.

Thirdly (91b1), he proves his proposal, namely, that such a proof involves begging the question. And he says that it does not follow from the fact that A follows on B and B on C, that the major extreme, A, is the *quod quid* of the minor extreme, C; what follows is simply that A is in C. And if it is further granted that A is the *quod quid* of something and is predicated universally of B, it does not yet follow that A is the *quod quid* of C: for it is plain that this, i.e., the *quod quid* of animal is universally predicated of this which is man's *quod quid*. For just as it is true that animal is universally predicated of man, so it is true that the definition of animal is universally predicated of the definition of man; but that does not mean that they are entirely one and the same.

And so it is clear that unless one takes the terms in such a way that the first is entirely one and the same with the middle, and the middle with the last, it will not be possible to syllogize that A, which is the first, is the *quod quid* of C—which is the last—and its essence. But if the terms are taken in that way, it follows that prior to its being concluded, the *quod quid* of C, namely, B, was assumed in the premises. From this it follows that there is not a demonstration but a begging or assuming of the question.

Lecture 4
(91b12–92a6)

WHETHER *QUOD QUID* CAN BE DEMONSTRATED BY THE METHOD OF DIVISION

b12. Nor, as was said
b25. For why should not
b26. Again, what guarantee

b28. The champion of division
b33. Nevertheless, we reply,

After showing that *quod quid* cannot be demonstrated with convertible terms, the Philosopher now shows that it cannot be demonstrated by the method of division. And in regard to this he does two things. First, he shows what he proposes. Secondly, he excludes a certain solution (91b28). Concerning the first he does two things. First, he shows what he proposes by using a reason common to all things which are syllogized. Secondly, he shows it with reasons proper to that which is *quod quid* (91a25).

He says therefore first (91b12) that just as the *quod quid* cannot be demonstrated by convertible terms, so neither by the method of division through which, as a matter of fact, nothing is proved syllogistically, as was established in *Resolutions Touching Figures*, i.e., in *Prior Analytics* I. For just as in the *Posterior Analytics* resolution to first principles is taught, so in the *Prior Analytics* resolution is made to certain first simple items which pertain to the arrangement of the syllogism in mood and figure.

That something cannot be syllogized by the method of division he proves from the fact that in this method, given the premises, the conclusion does not follow of necessity, which it should, considering the nature of a syllogism. Rather, the same thing happens in the method of division as happens in the method of induction. For one who induces through singulars to the universal does not demonstrate or syllogize from necessity. For when something is proved syllogistically, it is not necessary to make further inquiry concerning the conclusion or to ask that the conclusion be conceded; what is necessary is that the conclusion be true, if the premises laid down are true. But, as he shows with certain examples, this does not happen in the method of division. For the method of division consists in assuming something common which is divided into at least two members, so that, one being removed, the other is concluded. For example, if beings are so divided that on the one hand is animal and on the other lifeless things, then having established that man is not a lifeless thing, it is concluded that he is animal. But this conclusion does not follow, unless the hearer grants that man is either an animal or a lifeless thing.

It might be remarked here that he quite fittingly compared division to induction. For in both cases one is required to suppose that he has listed all the things contained under some general heading; otherwise, the person inducing could not conclude a universal from the singulars he assumed, nor could the person dividing conclude to one member just because the others have been eliminated. Thus it is obvious that one cannot in virtue of the fact that Socrates and Plato and Cicero run, induce of necessity the conclusion that every man runs, unless his audience concedes that nothing more is contained under man than the ones listed. In like manner, one who divides cannot, in virtue of having proved that this colored object is neither white nor grey, conclude of necessity that it is black, unless his audience grants him that nothing else is contained under *colored object* than the things mentioned in the division. And because a person investigating *what* man is must assume not only the genus which is animal but also the difference, he goes on to say in his example that if every animal is either of the land or of the water and it is established that because man is not a water animal, he is this whole which is land animal, that statement does not follow of necessity from the premises: rather it is further required that he suppose his audience to have granted him something, namely, that *animal* is sufficiently divided into those of the land and those of the water. And because in some cases several divisions are used in obtaining the *quod quid* of a thing, therefore, after laying down two divisions in his example, he adds that it makes no difference whether few or many are used. For the formality is the same in all. And thus he concludes once more that those who proceed by the method of division, even in matters that could be syllogized, do not use a syllogized proof.

Then (91b25) he induces two reasons proper to the *quod quid*. The first of these is that not everything which is truly predicated of something is predicated in *quod quid* or signifies its essence. Therefore, even if it be conceded that one has sufficiently proved by the method of division that this whole, namely, land animal, is truly predicated of man, it does not on that account follow that it is predicated of it in *quod quid* or that it shows the *quod quid erat esse*, i.e, that it demonstrates the essence of the thing.

Then (91b26) he gives the second reason. For the essence of a thing is declared through certain definite items which may neither be added to or subtracted from. But there is nothing to hinder one who proceeds by the method of division from adding something over and above the items which suffice for showing the *quod quid,* or from subtracting some of the things which are necessary for this, or from going beyond and exceeding the essence of the thing, as when it is more common than the thing itself —which happens when the ultimate differences which contract common things are removed. Hence the *quod quid* is not sufficiently proved by division. And this is what he concludes, namely, that in the method of division the above-mentioned conditions are not satisfied, i.e., the conditions that what is concluded be predicated in *quod quid* and that it neither exceed nor be exceeded.

Then (91b28) he excludes a certain solution. First, he proposes it. Secondly, he excludes it (91b33).

He says therefore first (91b28) that one might solve our objections by saying that when a division is made, one could be taking all the things that are predicated in *quod quid,* so that as a consequence of the division he accomplishes what was primarily intended, namely, that he obtains a definition signifying the *quod quid* and leaves out nothing which is required for defining. And if he does these two things, namely, if all the items he assumes in the division are predicated in *quod quid* and all such things are included in the division so that nothing is left out, then it is necessary that what is obtained be the *quod quid.* And the reason for this necessity is that in taking everything which is predicated in *quod quid* and leaving nothing out, that which is found must be something individual, i.e., the individual notion of such a thing, so that no further division is required for it to be appropriate to this thing.

Then (91b33) he excludes this solution, saying that even though under the aforesaid conditions something individual is necessarily obtained, as explained above, the method is nevertheless not syllogistic; although it might make one know the *quod quid* in some other way. And this is not unbecoming, namely, that something be manifested in a way other than by a syllogism: for one who uses induction does not prove anything syllogistically, but yet he does manifest something.

That one who reaches a definition by way of division does not achieve a syllogism he shows by something similar. For if a conclusion is induced from a major proposition, the second proposition being omitted, and the person concluding declares that this must follow from the premises, the hearer could ask why it is necessary—which is something that does not happen in a syllogistic proof. Hence such a method of arguing is not syllogistic. Similarly, in terms of division no syllogism is achieved, because the question *why* always remains. Thus, if someone wishing to disclose what man is were to assert by the method of division that man is a two-footed mortal animal, or one that has two feet but no wings, then as he adds one item to another in his division, he could be asked in regard to each one, why is it necessary. For one who sets out to manifest a *quod quid* by division will not only assert but also prove—in keeping with what he thinks—that everything which exists is mortal or immortal. And although it be granted that through this division he might be demonstrating his proposition, nevertheless it is not necessary that the notion so concluded be a definition; for perhaps the items out of which such a notion is formed are not predicated in *quod quid* or exceed the substance of the thing defined. But even though such a notion might happen to be a definition, it is nevertheless not proved by the syllogism to be a definition, as is clear from what has been established above.

Lecture 5
(92a6–b3)

WHETHER A *QUOD QUID* CAN BE DEMONSTRATED BY TAKING THAT WHICH IS REQUIRED FOR A *QUOD QUID*

a6. Can we nevertheless

a9. Or is the truth that,

a12. Further, just as in

a20. The following type

a23. The question is begged

a24. and as a premiss

a28. Again, both proof by

a34. How then by definition

After showing that the *quod quid* cannot be demonstrated either by convertible terms or by the method of division, the Philosopher here shows that it cannot be demonstrated by taking that which is required for a *quod quid*. In regard to this he does two things. First, he shows what he proposes. Secondly, he concludes from all of the foregoing that there is no way in which *quod quid* may be demonstrated (92a34). Concerning the first he does two things. First, he employs reasons proper to what he proposes. Secondly, he employs a reason common to what is now being said and to what was said above (92a28). Concerning the first he does two things. First, he shows that the *quod quid* cannot be demonstrated by taking that which pertains to the notion of its *quod quid*. Secondly, he shows that the *quod quid* of this thing cannot be demonstrated by taking the *quod quid* of some other thing (92a20). In regard to the first he does two things. First, he raises the question. Secondly, he argues for his proposal (92a9).

He asks therefore first (92a6) whether one might demonstrate what something is according to its substance by supposing that the *quod quid* of a thing can be obtained if one satisfies the conditions which are proper to the *quod quid:* for example, if one were to prove that two-footed land animal is the *quod quid* of man, having taken as middle the fact that this notion is converted with man and is composed of genus and difference; which are the only conditions required for a *quod quid.* Furthermore, this whole, which has been stated, is proper to the *quod quid* because it is the being or reality of it, i.e., of that which is *quod quid.* It is as though he were saying that being a convertible notion composed of a genus and difference is exactly the same as being the *quod quid.*

Then (92a9) he lodges two objections against the above question, showing that the *quod quid* cannot be demonstrated in the way it suggests. The first of these is that just as the previously mentioned ways of demonstrating failed because they assumed the very thing in question, so too in the present instance. For it, too, assumes the *quod quid erat esse,* as for example when it is assumed that every convertible notion composed of genus and difference signifies the *quod quid est;* consequently, the proof is not acceptable. For one must never take as middle the very thing the demonstration is intended to prove; rather it is necessary to demonstrate it through some other middle.

Then (92a11) he gives the second reason, which is based on a likeness to a syllogism. For when a person syllogizes, he is not required to use the definition of syllogism in order to syllogize; because the items from which a syllogism proceeds are such that each item is either a whole proposition, i.e., a universal or major proposition, or a part, i.e., a particular or minor proposition subsumed under the major one. Consequently, the definition of a syllogism is not one of the things from which a syllogism proceeds. In like manner if someone wishes to syllogize the *quod quid erat esse* of something, he is not required to mention what a *quod quid erat esse* is; but he must have this in reserve in his mind over and above the items which are put in the definition or in the syllogism. For these notions of a syllogism and of a definition function in defining and syllogizing as rules of art which an artisan must respect in his works. Now an artisan who makes a knife does not do so by establishing the rules according to which he works, but in the light of the rules he has in his mind he examines whether the knife was made well. So, too, a person who syllogizes does not mention the notion of a syllogism as he syllogizes, but in view of the notion of a syllogism he examines the syllogism he made, in order to see whether it is good.

Hence if a person should wonder, once a syllogism has been formed, whether it syllogized or not, the one who formed the syllogism can settle this doubt by showing that it does syllogize, on the ground that a syllogism is such and such a thing. So, too, a person who intends to syllogize the *quod quid erat esse* should have reserved in his mind the notion of what a *quod quid erat esse* is, so that if someone should say that a *quod quid erat esse* has not been syllogized, he can answer that it has, because such and such is put down as the *quod quid erat esse*. Thus, therefore, it is clear that a person who syllogizes a *quod quid erat esse* should not state what a syllogism is or what a *quod quid erat esse* is.

The (92a20) he shows that the *quod quid* of one thing cannot be demonstrated from the *quod quid* of another thing. Concerning this he does two things. First, he proposes what he intends. Secondly, he proves what he proposes (92a23).

He says therefore first (92a20) that the *quod quid* is not proved, if someone wished to prove it by supposing the *quod quid* of some other thing; for example, if someone were to proceed in such a way as to assume that the being or reality of divisible and of evil is the same, i.e., that division is the *quod quid* of evil, and then argued in the following manner: "In all things which have a contrary the *quod quid* of one contrary is a contrary; but the contrary of good is evil, and of divisible the contrary is indivisible: therefore, it follows that indivisible is the *quod quid* of the good." And these examples are taken according to Plato's opinion that the notion of the *one* and of the *good* are the same. For we notice that everything seeks unity as its own good. But one is the same as indivisible; and so in virtue of the opposition it follows that evil is the same as divisible. For everything shuns division of the self, because through division it tends to what is shattered and imperfect.

Then (92a23) he proves what he has proposed, namely, that the *quod quid* cannot be demonstrated: and this by giving two reasons. The first of these is that even according to this method one demonstrates by assuming the *quod quid erat esse*, and thus he assumes what he should have proved.

Then (92a24) he gives the second reason, saying that not only is it improper to take the *quod quid erat esse* when demonstrating, but this impropriety is compounded when one takes a *quod quid erat esse* to demonstrate a *quod quid erat esse*: because even in demonstrations in which this is proved of this, say a proper attribute of a subject, a *quod quid erat esse* is taken as middle; nevertheless the one so taken is not the very thing which was to be concluded or something which has the same notion and is converted. But good and indivisible, and evil and divisible, have the same notion; and each pair is converted, because one being posited, the other is posited, and vice versa.

Then (92a28) he presents a common reason against anyone who demonstrates from supposition and division. And he says that the same opposition is directed against both, namely, against one who tries to demonstrate the *quod quid* by division and against one who proceeds by laying down the *quod quid* in the syllogism. For clearly a definition signifies something which is one: hence to signify this oneness the items laid down in the definition should be arranged without a conjunction; thus one should say that man is a two-footed land animal, but not that man is an animal and two-footed. Hence if anyone desires to prove the *quod quid,* he must prove that one thing is formed from the things assumed. But it is not required, according to the above-cited methods of division and supposition, that one predicate be formed from these items which are taken for defining: since there might be several, for example, if one should state that man is grammatical and musical. It seems therefore that according to the ways mentioned above, the *quod quid* is not proved.

Then (92a34) he concludes from the foregoing that there is no way to prove the *quod quid,* saying: if then the *quod quid* cannot be proved either by convertible terms or division or opposition, how will the definer be able to demonstrate the substance of a thing or the *quod quid?* For it is now clear from the foregoing that he does not prove it according to the method whereby, in virtue of items that are *per se* known, one manifests that something else must follow through things which are said—which is required for a demonstration.

However, besides these three modes there is a fourth, namely, through induction. But it turns out that the *quod quid* cannot be proved by manifest singulars, namely, in such a way that something is predicated of all and is not anything that might be otherwise: because one who thus proceeds by induction will not demonstrate the *quod quid* but will demonstrate that something is or is not; for example, that every man is an animal, or that no animal is a stone.

But no other method is available for demonstrating the *quod quid,* save perhaps the method of demonstrating something to the senses, as when something is pointed out with the finger. But it is obvious that this method cannot be invoked in the present instance, because the *quod quid* is not an object of sense but of intellect, as it is stated in *On the Soul* III. It remains, therefore, that there is no way in which the *quod quid* can be demonstrated.

Lecture 6
(92b3–39)

WHETHER *QUOD QUID* CAN BE SHOWN BY DEMONSTRATION OR DEFINITION

b3. To put it another way:
b7. But further, if definition
b11. Then too we hold that
b18. Moreover it is clear
b26. Since, therefore, to define

b28. But that were
b30. all sets of words
b32. no demonstration can prove
b35. It appears then

After considering each of the ways in which something might be demonstrated and showing that none can demonstrate the *quod quid,* the Philosopher now shows what he proposes through common reasons. Concerning this he does three things. First, he lays down something which is necessary for proving what he proposes. Secondly, he shows what he proposes (92b7). Thirdly, he sums up what has been stated (97b35).

He says therefore first (92b3) that there does not seem to be any possible way for a person to demonstrate that some *quod quid* is man: and this because whoever knows a *quod quid* to be of man or of any other thing is required to know that the thing exists. For since there is no quiddity or essence of a non-being, it is impossible to know the *quod quid* of something which is not; but one might know the meaning of the name or have a notion composed of several names. Thus a person is capable of knowing the meaning of the word *tragelaphus* or *goat-stag,* because it signifies an animal composed of goat and stag, but it is impossible to know the *quod quid* of a goat-stag, because there is no such thing given in nature.

Then (92b7) from what has been established he goes on to prove what he proposed. In regard to this he does two things. First, he shows that the *quod quid* cannot be shown by demonstration. Secondly, that it cannot be shown by definition (92b26).

In regard to the first he presents three reasons, the first of which (92b7) is the following: Just as a definition is brought forward to manifest something which is one in the sense that from the parts of the definition something is formed which is one *per se* and not one *per accidens,* so a demonstration which employs a definition as its middle must demonstrate something which is one; for the conclusion must be proportionate to the middle. Consequently, it is clear that one cannot in virtue of one and the same definition demonstrate things that are diverse. But the *quod quid* of man is one thing and his being or existence is another—for it is only in

184

the First Principle of being, Who is being essentially, that *to be* and quiddity are one and the same; in all other things, which are beings by participation, the *to be* has to be other than the quiddity. Therefore, it is not possible to demonstrate both the *quid* and the *quia* with the same demonstration.

Then (92b11) he presents the second reason and it is this: According to a common opinion of wise men, it is necessary that *all* i.e., the whole demonstrated by a demonstration, be the *quia est,* unless perchance someone would want to say that the *quia est* itself is the substance of a thing. However, this is impossible. For the *to be* is not the substance or essence of anything existing in a genus; otherwise it would be required that *being* be a genus, because a genus is something predicated in *quod quia*. But, as it is proved in *Metaphysics* III, being is not a genus. For this reason God Who is His own essence is not in a genus.

Furthermore, if the *quia est* were the substance of any thing, then in the same breath that one shows the *quia est* he would be showing the *quid est;* consequently, the whole which a demonstrator manifests would not be the *quia est.* But this is false. Therefore, it is clear that demonstration manifests only the *quia est,* for it demonstrates some enunciation which signifies that something is or is not.

This is apparent also in the way a science proceeds. For geometry assumes what the name triangle signifies, and demonstrates *quod sit,* as when it demonstrates that an equilateral triangle has been formed on a given straight line. Therefore, if one demonstrated merely *what* a triangle is apart from the method of demonstrating which the sciences employ, he would not be demonstrating this whole which is that a triangle exists, but only what I call triangle. For just as, owing to the fact that *to be* is not the substance of a thing, one who demonstrates *to be* demonstrates that and nothing more, so if someone demonstrates the *quid est,* that is all he demonstrates. It would follow, therefore, that someone who knew the *quid est* in virtue of a definition would not know *an est* —which is impossible in view of what has been established above.

Then (92b18) he presents the third reason. Now this reason uses ordinary definitions as examples to manifest the same fact that was concluded in the previous reason, namely, that one who demonstrates the *quid est* is not demonstrating the *quia est.* Wherefore he says that it is clear not only in the light of the foregoing but also in view of the modes of terms, i.e., of definitions, which are presently in vogue that those who define do not manifest the *quia est.* For example, one who defines a circle as something all the lines from whose center to the circumference are equal, is still left with the question *why* there must be such a thing as he has defined, i.e., why it is necessary to posit that there exists such a thing as was defined; for example, why it is required to posit that there is a circle which is defined in the way mentioned. For it is acceptable to give a like description of a brass mountain by saying, for example, that it is a brass body which is lofty and extensive; but the task would still remain to establish whether there is such a thing in nature. And this because terms, i.e., defining notions, do not state that their counterpart either exists or is capable of existing; rather, whenever such a notion is formulated, it is legitimate to ask why such a thing should exist. Clearly then, it is impossible to demonstrate *quid est* and *quia est* simultaneously.

Then (92b26) by leading to something absurd, he shows that the *quod quid* cannot be shown by demonstration. First, therefore, he shows what would follow from this. Secondly, he shows that what does follow is unacceptable (92b28).

He says therefore (92b26) that since a definer might show either the *quid est* or merely what a name signifies, it follows that a definition does not necessarily manifest the *quod quid,* which belongs to definition in the proper sense; otherwise, it will follow that a definition signifying *quod quid* is nothing more than a statement signifying in the same way that a name does: for the only thing that a definition adds to such a notion is that it signifies the essence of some thing. Hence, if there is no thing whose essence the definition signifies, it will be no different from a statement explaining the signification of some name.

Then (92b28) he shows that it is unacceptable for a definition to be nothing more than a statement explaining the signification of a name: and this for three reasons. The first of these is that it happens that even things which are neither substances nor beings in a universal sense can be signified by a name. Now a name can be explained by some interpretation. Consequently, if a definition were nothing more than a statement interpreting a name, it would follow that a definition could be given of non-substances and of things that do not exist at all. But this is clearly false, for as it is shown in *Metaphysics* VII, definition bears principally on substance and on other things insofar as they are related to substance.

Then (92b30) he gives the second reason and it is this: To any notion, i.e., to any statement signifying something, it is possible to apply a corresponding name which is explained by that notion. Therefore, if a definition is nothing more than a notion explaining a name, it would follow that all notions were definitions. As a consequence, it would follow that when we dispute or converse with anyone, the disputations or our discussions are definitions; similarly, it would follow that the *Iliad,* i.e., Homer's poem about the Trojan War, is a definition.

Then (92b32) he gives the third reason and it is this: No science demonstrates that a given name signifies a given thing. For names are arbitrary signs; hence they must be used according to the will of the one inventing them. But it is obvious that definitions are given in every science. Therefore, it is obvious that definitions do not signify this, i.e., a mere interpretation of a name.

Then (92b35) he sums up what has been so far discussed disputatively. And he says that from the foregoing it is seen to follow that definition and syllogism are neither the same nor concerned with the same; and furthermore that a definition demonstrates nothing, since it is not concerned with the same thing as a demonstration. In like manner, it seems to have been shown that it is not possible to know *quod quid* either by a definition or a demonstration, bcause a definition merely shows the *what* and a demonstration the *quia*. But to know the *quod quid* a knowledge of *quia est* is required, as has been shown.

Lecture 7
(93a1–b21)

THE TWO WAYS, LOGICAL AND DEMONSTRATIVE, OF MANIFESTING *QUOD QUID*

a1. We must now start
a4. Now to know its
a16. —so let us begin
a21. Moreover we are aware

a24. As often as we have
a28. Let us then take
b15. We have stated then

After inquiring disputatively how the definition and the *quod quid* are known, the Philosopher here determines the truth. First, he states what his intention is. Secondly, he carries out what he proposes (93a4). Thirdly, he summarizes (94a13) [end of L. 8].

He says therefore first (93a1) that after the disputative process we must once more consider, but this time by establishing the truth, how much of the foregoing has been well stated and how much not well stated: and this both in regard to definition, by considering what a definition is, and in regard to *quod quid*, by considering whether it might somehow or other be manifested through a definition or a demonstration or not at all.

Then (93a4) he carries out what he has proposed. First, in regard to the *quod quid*. Secondly, in regard to definition which is a statement signifying it (93b28). Concerning the first he sets down two methods of manifesting the *quod quid*. First, the method of logical proof. Secondly, the method of demonstrative proof (93a16).

Regarding the first he reviews first of all (93a4) that which was established above, namely, that it is the same thing to know *quid est* and to know the cause involved in the question *an est*, just as it is the same thing to know *propter quid* and to know the cause involved in the question *quia est*. The reason for this, i.e., for the fact that it is the same thing

188 POSTERIOR ANALYTICS II

to know the *quid est* and the cause involved in the *si est*, is that there must be some cause of the fact that a thing exists, for something is referred to as *caused* by reason of the fact that it has a cause of its existing.

Now the cause of existing is either the same, i.e., the same as the essence of a thing, or something not the same: the same, indeed, as matter and form, which are parts of the essence; not the same, as agent and end, which two causes are somehow the cause of the form and matter, for the agent acts for an end and unites the form to the matter. And if we consider the cause which is other than the essence of a thing, sometimes it is such a cause that a demonstration can be formed in virtue of it, and sometimes not. For the effect does not follow of necessity from every efficient cause; but from the supposition of the end it follows that what is required for the end also exists, as is proved in *Physics* II.

So let us suppose that an effect exists which has as its cause not only the essence of the thing but also another cause such that something can be demonstrated through it; for example, we might say that if a man has attained happiness, it is necessary that virtue pre-exist. Now let us assume that the essence of virtue is a habit which operates according to right reason. Therefore, it can be demonstrated that there is a habit which operates according to right reason, if there is a habit conducive to happiness. Let that other cause, therefore, which is demonstrative, be taken as the middle, and let a syllogism be formed in the first figure (which must be done, because the *quod quid* must be universally and affirmatively predicated of the thing of which it is the *quod quid*): the syllogism then will be: "Every habit conducive to happiness is a habit operating according to right reason; but virtue is such a habit: therefore, ..." He concludes, therefore, that this method which is now being examined is one method of showing the *quod quid* through something else which is a cause. And this method is evidently suitable, because, as was established above, it is necessary that the middle taken for proving *quod quid* be the *quid est;* and similarly that the middle taken for proving properties be something proper.

But there is the further consideration that since the *quid est* is the cause of the very being of the thing, then according to the diverse causes of one thing, there are various ways of assigning the *quod quid* of the same thing. For example, the *quod quid* of house can be formulated in terms of its material cause, so that we might say that it is something composed of wood and stones; and also in terms of the final cause, namely, that it is an artifact constructed for habitation. Thus, therefore, it will occur that since there are several *quod quid's* of the same thing, one of them will be demonstrated and another not demonstrated but supposed. Hence it does not follow that there is a begging of the question, because one *quod quid* is supposed and the other proved. Nor is this a method proving the *quod quid* demonstratively, but of syllogizing it logically, because by this method it is not sufficiently proved that what is concluded is the *quod quid* of the thing of which it is concluded, but merely that it is in it.

Then (93a16) he shows how by demonstration the *quod quid* can be achieved. Regarding this he does two things. First, he shows how the *quod quid* can be manifested in certain instances through demonstration. Secondly, he shows that it is not so in all cases (93b22) [L. 8]. Concerning the first he does three things. First, he lays down certain things needed for showing what he proposes. Secondly, he manifests what he has proposed (93a28). Thirdly, he summarizes (93b15).

With respect to the first (93a16) he lays down three things. The first of these is a comparison between the *quod quid* and the *propter quid*. He says, therefore, that in order to show how it occurs that the *quod quid* can be achieved through demonstration, we must start once more from the beginning.

The first thing to be considered is the fact that a person may be in either of two states as regards knowledge of the *propter quid*. For sometimes we have the *quia* in our knowledge and are still seeking the *propter quid;* and sometimes both are manifest to us at one time. A third case is impossible, namely, that one know the *propter quid* of something before the *quia*. And the same holds for the *quod quid erat esse:* sometimes we know a thing to be without perfectly knowing the *quid sit;* sometimes we know both at once. Again, a third case is impossible, namely, to know *quid est* without knowing *if* it is.

Then (32a21) he lays down the second preliminary remark, saying that there are two ways in which we might know something to be without perfectly knowing the *quid est:* in one way, insofar as we might know one of its accidents, as for example, when by the speed of its motion we judge that something is a hare; in another way, by knowing something of its essence. This of course is possible in the case of a composite substance, as when we comprehend something to be a man in virtue of the fact that it is rational, without yet knowing the other items which complete the essence of man. However, in simple substances this does not occur, because one cannot know anything concerning the substance of a simple thing without knowing the entire essence, as is clear from *Metaphysics* IX.

At any rate, a person who knows some thing to be must know it through something of that thing, namely, something outside the essence of the thing or something pertaining to its essence. And he clarifies this with the example of knowing thunder to be, because we perceive a sound in the clouds—which of course pertains to the essence of thunder, albeit not the entire essence, because not every sound in the clouds is thunder—or of knowing a defect, i.e., an eclipse, of the sun or moon to be, because there is a failure of light—although not every failure of light is an eclipse. And the same applies if someone perceives a man to be, because there is an animal; or a soul to be, because something is moving itself.

Then (93a24) he sets forth the third preliminary remark, saying that those things which we know to exist through some accident belonging to them are such that there is no correlation between this knowledge and knowledge of their *quid est,* because in virtue of such accidents we do not even truly know that they are. We do of course know these accidents to be theirs, but because the accidents are not the things themselves, we do not thereby know that the things themselves exist. Moreover, it is fruitless to seek the *quid est* if one does not know *quia est;* but those things which we know to exist through something of their own can be more easily known by us as to what they are. Hence it is plain that as we are in regard to knowing that something is, so we are in regard to knowing what it is.

Then (93a28) in the light of the foregoing he manifests what he proposed. And he says that in regard to a thing which we know exists because we know something of its essence, let us consider the following example in which A, the major extreme, is *defect,* i.e., eclipse; and in which C, the minor extreme, is *moon;* and *interposition of the earth between sun and moon* is B, the middle. In this case, therefore, to ask whether the moon is eclipsed or not is the same as to ask whether B exists or not; but to ask whether B exists or not is to ask if there is some reason for that eclipse. For B, i.e., the interposition of the earth, is the reason for the moon's eclipse; and if there is an interposition of the earth we say that the other exists, i.e., the eclipse of the moon. Or, similarly, if we should seek the reason for one side of a contradiction, i.e., does it lie in having or in not having two right angles.

But when we find that what we seek exists, for example, that there is an eclipse, then we know the *quia* and the *propter quid* together, if what is sought is found through an appropriate middle which is the cause; and if not, but it is found through something extrinsic, we will know the *quia* and not the *propter quid.* For example, let the moon be C and the eclipse A, and let us take as middle, i.e., B, the fact that the moon, although it is full, is now unable to cause a shadow when we put an object between it and us. For the moon, whenever it is not eclipsed, causes a shadow if some body is interposed; yet the fact that it is now unable to cause a shadow is not the cause of the eclipse, but rather its effect. Therefore, if B be predicated of C (i.e., that the moon is now unable to produce a shadow of an object which is interposed), and if moreover A is true of that middle (i.e., if we assume that whenever this happens, the moon is eclipsed), it will be plain that the moon is eclipsed. But it will not yet be clear why the moon is eclipsed. Similarly, we will know that there is an eclipse but not know what an eclipse is, when we know that A is in C, i.e., that the moon is eclipsed.

Now just as in this example neither the *propter quid* nor the *quid* is known, so to inquire why [i.e., *propter quid*] something is, is the same as to inquire [*quid*], i.e., what it is. Thus, if we should ask *propter quid*, i.e., why the moon is eclipsed, namely, is it because the earth is between the sun and moon, or because the moon has turned, i.e., because the dark side of the moon has been turned toward us, as some say, or even because the light of the moon has been extinguished in something moist: to ask whether it is due to any of these causes that the moon is eclipsed is nothing more than to ask whether the eclipse of the moon consists in the interposition of the earth, or the turning of the moon, or the extinction of its light. And this middle is the reason of the other extreme: thus, in the foregoing example, it is the reason for A which is the major extreme, because the eclipse of the moon is nothing more than the moon's light being blocked by the earth.

He gives a further example, namely, inquiring what is thunder. According to the opinion of Anaxagoras and Empedocles it is the quenching of fire in a cloud; although according to his own opinion in *Meteorology* II, thunder is caused by a dry exhalation in a cold environment beating against a cloud. But he frequently uses the opinions of others in his examples. So, if according to the above-mentioned opinion, one should ask why it thunders, the answer might be given that it is because fire is being quenched in a cloud. Therefore, let the *cloud* be C, the minor extreme, and *thunder* A, the major extreme, and the *quenching of fire* B, the middle. Then we may syllogize in the following manner: "In C is B, i.e., in the cloud is a quenching of fire; but every quenching of fire is a sound: therefore in the cloud is a sound of thunder." And thus it is clear that to arrive at the *propter quid* through demonstration, we take the *quid est*, because the very middle which shows the *propter quid* is a statement defining the first term, i.e., defining the major extreme. But if we had to take some other middle to demonstrate this, it would be taken from the remaining statements, i.e., from the definition of the minor extreme and of other extrinsic causes. For since the subject is the cause of its proper attribute, it is required that the definition of the proper attribute be demonstrated by the definition of the subject. And this is clear in the other example; for since the moon is a body fixed by nature to move in such and such a way, it is necessary that at some time the earth be interposed between it and the sun.

Then (93b15) he sums up what has been said, saying that we have shown how the *quod quid* is taken and made known, namely, by taking the *propter quid*. We have also said that there is neither syllogism nor demonstration of the *quid est* in the sense of properly syllogizing or demonstrating the *quod quid*, although the *quod quid* is manifested by syllogism and demonstration, insofar as the middle in a *propter quid* demonstration is the *quod quid*. Hence, it is clear that a *quod quid* having another cause cannot be known without a demonstration, but the demonstration is nevertheless not of the *quod quid,* as was proved in the objections. And according to this the above objections are true.

Lecture 8
(93b22–94a19)

TO ATTAIN *QUOD QUID* THROUGH DEMONSTRATION IS NOT POSSIBLE IN ALL CASES

RELATION OF DEFINITION TO DEMONSTRATION

b22. Now while some things
b28. Since definition is said
b38. Another kind of definition
b39. Thus the former signifies

a2. For there is a difference
a9. On the other hand
a13. Our discussion has therefore

After showing that in some instances the *quod quid* is acquired through demonstration, the Philosopher now shows that this is not possible in all. And in order to show this he repeats (93b22) that of some things there is a cause other than the thing, but of other things not. Therefore, because the *quod quid* is acquired by a demonstration whose middle is a cause, it is manifest that there are certain things whose *quod quid* must be taken as an immediate principle, in the sense that one must suppose both the *to be* and the *quid* of that thing, or manifest it by some means other than demonstration, say by an effect or by a likeness or some other way.

Here it should be noted that his statement that some things have a cause not distinct from themselves can be understood in three ways. In one way, it means that it simply and absolutely has not a cause of its being. And this is proper to the First Principle alone, which is the cause of the being and truth of all things. For there is nothing to prevent even things which exist of necessity from having some cause of their necessity, as is stated in *Metaphysics* V. And therefore, although the Philosopher is speaking in the plural here, his words should not be taken to mean that there are several things which have no cause of their being.

In another way it can be understood as referring to the order of the causes of one thing. For it is clear that in things which have four causes, one cause is somehow the cause of another one. For since matter is for the sake of form and not vice versa, as is proved in *Physics* II, a definition which is based on the formal cause is the cause of the definition which is taken from the material cause of the same thing. And because the thing produced obtains a form in virtue of the action of the generator, it follows that the agent is somehow the cause of the form, and the definition the cause of the defined. Furthermore, every efficient cause acts for an end; hence, too, the definition taken from the end is somehow the cause of the definition which is taken from the efficient cause. Beyond this it is impossible to go in the genera of causes: hence the dictum that the end is the cause of the causes. Yet in the individual genera of causes one can proceed from the subsequent to the prior; but definitions should be given through proximate causes.

And according to this interpretation we find it stated in certain books that definitions which are made in terms of the species have no middle by which they might be demonstrated: but that definitions made in terms of matter can have a middle, in the sense that definitions which are given according to the material cause, can be demonstrated by those which are given according to the formal cause. But a definition which is given according to formal cause cannot be further demonstrated by an intrinsic principle of the thing which belongs in a proper way to the *quod quid* as entering into the essence of the thing. But if it were to be demonstrated by the efficient and final cause, one would have to say that a higher cause is related as formal to the lower. However, these words are not present in the Greek version; hence they seem to be a Gloss introduced into the text by a copyist's error.

Thirdly, they could be understood in the sense that there are some things which do not have a cause in the generic subject of some science; as in the genus of number, with which arithmetic is concerned one arrives at unity, which has no principle in this genus. And this sense concurs with the example which the Philosopher adds when he states that the arithmetician accepts *what* unity is and *that* it is. And just as in the case of things that do not have something else as cause, so too in the case of things which can have a middle and whose cause is something else, their *quod quid* can be manifested; in such a way, however, that the *quod quid* is not demonstrated, but rather that the middle of demonstration is taken as *quod quid*.

Then (93b28) having shown how the *quod quid* is related to demonstration, he shows how definition is related to demonstration. Concerning this he does two things. First, he shows how a definition is related to demonstration. Secondly, he uses an example to manifest what he has stated (94a2). In regard to the first he does three things. First, he lays down one type of definition which signifies *quid est*. Secondly, another type which signifies *propter quid* (93b38). Thirdly, he shows how each of these definitions is related to demonstration (93b39).

In regard to the first he supposes first of all (93b28) that definition is a statement signifying the *quod quid*. But if no other notion could be had of a thing except the definition, it would be impossible for us to know that some thing is, without knowing the *quid est* of it; because it is impossible for us to know that a thing is except in virtue of some notion of that thing. For in regard to a thing completely unknown to us, we cannot know if it is or not. But we do find some other notion of a thing besides the definition, namely, a notion which explains the signification of a name, or a notion of the very thing named; which notion, however, is distinct from the definition, because it does not signify the *quid est* as does a definition, but perhaps some accident. Thus one might find some notion which explains what the word *triangle* means. Then having the *quia est* in virtue of this notion, we would seek the *propter quid* in order that we might thereby arrive at the *quod quid*. But, as stated above, it is difficult to arrive at this in the case of things whose existence we do not know. Furthermore, the cause of this difficulty was mentioned above, namely, because when we do not know a thing to be by means of something of that thing, we do not know absolutely if it is or is not, but only according to an accident, as was explained above.

Then in order to distinguish the notion signifying the *quid est* from the other notions, he adds that there are two ways in which a notion can be said to be one. For some are one by junction only: in this way even the *Iliad*, i.e., the poem of the history of Troy, possesses a unity. And this is the way the notion which explains a name or describes the thing named through its accidents is one, as when it is stated that man is a risible animal capable of discipline. But a notion is also one insofar as it simply signifies one thing about one thing of which it is the notion, and this not in virtue of some accident. And such a notion is the definition signifying *quid est*, because the essence of anything is one. Thus, therefor, he concludes that what has been said, namely, that a definition is a notion of the *quod quid*, is one definition of a definition.

Then (93b38) he lays down another type of definition, saying that another definition of definition is that it is a notion manifesting the *propter quid*.

Then (93b39) he shows how each of these definitions is related to demonstration, concluding from the foregoing that the first definition merely signifies, but does not demonstrate the *quod quid*; whereas the second definition is, as it were, the definition of the *quod quid* and differs from a demonstration by position alone, i.e., in the ordering of the terms and propositions.

Then (94a2) he uses examples to manifest what he had said. In regard to this he does two things. First, he shows by examples what has been said. Secondly, from the foregoing he gathers the various kinds of definition (94a9).

He says therefore (94a2) that it is one thing to say *why* it thunders and another *what* thunder is: because according to the opinion of those who state that the quenching of fire in a cloud is the cause of thunder, one is giving the *propter quid* when he asserts thunder to be due to the fact that fire is quenched in a cloud; whereas one who asserts that thunder is the sound of fire being quenched in a cloud is stating *what* thunder is.

Now each of these signifies the same notion but not in the same way. For when one states that it thunders because fire is being quenched in a cloud, the notion is signified after the manner of a continuous demonstration, i.e., not broken down into explicit propositions; yet all the terms of a demonstration are continually being taken. But when it is asserted that thunder is the sound of fire being quenched in the clouds, the notion is signified after the manner of a definition. But if we were to say that thunder is the sound in the clouds, no mention being made of the quenching of fire, it will be a definition signifying *quid est,* and will be merely the conclusion of a demonstration.

Then (94a9) he gathers together from the foregoing how many modes of definition there are insofar as they are relevant to demonstration.

First, he repeats something previously stated, namely, that in the case of things which do not have a cause, their definitions are to be taken as immediate principles. Hence he says here that the definition of "immediate things," i.e., of things not having causes, is as an indemonstrable positing of the *quod quid.*

From this, therefore, he concludes that there is a threefold genus of definition when considered relative to demonstration. For there is one definition which is an indemonstrable notion of a thing's *quod quid:* this is the one which he said concerns immediate things. Another definition is that which is, as it were, a demonstrative syllogism of a thing's *quod quid* and differs from a demonstration merely by structure, i.e., by a different acceptance and position of the phrasing, as when it is stated that thunder is the sound of fire being quenched in the clouds. The third is the definition which only signifies *quod quid* and is the conclusion of a demonstration.

Then (94a13) he summarizes what has been said, declaring that it is plain from the foregoing in what way there is demonstration of the *quod quid* and in what way not; namely, that the *quod quid* can be taken from a demonstration but cannot be demonstrated. The things have also been pointed out in which there can be demonstration of the *quod quid* according to the manner indicated (namely, in things having a cause) and those in which there cannot be (namely, in things not having a cause). It has also been indicated in how many ways definition is said to be: namely, that some signify *quod quid,* and others even the *propter quid.* It has also been stated how *quod quid* is demonstrated, namely, so far forth as this is signified by a definition which signifies only *quod quid;* and how it is not demonstrated, namely, insofar as in virtue of the definition not only the *quid* but also the *propter quid* are taken. It has also been pointed out how definition is related in various ways to demonstration; and how it comes about that there is demonstration of the definition of a same thing, and how this does not come about.

Lecture 9
(94a20–95a9)

PROPTER QUID CAN BE MANIFESTED IN FOUR GENERA OF CAUSES

a20. We think we have	b23. Incidentally, here the order
a24. for (a) though the	b27. The same thing may exist
a28. The following example	b35. Indeed, there are
a35. Moreover, the formal cause	a3. Of the products of man's
a36. Why did the Athenians	a7. and the end is consequently
b8. This is no less	

After showing how the *quid est* functions relative to demonstration, the Philosopher now shows how the *propter quid,* which signifies the cause, functions relative to demonstration. In regard to this he does two things. First, he shows how causes are taken in a demonstration. Secondly, how diversely in diverse things (95a10) [L. 10]. Concerning the first he does two things. First, he proposes what he intends. Secondly, he manifests what he has proposed (94a24).

He says therefore first (94a20) that, as was established in the first book, because we think we know in a scientific manner when we know the cause, and a demonstration is a syllogism causing us to know in a scientific manner, the consequence is that the middle of a demonstration is a cause.

But there are four genera of causes as is more fully explained in *Physics* II and *Metaphysics* V. One of these is the *quod quid erat esse,* i.e., the formal cause, which is the completeness of a thing's essence. Another is the cause which, if placed, the caused must also be placed: this is the material cause, because things which follow on the necessity of matter are necessary absolutely, as is established in *Physics* II. The third is the cause which is the source of motion, i.e., the efficient cause. But the fourth is that for the sake of which something is performed, namely, the final cause. And so it is clear that through the middle in a demonstration all these causes are manifested, because each of these causes can be taken as the middle of a demonstration.

Then (94a24) he manifests what he had said. In regard to this he does two things. First, he shows how the various causes are taken as middles of demonstration in various things. Secondly, he shows how there can be various causes of the same thing (94b27). Concerning the first he does four things. First, he shows how the material cause is taken in demonstration. Secondly, he manifests his point in regard to the formal cause (94a35). Thirdly, he does the same in regard to the efficient cause (94a36). Fourthly, in regard to the final cause (94b8). Regarding the first he does two things. First, he sets forth the way in which the material cause is taken in a demonstration; a way, namely, that applies also to the other causes. Secondly, he presents an example (94a28).

He says therefore first (94a24) that that which once it exists, something else must also exist, namely, a material cause, is not to be so taken that something follows of necessity if one proposition alone is taken; rather, one must take at least two which are so related that they communicate in one middle. Therefore, if one middle which is the material cause be taken in two propositions, a conclusion follows of necessity; as if we were to say: "Everything composed of contraries is corruptible; but a stone is such: therefore, a stone is corruptible." Now it is required that two propositions be taken, not only because the syllogistic form demands it, but also because not all things which are from matter have necessity from the matter, as is proved in *Physics* II. And therefore, besides the proposition in which it is stated that this has matter, another must be taken which declares that from such matter something follows of necessity.

Then (94a28) he presents an example from mathematics. Now this does not conflict with the statement in *Metaphysics* III that mathematical sciences do not demonstrate through material cause: for although mathematics abstracts from sensible matter, yet not from intelligible matter, as it is stated in *Metaphysics* VI. This matter is considered intelligible precisely insofar as something divisible is taken in numbers or in continua. Therefore, in mathematics whenever something is demonstrated of a whole through the parts, it seems to be a demonstration through material cause: for the parts are compared to the whole according to the notion of matter, as is stated in *Physics* II. And because matter is more properly said of sensible things, he preferred not to name it material cause, but a cause of necessity.

To understand the example in the text it should be noted that every angle inscribed in a semicircle is a right angle, as is proved in *Euclid* III in the following way: Given a semicircle ABC such that its chord, namely, the diameter of the whole circle, is cut in half at the point D which is the center of the circle. From this point D draw a perpendicular line which touches the circumference of the circle at point B, from which are drawn two lines, one to point A and one to point C. He says, therefore, that angle ABC which falls within the semicircle is a right angle. And the proof is this: Triangle BDC has three angles equal to two right angles; but its angle BDC is a right angle, because BD is perpendicular to DC. Therefore, its other two angles, namely, DBC and BCD are equal to one right angle. But these two angles are equal, because the lines BD and DC are equal; since they proceed from the center to the circumference. It follows therefore that angle DBC equals one half a right angle. In the same way it is proved that angle ABD equals one half a right angle. Therefore, the entire angle ABC is a right angle.

This, proof, therefore, the Philosopher uses here, saying that in this way is shown why "that is right which falls in a semicircle," i.e., why the angle which falls in a semicircle is a right angle, when that is given which, when it exists, it follows that it is a "right." Therefore let *right angle* be A, the major extreme; *the half of two right angles*, the middle, be B; and *angle falling in a semicircle*, the minor extreme, be C. Now the cause of A's being in C, i.e., of the angle in the semicircle's being right is B, namely, that the angle of a semicircle is half of two right angles. For this half is by conversion equal to A; in like manner, C is equal to B. For B consists in being the half of two right angles. Therefore, since this is the case, it is necessary that A be in C, which is nothing else than for the angle of a semicircle to be right. He further adds that this method of demonstration can also pertain to the formal cause (which he called *quod quid erat esse*) on the ground that being half of two right angles can be taken as an expression signifying the *quod quid* of a right angle.

Then (94a35) he returns to what has been previously established and states that it was shown there how the formal cause which is the *quod quid erat esse* pertains to the middle of demonstration.

Then (94a36) he gives an example of the movent cause, touching on an event from the history of the Greeks, namely, that the Athenians, allying themselves with certain other Greeks, once invaded the Sardians who were subject to the king of the Medes; and for that reason the Medes invaded the Athenians. He says, therefore, that one might ask *propter quid* [i.e., why] the war of the Medes with the Athenians occurred; and this *propter quid* would be the cause why the Athenians were attacked by the Medes, namely, because the former along with certain allies, namely, the Eretrians, made an assault upon the Sardians: for this was the first motive of the war. Therefore, let *war* be the major extreme, A, and *the first to attack* be the middle, B, but *Athenians*, the minor extreme, C. Therefore B is in C, so far forth namely as it belongs to the Athenians that they were the first to make an assault. But A is in B, because namely the ones who were first to work an injustice were in turn warred upon. Thus, therefore, A is in B, inasmuch as they were attacked who first launched the war. But this, namely, B, which is the middle, pertains to the Athenians who first began the war. And thus it is clear that in this example the cause which first moved is taken as middle.

Then (94b8) he manifests the same thing in the final cause. Concerning this he does two things. First, he sets forth an example in final cause. Secondly, he shows the difference between the final cause and the cause which is the source of motion (94b23).

He says therefore first (94b8) that it happens in like manner in all cases where the cause taken is the end for the sake of which something is done: for example, if we should state *propter quid* [i.e., for what purpose] someone walks after dinner, namely, to be made healthy; and again *propter quid* [i.e., for what] does a house exist, namely, so that the vessels, i.e., a man's belongings, may be kept safe. Thus, therefore, this, namely, walking after dinner is done for the sake of health; this other, namely, the building of a house is for the sake of keeping belongings safe. Thus, there is no difference in saying *propter quid* [i.e., for what purpose] one should walk after dinner and that for the sake of which this is necessary. So let *walk after dinner* be C, the minor extreme; but *food not to rise to the entrance of the stomach* be B, the middle; and *be made healthy* be A, the major extreme. Hence let B be in C, because walking after dinner brings it about that food does not rise to the entrance of the stomach; and for this reason one is made healthy, which is for A to be in B. For it is seen that to C which is *walk* belongs B, which is that *food does not rise to the entrance of the stomach*. From this follows A, which is *to be made healthy*. Thus, therefore, it is clear that B, namely, that the food does not rise to the entrance of the stomach is the cause why C is A, i.e., why walking after dinner is healthful: and this, namely, that foods do not rise to the entrance of the stomach is involved in the notion of being kept healthy. For A, i.e., to be healthful, will be thus explained, i.e., made known. But the fact that B is in C is *propter quid*, namely, because to be healthy consists in being in such a state that foods do not rise to the opening of the stomach. And in order that each of these be better understood one should arrange the reasons, so that the middle will be taken as the reason of the major extreme, as appears in the above example.

Then (94b23) he shows how the situation is otherwise in the cause which is the principle of motion. For in the order of generation the final cause and the cause which is the principle of motion behave in contrary ways. For there, namely, in the demonstration which is based on the cause which is the principle of motion, the middle must eventuate first, i.e., be first in the order of generation, just as the Athenians assaulted the Sardians before being attacked by the Medes. But here, in the demonstration which is based on final cause, the first to be taken in the order of generation is C, which is the minor extreme; and the last, the effect of the final cause. But in the way of generation the last thing is the end for the sake of which something is done. For it is obvious that one first of all walks after dinner, and on that follows the fact that foods do not rise to the entrance of the stomach, upon which further follows the man's health which is the chief end.

Then (94b27) he shows how for the same effect several of the aforesaid causes can be taken. In regard to this he does two things. First, he manifests that there are several causes of a same thing. Secondly, he shows the cases in which this is applicable (94b35).

He says therefore first (94b27), that it happens that one and the same effect exists because of an end or for its sake, and also from the necessity of some prior cause: thus, the fact that light appears through the skin of a lantern comes about of necessity; for it is necessary that a tiny body pass through pores that are larger. Now this is said according to the opinion of those who posit light as a subtle body, and the appearance of light through a transparency as occurring because of the size of the pores which are regarded as openings. But a subtle body seems to be comprised of tiny parts. And because this is not according to his own opinion, he adds that this arises from that sort of necessity, namely, if light does appear by passing through, i.e., by the passing of its parts through the pores of the transparency. But the appearing of light through the skin of a lantern occurs for some end, namely, in order that with the help of the light we might walk at night without stumbling.

In such cases, therefore, it is possible to argue in two ways: in one way from a pre-existing cause, as when we say that if this occurs then this other will occur; for example, if a light is set in a lantern, it follows that it will be diffused through the pores of the skin. In another way from a posterior cause which is posterior in the order of becoming. According to this, one will argue that if some ultimate end comes to pass, it is required that those items precede through which the end is attained, as is clear in thunder; which if it is quenched fire, it is necessary that it hiss, i.e., make the sound and roar of fire being quenched. And if the opinion of the Pythagoreans is true that thunder takes place to strike terror into the denizens of Tartarus, then one should say that thunder takes place to the end that the men in Tartarus shudder.

Then (94b35) he shows in which things this occurs that has been said. In regard to this he does three things. First, he shows how this is in regard to things which are from nature. Secondly, with things that are done intentionally (95a3). Thirdly, he draws a corollary (95a7).

He says therefore first (94b35), that very many of these, namely, which are from necessity and are done for an end, are found chiefly in things which subsist by nature and in things which are constructed by nature. For nature makes certain things, acting for an end, and certain things it makes from the necessity of prior causes. This latter is twofold: one, according to nature, which is according to the condition of the matter; the other, according to movent cause, as a stone is moved by necessity sometimes upwards and sometimes downwards, but not on account of the same type of necessity: it is moved downward on account of a necessity of nature, but upward on account of a necessity of the mover, i.e., of the one casting it.

Then (95a3) he shows how this is in regard to things that proceed from intention. And he says that in things that are done through reason (as works of art are), some are such that they never occur by chance; for example, a house and a statue, and never from the necessity of nature: but they are always done for an end, because they are always done by reason, which does not act without intending an end.

However, there are certain things which can indeed be produced from the reasoning of art, but can also come about through fortune: as in the case of health, which can sometimes be produced by the art of medicine; but because it can occur from a natural cause, it can happen that someone be healed not intending it, as if a leper should be healed from eating a serpent which he ate to die. The same can happen in regard to safety, namely, when a person entering a house for some other purpose is saved from the hands of enemies hunting him. And this happens mainly in all cases in which something can happen one way or another, when it is not due to fortune, i.e., when a same effect might happen without fortune from various causes. For example, a person might enter a house not by chance in order to be saved from the hand of his enemies or to eat or to rest. Hence, if in intending one of these something else occurs, it will be from fortune. But a house and a statue cannot be produced except by identical causes and therefore such things cannot be done by fortune.

Then (95a7) he concludes from the foregoing that arrival at a good is either by nature or by art. For art and nature operate in similar fashion for an end, as is stated in *Physics* II. But what is done by fortune is not done of set purpose. He says this because even though fortune may be involved in things that are being done for something, as it is stated in *Physics* II, nevertheless that which is said to be done by fortune is not intended as an end, but happens outside one's intention.

Lecture 10
(95a10–b1)

HOW SOMETHING IS DEMONSTRATED THROUGH A CAUSE NOT SIMULTANEOUS WITH ITS CAUSED

HOW A CAUSE NOT SIMULTANEOUS WITH ITS EFFECT IS TAKEN AS MIDDLE IN DEMONSTRATING

After showing how the four genera of causes are used as middles in demonstrating, the Philosopher now shows how in different cases something is demonstrated through a cause. But there are two differences to be noted in this regard: the first difference is whether the cause is or is not simultaneous with its effect; the second difference is whether the cause produces its effect always or only as a general rule—this second difference will be discussed later (96a8) [L. 12].

Concerning the first he does two things. First, he shows how something is proved through a cause which is simultaneous with that of which it is the cause. Secondly, how something is demonstrated through a cause which is not simultaneous with that of which it is the cause (95a23).

In regard to the first point it should be noted that since one is involved with the notions of prior and subsequent when he analyzes motion, so too in considering the causes of motion one must take into account that the cause and the caused are related as prior and subsequent. For it is obvious that a natural agent causes its effect by moving something. Furthermore, just as the movable object is brought to the terminus of its motion by virtue of the entire motion, so by virtue of the first part of that motion it is brought to the second part, and so on. Hence, just as the entire motion is the cause of the subsequent state of rest, so the first part of the motion is the cause of the subsequent part, and so on.

This analysis is true whether we confine ourselves to one object which is being moved without interruption from beginning to end, or to several objects the first of which moves the second and the second the third. And although at the same time that the first mover is moving its object that object is being moved, nevertheless the object thus moved continues

202

to act as mover even after it stops being moved. Consequently, while it is acting as mover, another object is being moved. In this way several moveable objects are successively moved in such a way that one is the cause of the motion of another, and so on, as happens in the case of thrown objects whose motion the Philosopher explained in *Physics* VIII. Therefore, in this example it turns out that the cause is not simultaneous with that of which it is the cause, namely, inasmuch as the first part of the motion is the cause of the second part, or the first moved object moves the second.

But although the motion has succession in its parts, it is nevertheless simultaneous with its movent cause. For the moveable object is moved at the same time that the mover acts, inasmuch as motion is nothing else than the act existing in the moveable object from the mover, such that in virtue of that act the mover is said to move and the object is said to be moved. Indeed, the requirement that the cause be simultaneous with what is caused must be fulfilled even more in things that are outside of motion whether we take something outside of motion to mean the terminus of the motion—as the illumination of air is simultaneous with the rising of the sun—or in the sense of something absolutely immovable, or in the sense of essential causes which are the cause of a thing's being.

Concerning the first point, therefore, he does two things. First, he states what he intends to establish. Secondly, he clarifies this with examples (95a13).

He says therefore first (95a10) that whenever the cause is simultaneous with its effect, it is necessary to take the same cause for the coming to be or the "having come to be" or the future existence, as is taken for the actual existence: for if the cause is simultaneous with that of which it is the cause, then just as it is necessary that when the cause exists, the effect be, so it is necessary that when the cause is coming to be, the effect be coming to be; and when the cause has come to be, the effect should have come to be; and when the cause will have been, the effect will have been. Nor does it avail to object that when a builder is coming to be— while he is learning the art of building—the edifice is not yet being constructed: for "builder" does not stand for the cause in act of the edifice, but for the cause in potency, or as possessed of the skill. But "someone building" denotes the cause in act: it is this cause that must be simultaneous with that of which it is the cause, as it is stated in *Physics* II. There is identity in the sense that in all these cases the middle is the cause. However, this must be taken according to a due pro-portion, namely, so that the *to be* of the cause corresponds to the *to be* of the effect, and the coming to be of the cause to the coming to be of the effect, and the "having come to be" of the cause to the "having come to be" of the effect, and the future being of the cause to the future being of the effect.

Then (95a13) he clarifies what he had said with two examples, the first of which concerns the eclipse of the moon. For we say that there was an eclipse of the moon yesterday, because the earth was interposed between the sun and the moon yesterday; and that an eclipse of the moon is now coming to be, because such an interposition is now coming to be; and that tomorrow there will be an eclipse of the moon, because the earth will be between then; and that there is now an eclipse of the moon, because the earth is now interposed.

The second example concerns ice. Thus we might state what ice is and take as its definition that it is rigidly congealed water. Therefore, let C be *water*, i.e., the minor extreme, and A be *congealed*, i.e., the major extreme, and take B as the middle, i.e., *that which completely lacks heat*. For when that which is moist gives off heat it congeals; hence when it intensely gives off heat, the moist object becomes very thick and hard. Bringing this into syllogistic form, therefore, we shall say that B is in C, namely, because ice involves a complete giving up of heat; but A is in B, because that which completely lacks heat is congealed. Therefore, just as the fact that it has a deficiency of heat is the cause of ice's being water which is completely congealed, so the cause of ice's coming to be is that B is coming to be. And the same holds for having come to be and for future coming to be. And so he concludes that if the cause and the caused are taken to be simultaneous, it is necessary that they be simultaneous in coming to be, in being, in having come to be, and in future coming to be.

Then (95a23) he shows how a cause which is not simultaneous with its effect is taken as the middle of demonstration. First, in things that come to be in a direct line. Secondly, in things that come to be reciprocally (95b38) [L. 12].   Concerning the first he does three things. First, he states the question. Secondly, he interjects something that must be known in order to solve the question (95a27). Thirdly, he settles the question (95b1) [L. 11]. In regard to the first he does two things. First, he proposes the question. Secondly, he elucidates it (95a24).

First therefore (95a23) he proposes the question, namely, whether in the case of causes which are not simultaneous with what they cause, one should say that what is caused follows upon its cause according to a continuous temporal succession, or not?

Then (95a24) he restates the question more plainly. For we see that some causes of things do not exist at the same time as those things: thus the cause of a "having come to be" is something prior to it, namely, a "coming to be"; and the cause of a "shall have come to be" is a "shall be coming to be"; and again the cause of a "coming to be" is a previous "has come to be." Therefore, the question is this: Do these causes which follow one upon the other exist in a continuous span of time or not? For it is necessary that the demonstrator know this, because if there is no continuity in these causes, it will not be possible to employ an immediate principle, because between any two discontinuous *now's* it is always possible to take something intermediate. Consequently, if that *now* during which the effect exists is not continuous with that *now* in which the cause exists, it will be possible to find a cause between them, and so on to infinity.

Then (95a27) he explains something that must be understood in order to solve this question. First, he proposes what he intends. Secondly, he proves what he has proposed (95a32).

In regard to the first (95a27) it should be noted that just as a line is a continuous thing, but a point is an indivisible which terminates and divides the line, so the process of becoming or of being moved is something continuous, but the fact of having been moved or having come to be is something indivisible which can be taken either as terminating an entire motion or as dividing the motion, in the sense of being the end of the first part and the beginning of the second part of the motion, just as in the case of a point which divides the line.

In this way, therefore, a "having come to be" is both a cause which precedes a "coming to be" of which it is the principle, and an effect following the "coming to be" of which it is the terminus. Therefore, if we are to demonstrate, the demonstrative syllogism must proceed from a subsequent "having come to be" to a previous "coming to be." Thus, we would say: "This has come to be; therefore that was previously coming to be." But because the very "having come to be" is the principle of the "coming to be" (or the things that have come to be are the cause of those that are coming to be), it follows that the former is similarly related to the things that are coming to be, namely, that one may syllogize from a subsequent "coming to be" to a prior "having come to be," as though we were to say: "The sun is being moved to the midst of the heavens; therefore it was previously moved to a point in the east." But one may not syllogize from what is prior to what is later and say, for example, that because this has first come to be, it follows that what is later is coming to be or has come to be. And what is true of the relationship between coming to be and having come to be applies to what shall have come to be and what will be coming to be.

Then (95a32) he proves what he had said. In regard to this he does two things. First, he proves his proposition with a reason based on the notion of time considered absolutely. Secondly, with a reason based on the time that intervenes between a cause which is prior and an effect which is subsequent (95a39).

He says therefore first (95a32) that the reason why one may not syllogize from what is prior to what is subsequent is that the prior having been posited, it is not necessary that the subsequent follow either at some definite time or at some indefinite future time.

First, therefore, he manifests this in regard to a definite time, as in the case where we might say: "The patient has drunk the medicine; therefore he will be cured on such and such a day." For if one could syllogize from a previous fact to something which will occur later at a definite time, it would be possible to conclude that because it is true to say that this has happened, namely, that the patient has drunk the medicine, it will also be true to say that what is subsequent has come to pass, namely, that he has been cured. But this does not follow: because it is possible to discover some time in which it is true to say that he has drunk the medicine but not yet true to say that he has been cured, say the time between the taking of the medicine and the attainment of the cure.

And this is what he says, namely, that the reason why the aforesaid conclusion does not follow is because during the interim it is false to say that this has taken place, namely, that he has been cured, although the other has already taken place, namely, that he has drunk the medicine. The same reasoning holds in regard to the future. For we cannot conclude, "He is now drinking the medicine; therefore he will be cured," referring to some definite time; because this will not be true for each subsequent period of time, namely, not in the intervening time.

Secondly (95a35), he proves the same point in regard to an unspecified future time, as when we might say, "He is drinking the medicine; therefore he will be cured." For it does not follow that because this has taken place, namely, that he has drunk the medicine, that this will be, namely, that he will be cured. For it has already been established that a cause which necessarily infers its effect is simultaneous with its effect. Furthermore, the middle which is taken is homogeneous, i.e., of one genus. For example, to prove that certain things have come to be in the past, one takes as the middle and cause something which has taken place in the past; likewise, for things of the future, something which is future, and for things that are in the process of coming to be, one takes that which is coming to be, and for things that exist, one takes that which exists. However, when one syllogizes, "This has taken place; therefore this will be," the middle taken is not of one genus, but one middle is prior and the other subsequent. Therefore, having posited what is prior, the subsequent does not follow of necessity in those cases in which the effect of causes can be impeded.

Then (95a39) he presents another argument which is based on the intervening time. And he says that just as on the part of time considered absolutely, it is obvious that one may not syllogize from what is prior to what is subsequent either according to a specified time or according to an unspecified time; so neither on the part of the intervening time is it possible to assume a specified or an unspecified time in which that which is subsequent can be concluded from what is prior. For it has already been established that during the entire intervening time it is false to say that the subsequent exists, even though that which is prior has already occurred.

Lecture 11
(95b1–37)

HOW A CAUSE WHICH IS NOT SIMULTANEOUS WITH ITS EFFECT MAY BE TAKEN AS A MIDDLE IN DEMONSTRATION

b1. We have also to inquire   b25. The like is true
b12. The following must suffice   b31. And in the world of fact
b23. or since, as we said,

After stating the question whether in things that do not come to be simultaneously the subsequent according to temporal continuity follows the prior, and after interjecting something necessary, namely, that one may not syllogize from what is prior to what is subsequent, the Philosopher now undertakes to settle the question he raised. Concerning this he does two things. First, he shows how coming to be and having come to be are related according to continuity of time. Secondly, he proves his proposal (95b12).

He says therefore first (95b1), that in order to prove the proposal it is necessary to investigate what it is that joins or forms a continuity between a "having come to be" and a "coming to be," so that one might follow the other without interruption.

In regard to this he says first of all that it is obvious that a "coming to be" is not *had,* i.e., is not consecutive to a "having come to be." (Those things are said to be consecutive which have no member of their genus between them; for example, two soldiers in a line or two clerics in their choir stalls. *Had,* however, adds the notion of contact to that which is consequent, as it is stated in *Physics* V). Thus, therefore, he is saying that a "coming to be" cannot be consecutive or contiguous to a "having come to be."

Then he proves this, because not even a "having come to be" is contiguous in the sense of consecutive to any other "having come to be": for two instances of "having come to be" are related in the way that two indivisible boundaries of time are related, or as two points in a line. Hence just as two points are not consecutive to one another, so neither are two instances of "having come to be": for the points and the instances of "having come to be" exist as indivisibles, and such things are not consecutive in their continua, as is proved in *Physics* VI. And since two instances of "having come to be" are not consecutive, it is therefore obvious that a "coming to be" and a "having come to be" are not consecutive. For a "coming to be" is something divisible, just as a "being moved" is; but a "having come to be" is something indivisible, just as a point is. Therefore, as the line is to the point, so the "coming to be" is to the "having come to be." For there is an infinitude of "having come to be's," just as there is potentially an infinitude of points in a line. And this is the cause why it is impossible to take two points that are consecutive in a line, namely, because between any two points there is still another point to be taken; likewise, between any two "having come to be's" there is another to be taken. Hence two "having come to be's" are not consecutive.

Furthermore, because a "having come to be" is the terminus of a "coming to be," it follows that not even a "coming to be" is consecutive to a "having come to be"; otherwise two "having come to be's" would be consecutive. Rather a "coming to be" is terminated immediately at a "having come to be," as a line is terminated at a point. This matter is treated at greater length in the analysis of motion, i.e., *Physics* VI.

Then (95b12) he shows in the light of the foregoing how the effect can be taken as being immediate or mediate to the cause in cases where they are not simultaneous. First, he proves his proposal. Secondly, he elucidates it with examples (95b31). Concerning the first he does two things. First, he shows his proposal in regard to the past. Secondly, in future things (95b25). Concerning the first he does two things. First, he shows his proposal. Secondly, he excludes an objection (95b23).

He says therefore first (95b12) that from what has been established it is possible to gather how a cause which is taken as a middle in demonstration may be consecutive to that which is in the process of becoming or of being generated: because even in these demonstrations which syllogize about things that are in a "coming to be," it is necessary to admit a middle and a first which are immediate, as when we conclude that A has come to be because C has come to be, so long, namely, as C has come to be subsequently and A previously. For example, if we should say, "He has been cured; therefore he drank the medicine": for the syllogism would not follow if we began with what is prior, as we have established above; but C is taken as a principle, although it is later in coming to be, owing to the fact that it is closer to the present *now* than A.

But the present *now* is a principle of time because according to it the past and future are distinguished; hence it is necessary to take the present *now* as the principle for making known the succession of time. For in the realm of the past, something is more subsequent in becoming, the closer it is to the present *now*; but the converse is true in regard to the future. Therefore, just as C is taken as the principle of syllogizing, since it is more subsequent in coming to be than A and closer to the present *now*, so we may take D as nearer to the present *now* than C, and conclude that if D has come to be, C came to be previously: for example, if he performs the tasks of a healthy man, then previous to that he was cured.

Therefore, we can conclude that if D has come to pass, it is necessary that A have previously come to pass; and we take as cause that which was in the interim, namely, C. For D having come to be, it is necessary that C previously have come to be; and C having come to be, it is necessary that A have previously come to be. Therefore, D having come to be, it is necessary that A have previously come to be. For example, if this person now accomplishes the tasks of a healthy man, it follows that previously he had been cured; and if he has been cured, it is necessary that previously he have drunk the medicine. Therefore, by always taking a middle in this way, for example, something else between C and A, as C was taken as middle between D and A, one will come to rest somewhere at something immediate.

Then (95b23) he presents an objection. For someone can say that something immediate will never be reached, but it will always be necessary to take something between two "having come to be's" on the ground that in every instance of coming to be there is an infinitude of "having come to be's," since one "having come to be" is not consecutive to another, as has been said. But he excludes this objection because although there is an infinitude of "having come to be's" in one case of coming to be, nevertheless it is necessary to begin at some middle, namely, from a *now* as from something first: for it has been established that that which is subsequent is a principle of syllogizing. But in relation to all things that have come to be in the past, the latest is the present *now;* hence it is necessary to take the present *now* as the first and immediate principle. However, any other "having come to be" is taken as a mediate principle.

Then (95b25) he shows the same for future things, saying that as the case was in that which has come to be, so it is in that which will have come to be: because if it is true that D will be, it is necessary that it previously be verified that A exists; and the cause of this will be taken to be C, which falls as middle between D and A. For if C will be, it is necessary that prior to it A will be.

In this case, too, the objection concerning the infinite division of the future into instants, or of motion into moments can be lodged: because, as in the case of past things, so also in future things, the indivisibles are not consecutive. Nevertheless here too, something must be taken as an immediate principle, as was done in things which came to be in the past. For although one cannot take two consecutive "having come to be's" either in the past or in the future, nevertheless something terminal can be taken in both, and this will be taken as the immediate principle.

Then (95b31) he elucidates what he had said with examples, saying that the manner of arguing employed above can be considered in regard to human works. Thus, let us take the "having come to be" of a house as something terminal; from this it is concluded, as something first, that it is necessary that the stones have previously been cut; and we shall take as middle the laying of the foundation: because if the house has been constructed, it is necessary that previously the foundation has been laid; and if the foundation has been laid, it is necessary first that the stones have been cut. And what was taken in regard to the past must also be taken in regard to the future: for example, if a house will exist, it is necessary that first the cutting of the stones will occur, and that this be demonstrated through some middle, which is the laying of the foundation.

Lecture 12
(95b38–96a20)

HOW IN THINGS THAT COME TO BE RECIPROCALLY, A CAUSE WHICH IS NOT SIMULTANEOUS WITH THE EFFECT IS TAKEN AS MIDDLE IN A DEMONSTRATION.–HOW ONE DEMONSTRATES THROUGH CAUSE DIFFERENTLY IN THINGS THAT OCCUR ALWAYS AND IN THINGS THAT OCCUR AS A GENERAL RULE

b38. Now we observe in Nature
a2. In actual fact
a8. Some occurrences are universal

a12. For if A is predicated
a20. We have already explained

After showing how one must take the middle, which is the cause, in things that come to be in a direct line, the Philosopher now shows how one should take it in the case of things that come to be in reciprocal generation. First, he proves his proposal. Secondly, he elucidates it with examples (96a2).

In regard to the first it should be noted that because the circular movement of the heavens is the cause of generation in sublunar things, it is stated in *On Generation* II that a kind of circular reciprocity is found in generation in the sense that earth is generated from water, and water in turn from earth.

He says therefore (95b38) that since we observe a certain pattern of generation in things that are generated *circularly*, it is possible in these cases also to follow what has been established above, namely, to syllogize from what is subsequent, provided that the terms of the demonstration are taken in such a way that middle and extremes follow one upon the other: because in the case of things that are generated in that way, there is a kind of circular conversion in the sense that one passes from the first thing to the last thing, and then a return is made from the last to the first; although these things are not numerically but specifically the same, as is explained in *On Generation* II. Hence it does not follow that the same numerical thing is prior and subsequent, or is cause and effect.

And this is suitable to the process of demonstrations, for, as has been established in the foregoing, whenever conclusions are converted, i.e., whenever some of the premises can be syllogized from them, this is a circular demonstration. And although this is not fitting if the very same thing which was first the conclusion is later the principle of the same numerical thing (otherwise the same thing would be at once better known and less known), nevertheless if they are not entirely the same, as happens in things that are circularly generated, there is nothing unfitting.

Then (96a2) he uses examples to elucidate what he has said, saying that a circular process is seen to occur in the works of nature. For if the earth is saturated with rain, it is necessary that the action of the sun release vapors from it; when these are released and borne aloft, it is necessary that clouds be formed; and after they are formed, it is necessary that rain water be formed; and when this is formed, it is necessary that in falling upon the earth it saturate it. Now this saturation of the earth was the very thing we took as being first; however, it is not the same saturation as the one from which we first began.

Thus it is clear that a cycle has been achieved in the sense that with one of them existing, another comes to be; and that other existing, still another comes to be; and that one existing, a return is made to the first, which is not numerically the same, but specifically the same. Yet this cycle of causes cannot be found according to the order which is found in *per se* causes; for in *per se* causes it is necessary to reach some one thing which is first in each genus of causes, as is proved in *Metaphysics* II. But the fact that water is generated from fire, and fire in turn from water, is not *per se* but *per accidens*. For being is generated *per se* not from actual being but from potential being, as it is stated in *Physics* I. Therefore, if we proceed from cause to cause in *per se* causes, there will not be a cycle. For we will accept as the efficient cause of the rain-soaked earth, the heat of the air which is caused by the sun, but not vice versa; but the material cause we take as water, whose matter is not vapor but the common matter of the elements.

Then (96a8) he shows how one demonstrates through the cause differently in things which occur always and in things which occur as a general rule. Concerning this he does three things. First, he proposes what he intends. Secondly, he proves what he has proposed (96a12). Thirdly, he sums up (96a20).

He says therefore first (96a8) that there are some things which come to be universally both as to time, because always, and as to subject, because in all cases; either because they maintain themselves as unchangeable things which are not subject to coming to be, or because they come to be as changeable things which always follow a uniform pattern, as in the case of heavenly movements. Again, there are other things which do not occur in the sense of always, but as a general rule. An example of this is that every human male develops a beard as a general rule, although it does not occur always. Therefore, just as in the case of things that occur always, it is necessary to take a middle which is always, so in the case of things which occur as a general rule, it is necessary to take a middle that occurs as a general rule.

Then (96a12) he proves that if one is to conclude to something that occurs as a general rule it is necessary to take a middle which occurs as a general rule. For if one were to assume the opposite by taking a middle which occurs universally and always; for example, if A, which is the major extreme, is predicated universally of B, which is the middle, and B of C, which is the minor extreme, then it follows of necessity that A is predicated universally of C both as to time and as to subject, which is the same as being predicated always and of each thing. Hence, we are now saying that for something to be predicated universally is the same as being predicated of all and always. But it has been assumed that A is predicated of C as a general rule. Therefore, it is necessary that the middle, which is B, should be taken as existing as a general rule.

Thus it is obvious that certain immediate principles of things which occur as a general rule can be taken, such that those principles exist or come to be as a general rule. Yet such demonstrations do not enable one to know that what is concluded is true absolutely but only in a qualified sense, namely, that it is true in the majority of cases. And this is the way that the principles which are taken possess truth. Hence sciences of this kind fall short of sciences which deal with things absolutely necessary, so far as the certitude of demonstration is concerned.

Then (96a20) he sums up what has been said, saying that we have now established how the *quod quid* which is practically identical with the *propter quid* is assigned among syllogistic terms, inasmuch as we have shown how the several genera of causes are middles of demonstration according to the respective diversities of things. We have also shown in what sense there is or is not demonstration or definition of the *quod quid*.

Lecture 13
(96a22–b14)

CHARACTERISTICS WHICH SHOULD BE PRESENT IN THE ITEMS WHICH CONSTITUTE THE DEFINITION SIGNIFYING THE ESSENCE OF A THING

a22. so let us now discuss
a24. Now of the attributes
a32. It is such attributes

a34. For example every triad
b2. Now since we have shown
b6. Further, that the synthesis

After showing how the *quod quid* and *propter quid* are related to demonstration, the Philosopher now shows how they can be investigated. First, how the *quod quid* should be investigated. Secondly, how the *propter quid* ought to be investigated (98a1) [L. 17]. Concerning the first he does two things. First, he states his intention. Secondly, he pursues it (96a24). He says therefore first (96a22) that after stating how *quod quid* is recognized and how the *quod quid* or *propter quid* is taken as a middle in demonstration, we must now point out how to investigate those items which are predicated in *quod quid*. Then (96a24) he states his proposal. First, he indicates what characteristics should be present in things which are accepted as constituting the *quod quid*. Secondly, how to investigate them (96b15) [L. 14]. Concerning the first he does three things. First, he presents a certain division. Secondly, he proposes what should be the characteristics of things which are taken as constituting *quod quid* (96a32). Thirdly, he proves (96b2).

In regard to the first (96a24) it should be noted that things predicated in *quod quid* must be such that they are predicated always and universally, as has been established above. Then taking those things which are predicated of each thing in the sense of always, he says that we find among them certain ones which apply to more than that in which they are present, but not to the extent of being found outside that genus.

(He explains what is meant by *apply to more*, saying that those things are said to apply to more which are indeed universally present in something, but are not solely in it but in other things also). This would imply that there is another and opposite member which applies to more, but is outside the genus. He gives an example of the first one, saying that there is something which is present in every *three*, as well as in *non-three's*, as is obviously true of *being*, which is universally present not only in *three* but in other things; and not only in the genus of number, but even in things outside the genus of number. *Odd*, however is found

213

in every three and in more things, because it is found also in *five's;* however, it is not found outside the genus of *three,* namely, number, because even *five* is in the genus of number. For nothing outside the genus of number can be called *odd.*

Then (96a32) he shows what should be the characteristics of things that are taken as constituting the *quod quid.* First, he proposes his intention. Secondly, he clarifies it with examples (96a34).

He says therefore first (96a32) that in order to manifest the *quod quid,* we must take items which are both always and *applicable to more* (but not outside the genus), until the term is reached. And they should be so selected that each item when first taken should be applicable to more, but when all are taken together the combination does not apply to more, but is converted with the thing whose *quod quid* is sought. For the *quod quid* of a thing must signify its essence.

Then (96a34) he manifests what he had said with an example. Let us, therefore, take those four, namely, *number, odd,* and *prime* in both its senses. For there are two senses in which a number is said to be *prime:* in one way because it is not divided by any other number, as opposed to *four,* which is not a prime number, since it can be divided by *two; three,* however, is a prime number, because it is not divided by any other number except *one.* In another way a number is called *prime* because it is not composed of other numbers, as opposed to *seven,* which is prime in the first way, because it is not divided by any other number except *one,* but is not prime in the second way, for it is composed of *three* and *four. Three,* however, is not composed of several numbers, but only of the number *two,* and *one.*

And so it is obvious that each of the four aforesaid notions belongs universally to every *three,* although each of them is also found in other things in the genus of number. For *number* and *odd* are found in all odd numbers; but the fourth, i.e, being *prime* in both ways, belongs also to *two,* which is neither divided by any other number nor composed of numbers, but only of units; hence, when they are all assembled they signify the *quod quid* of *three.*

But the requirement that each particle of the definition apply to more than the definition seems superfluous. For the Philosopher says in *Metaphysics* VII that when the ultimate differences are reached, those differences will be equal to the species; therefore, it is not required that the difference apply to more things than the species does. This can also be proved with an argument. For the Philosopher says in *Metaphysics* VIII that a formality which is based on differences seems to be of the species and of the act, i.e., of the form; because, as he says in the same place, the difference corresponds to the form. But each species has its own appropriate form which belongs to no other species. Therefore, it seems that the ultimate difference does not exceed the species.

Furthermore, the Philosopher in *Metaphysics* VII says that there is no more in a definition than genus and differences, and that it is possible for a definition to be formed of two things, one of which is a genus and the other a difference. But a difference cannot be found outside its appropriate genus; otherwise it would not divide the genus *per se* but *per accidens*. Therefore, it seems that the difference does not exceed the species.

But it should be answered that if one were able to discover the difference which would make known the substantial form of the species, then, as the arguments prove, the ultimate difference would not apply to more things than the species does. But because the essential forms are not known to us *per se,* they must be disclosed through certain accidents which are signs of that form, as is stated in *Metaphysics* VIII. However, one should not take the proper accidents of that species, because they are the ones that will be demonstrated by the definition of the species; rather the form of the species must be made known by certain accidents that are more common. Hence according to this, the differences which are used are indeed called substantial, inasmuch as they are adduced in order to declare the essential form; but they are more common than the species, inasmuch as they are taken from signs which follow upon higher genera.

Then (96b2) he explains what he had said above. First, the statement that the items mentioned above should be predicated universally and necessarily of *three*. Secondly, that the very essence of *three* is constituted by those items (96b6).

He says therefore first (96b2) that since it has been established above that items which are predicated in *quod quid* are present of necessity, and whatever is present of necessity is predicated universally, it follows that whether those items which are taken in the manner above indicated be predicated as *quod quid* of *three* or of any other thing, it is necessary that they be predicated necessarily and universally.

Then (96b6) he shows that from things which are taken in the above-mentioned way the essence of *three* or of anything else is constituted; for it is necessary, if the items mentioned above are not the substance of *three,* that they be its genus, either named or unnamed, since they are predicated in *quod quid.* For not every formality has a name. That is why there are many genera and species without names. However, the reason why the above formality is the genus of *three,* if it does not signify its essence, is that whatever is predicated in *quid* is either the genus or the definition signifying the essence. Yet it cannot be the genus; otherwise it would apply to more things than *three's:* for we assume a genus to be something which potentially contains several species under it. But we have established that the aforesaid formality applies only to the atoms, i.e., to the individuals contained under *three.* What remains, therefore, is that the formality in question is the definition signifying the essence of *three*. For the essence of a thing is supposed to be that which is found in the individuals of that species ultimately, according to the manner of predication described above. And what has been said of *three* is also understood of any other things regarding which something is demonstrated to be the same in the manner indicated above.

Lecture 14
(96b15–97a6)

DIVIDING THE GENUS TO INVESTIGATE WHICH ITEMS SHOULD BE PUT IN A DEFINITION

b15. The author of a hand-book   b30. But, in fact, the order
b18. After that, having   b35. Again, division is the only
b25. Divisions according to

After showing what should be the characteristics of the items which constitute the definition signifying the essence of a thing, the Philosopher now shows how they should be investigated. Concerning this he does two things. First, he proposes the most suitable method of investigating the items to be put in the definition, namely, by division of the genus. Secondly, he sets forth another method, namely, by similarities and differences (97b7) [L. 16]. Concerning the first he does two things. First, he shows that one should employ division of the genus for investigating the particles of the definition. Secondly, he shows what to look for in such an investigation (97a23) [L. 15]. In regard to the first he does two things. First, he shows the truth. Secondly, he excludes an error (97a6) [L. 15]. Concerning the first he does three things. First, he shows how the particles of a definition are investigated by the method of dividing the genus. Secondly, how the process of division is useful for this task (96b25). Thirdly, how to avoid pitfalls which can invalidate this process (96b30). Concerning the first he does two things. First, he shows that one should employ division of the genus for defining. Secondly, how one should take the differences (96b18).

He says therefore first (96b15) that when someone wishes to deal with some whole, i.e., a universal, in order to define it, it is recommended that he first divide the genus into the first parts of that genus, i.e., those that are not further divisible into species; for example, he should divide number into *two* and *three*. Having accomplished this division through which the genus is known, he should then try to obtain the definition of each species as is done in other matters, say in the matter of straight line and circle and right angle. For all these are fittingly defined after one has divided the genus.

Then (96b18) he shows how to obtain the differences, saying that after we have learned what the genus is by dividing the genus into its species, for example, whether it is in the genus of quality or quantity, the next step is to investigate the differences by considering the proper attributes which, as has been said, are signs manifesting the forms proper to the species. And this should first be done by means of certain common items. For if we assemble the accidents from the more common genera (which he here calls *indivisibles,* because they are not resolved into prior genera), then from their definitions the things we are searching for will be immediately obvious. For "the basic element of all definitions must be something simple," i.e., a common genus; furthermore, it is only in such simple things that the accidents inhere *per se* which are commonly found in many, but they are found in all other things in virtue of those simple genera. For example, black and white belong *per se* to terminated body; and in virtue of this common characteristic they belong also to man and horse and other things. Hence if one is to obtain the definition of something to which white belongs universally, say the definition of snow, he must have recourse to the more common genus, such as terminated body, and obtain from it the cause of whiteness; and according to this we would learn why snow is white universally. And that cause could pertain to the *quod quid* of snow: for example, the solidifying of a moist element which makes it be terminated, some light being preserved.

Then (96b25) he shows how the above method is useful in definitions. And he says that when someone seeks to define according to the above method, i.e., by dividing the genus into species, the benefit it confers is that it accomplishes the division of the genus through differences. How this method reveals the *quod quid* has been indicated above. Furthermore, these divisions are useful for achieving the *quod quid* solely in the manner described above; they seem to contribute nothing to the syllogizing of the *quod quid,* as we said earlier. Rather it seems that upon dividing, one immediately obtains everything without syllogizing, as though he knew them from the beginning before he divided.

Then (96b30) he shows what to avoid if this method is not to fail. Concerning this he does two things. First, he shows that one must avoid improper order. Secondly, one must avoid diminution (96b35).

He says therefore first (96b30) that it makes a great difference, when arranging the items present in a definition, which items are mentioned first and which are mentioned later. For it is possible to state that man is a gentle animal which is two-legged, or to state that man is a two-legged animal which is gentle. That the order of terms does make a difference in defining is clear from the fact that anything which is defined should be composed of two things, namely, a genus and a difference. Therefore, if "gentle" is taken as a difference of animal, it is required that "gentle animal" be some one thing which can be taken as a genus from which, with the addition of the difference "two-legged," man is constituted. And the same reason holds for anything else which is formed from several things into a unit which is *per se* and not *per accidens*.

Therefore, just as it does make a difference whether this or that be taken for the genus or the difference, or whether something is taken as a difference constituting the genus or as dividing it, so it makes a difference in defining just how the parts of the definition are ordered. For if I say that man is a two-legged gentle animal, "animal" will be taken as the genus, "gentle" as the difference constituting a genus, and "two-legged" as the difference dividing it. It will be the opposite if I say that man is a gentle two-legged animal. Therefore, since a variation in order makes a difference in *quod quid,* the consequence is that one who divides should not only suppose the things which are taken for defining, but should take care about the ordering of those things. And so it is clear that a definition does not syllogize the *quod quid.*

Then (96b35) he teaches that one should avoid diminution, pointing out how to make certain that nothing required for the *quod quid* be omitted. And he says that the only way this can be avoided is by following the method he will indicate.

To understand this it should be noted that all the differences of higher genera pertain to the *quod quid* of some species. For the lower genus is constituted by the difference which divides the higher genus. Therefore, to avoid diminution it is necessary that none of these differences be overlooked. But they are overlooked if someone, after taking the supreme genus, were to take a difference which divides not that supreme genus but some lower genus. But this can be recognized in the following way: when animal is taken as a supreme genus, if someone then takes the division of something pertaining to lower genera, not everything which is contained under the higher genus will fall into that division.

As an example of this he says: for example, not every animal is either whole-winged or possessed of divided wings. (An animal is said to be whole-winged if its wings are each a continuous whole, as in a bat; but an animal is said to be possessed of divided wings if its wings are composed of distinct feathers, as in a hawk or raven). But neither of these belongs to a non-winged animal. However, any animal that flies is contained under one or other of these differences, because it is according to the above differences that this genus, *flying animal,* is divided. But the first and immediate difference of animal is such that every animal falls under the division. And the same applies to all other genera, whether we are dealing with genera extrinsic to animal, such as stone and plant, or those which are contained under animal, such as bird and fish. Yet the first difference of bird is such that every bird is included; and the same is true of fish.

He concludes, therefore, that if someone proceeds to divide according to this method, namely, that the totality which is divided is contained under the parts of the division, he will be able to know that nothing necessary for defining has been omitted. But if he proceeds some other way, he is bound to omit something; and he will not be sure that he has defined integrally.

Lecture 15
(97a6–b6)

TWO ERRORS ARE EXCLUDED.—WHAT IS REALLY REQUIRED FOR CONSTITUTING A DEFINITION ACCORDING TO THE METHOD OF DIVISION?

a6. To define and divide
a7. Yet some hold it
a11. Now first of all
a13. Secondly, when one
a19. Moreover, to postulate

a23. In establishing a definition
a25. The first is feasible
a28. The right order will
a34. Our procedure makes it
b1. For it is clear

After presenting the truth concerning the division of the genus which is used in defining, the Philosopher here excludes two errors. In regard to the first one he does three things:

First (97a6) he excludes the error and says that it is not necessary that one who defines by dividing should know all the things which exist in the world.

Secondly (97a7) he sets forth the opinion of those who make this error. For some have said that it is not possible to know the difference between one thing and everything else, unless everything else is known, as is plain in regard to any two given things, whose difference we cannot know unless we know both things. However, they added that the *quid est* of something cannot be known, unless the difference between it and everything else is known. For that wherein something is not different is identical with it, whereas that by which something differs is other than it. But we cannot know what a thing is, unless we know what is the same as it and what is other than it. According to this, therefore, they concluded that something cannot be known unless everything is known.

Thirdly (97a11) he disproves what they say in two ways. First, he destroys the statement according to which it is said that that by which something differs is something other. For we are now speaking about what is the same and what is other according to the essence which the definition signifies. But it is obvious that even in the same species there are many accidental differences which neither diversify the substance of the species which the definition signifies, nor are in it *per se*. Hence it follows that not every difference makes something other in such a way that it must be known if one is to define.

Secondly (97a13), he disproves it another way. For since one who proposes to define by dividing must take opposing differences in such a way that everything contained under the divided whole falls under this member or that member of the division, and must subsume under one or the other of the members that whose definition is sought (if he knows that the thing he intends to define is contained under that member of the division), then it makes no difference, so far as his intent is concerned, whether he knows or does not know the things of which the opposing differences might be predicated. For example, if I divide animal into rational and irrational, and assume that man is contained under animal in the way we have proposed, it is not required that I know the things of which irrational is predicated or how they differ from one another. For it is obvious that if someone proceeds in this way, namely, by dividing the genus into its first differences and taking the definitum [thing being defined] as subsumed under one of the members and then dividing until certain items are reached that cannot be further divided by essential differences, then by proceeding in this manner he will have the definition of the substance which he was seeking.

Therefore, the persons mentioned above were deluded for failing to distinguish between something in common and in detail. For it is required of one who knows what something is, that he know all things in common but not in detail. For example, one who knows what man is must know that it is through being an animal that man is distinguished from all things that are not animals, and through being rational that man is distinguished from all things that are not rational. But it is not required that he know anything more about these others than is included in the general notion of *non-animal* or *irrational*.

Then (97a19) he excludes the second error. For someone might believe that whoever uses division for defining must assume that the entire whole is contained under the members of the division. But he says that this is not necessary, if the opposites through which the division is made are immediate; because the divided whole is necessarily contained under one of the opposites, provided the first differences of the genus were taken. For differences which are immediate when compared to a lower genus are not immediate if compared to a higher genus. For example, *even* and *odd* are immediate if compared to number of which they are proper differences, but not if they are compared to quantity.

Then (97a23), after rejecting things which are not required in the divisions of the definitum, he shows what is really required. First, he proposes what he intends. Secondly, he manifests his proposal (97a25).

He says therefore first (97a23) that in order to achieve a term, i.e., a definition, by the method of division three things must be observed: first, that the things which are taken be predicated in *quod quid;* secondly, that they be arranged according to what is first and what is second; thirdly, that everything taken pertain to the *quod quid* and that nothing be omitted. Then (97a25) he manifests his proposal. First, he shows how these three rules can be observed. Secondly, he shows that it is enough to observe those three rules (97b1).

In regard to the first point he does three things. First (97a25), he shows how the first rule is observed, saying that this one (namely, that one take things which are predicated in *quod quid*) is observed, first of all, by the fact that a person can form syllogisms to show that what is assumed is in the thing (as is done when there is dispute about whether something is an accident); secondly, to show that it is predicated in *quod quid* (as is done when there is dispute about a genus).

Secondly (97a28), he shows how the second rule is observed, namely, that there be a correct ordering of the parts. And he says that the parts of a definition are arranged as they should, if one takes what is first—and he will do this, if he first takes that which is implied by the other things that are taken later, and not conversely. For this is more common and prior. But such a thing must be taken in the definition as a genus, as when it is stated that man is an animal, two-legged and walking. For if he is a two-legged walker, he is an animal; but not vice versa. Therefore, when I have taken animal as first, the same method must be observed in arranging the other items. For the second item to be employed in the definition will be that which according to the foregoing description will be first among all the others; likewise, the third item to be taken will be that which is first in respect of the items *had,* i.e., following. For it will always turn out that when the more general item has been removed, that which is *had,* i.e., that which immediately follows, will be true in regard to all the other items, say a fourth and a fifth, if that many parts are needed for the definition.

Thirdly (97a34), he shows how the third rule can be observed. And he says that it will be obvious that all items pertaining to the *quod quid* are present in the definition according to the aforesaid method, because when we divide the genus, we take its first differences, under which the divisum is universally contained; for example, that every animal is this or that, i.e., rational or irrational, and we assume that what we intend to define is this, i.e., rational. And again we take this whole, namely, rational animal, and divide it by its proper differences; but when we arrive at the ultimate difference, it will be impossible to divide by other specific differences, but as soon as the ultimate difference is added, the thing whose definition is being sought will differ in no way from the assembled whole, i.e., from the description formed by all the parts that were taken. Thus, man does not differ specifically from any of those of whom rational mortal animal is predicated.

Then (97b1) he shows that the observance of the three aforesaid rules is sufficient for defining, because the definition will have neither more nor less than it should. That no more has been assigned than it should have is obvious from the first rule, namely, because the only things accepted are items predicated in *quod quid;* and it was necessary to accept such things. Likewise it will be clear that nothing has been omitted. For either the genus or the difference might be missing. But that the genus is not missing is clear from the second rule; for the first thing taken was the item without which the others do not exist, and which can exist without the others: and this is the genus. And with the genus the differences were then taken. But that all the differences have been taken is obvious from the third rule, since there can be no further subsequent difference taken after the one concerning which we have said that it has no difference; otherwise it would follow that what had been admitted to be the last would still differ with an essential difference, whereas it had been said that it does not have a difference.

Similarly, it is obvious from the foregoing that no difference has been left out in the meantime, namely, because first differences are always taken. Hence it remains that for defining it is sufficient that the three aforesaid rules be observed.

Lecture 16
(97b7–40)

HOW TO SEARCH FOR THE DEFINITION OF A THING BY EXAMINING THINGS SIMILAR TO IT AND DISSIMILAR

b7. To resume our account
b15. I may illustrate
b26. Besides, every definition

b28. It is also easier
b31. Indeed, perspicuity is
b38. We may add that if

After teaching how to investigate the *quod quid* according to the most suitable method which is by division of the genus, the Philosopher now teaches another method. Concerning this he does three things. First, he describes the method. Secondly, he gives examples (97b15). Thirdly, he proves that this method is satisfactory (97b26).

He says therefore first (97b7) that if someone is searching for the definition of some thing, he should examine things which are similar to it as well as things which are different from it. He shows how this should be done when he says that in those things which are similar, one should consider some item that is the same in all; for example, what is found to be the same in all men is that they all coincide in being rational. After that, one should investigate the things which agree with the first things in genus and are specifically the same among themselves, although specifically different from the things first taken, as horses from men. It is also necessary to investigate what is the same in these things, namely, these horses; say neighing.

Then having taken what is the same in all of the former, i.e., men, namely, rational, and what is the same in the others, i.e., horses, namely, neighing, the next step will be to consider whether anything is the same in those two, namely, in rational and neighing. And this method of investigating must be continued until one common formality is found. For this will be the definition of the thing. However, if such an investigation does not uncover one common formality, but leads to two or even several diverse formalities, it will be obvious that the thing whose definition is being sought will not be one thing according to essence but several. Consequently, it will not have one definition.

Then (97b15) he elucidates what he had said with an example, saying that if we would investigate what magnanimity is, we should first of all consider certain magnanimous persons, in order to learn what is the one item they have insofar as they are magnanimous. Thus, Alcibiades was said to be magnanimous, and so were Achilles and Ajax; all of whom have one item in common—not to tolerate insults. The sign of this is that Alcibiades fought rather than accept insults; Achilles went mad from anger; Ajax committed suicide. Then we should consider this in others who are said to be magnanimous, say in Lysander and Socrates. For they have this in common that they were unmoved by good fortune or bad, but were indifferent to both.

Therefore, let us take these two items, namely, equanimity in the face of the vicissitudes of life and intolerance of insults, and see if there is anything common to them. For in this consists the notion of magnanimity. For example, we might say that these two things are due to the fact that a person considers himself worthy of great things. For it is from this attitude that a man does not tolerate insults and it is also from this attitude that he scorns fluctuations affecting external goods as being trifles. But if nothing common is to be found in the two items taken, the species of magnanimity would not be one but two. Hence one common definition could not be given.

Then (97b26) he shows that the above method is well adapted to finding the *quod quid*. Concerning this he does two things. First, he shows that the method is suitable. Secondly, he shows what should be avoided in this method (97b38). Concerning the first he does two things. First, he shows that the above method is suitable as to its result, namely, as to arriving at something common. Secondly, as to its procedure, namely, inasmuch as it starts with particular cases (97b28).

He says therefore first (97b26) that it was said advisedly that one who is investigating the *quod quid* must reach something common, because every definition of something is given insofar as that thing is considered in its universality, and not as it is considered in this or that individual. For a physician does not define health as it exists in this eye of this man, but either as it is universally and absolutely in regard to all men, or he distinguishes health according to various species; for example, when he says this to be health for the cholerics, or for the bilious.

Then (97b28) he shows that this method is satisfactory as to procedure, inasmuch as it proceeds from the less common to the more common. And this in two ways: first, by reason of facility. For a discipline begins from the easier things. But it is easier to define something singular, i.e., something less common, than something universal, which is more common; inasmuch as equivocations are less likely to be detected in universals, because they are less determinate, than in things which are undifferentiated, i.e., in things which are not divided by specific differences. Accordingly, one must define by ascending from singulars to universals.

Secondly (97b31), he shows the same thing by reason of evidence. For just as in demonstrations one should syllogize by presupposing something which is evident and obvious, so too in *terms*, i.e., in definitions. For no one can pass to a knowledge of something which is unknown except by means of something known, whether he intends to know *quia est*, which is made known through demonstration, or *quid est*, which is done by definition.

But this happens, i.e., something evident preexists, if it is defined or happens to be defined separately, i.e., distinctly, by means of items that are predicated singularly, i.e., which belong to this or that thing properly and distinctively. Thus, if someone desires to know what *similar* is, he will not examine every single thing which can be called similar, but only some similar things; for example, how things are similar in color, and how something is accounted similar in figure. For it is from the unity of color that things are said to be similar in color; but in the realm of figure, two things are similar because corresponding angles are equal and the sides proportional. Likewise in other things: if someone desires to define *sharp*, he will not examine everything which can be called sharp, but he will consider *sharp* as applied to a sound.

Hence it is clear that one who follows this method when he defines is automatically avoiding the possibility of equivocation. Consequently, it is clear that this is a practical method of defining, i.e., the method of passing from the less common to the more common, inasmuch as it is easier in special things to define what is special, and univocation can be more easily recognized in such things.

Then (97b38) he excludes a certain method of procedure in definitions, saying that just as one may not dispute by metaphors, so he may not define by metaphors; for example, by stating that man is an inverted tree. Furthermore, in definitions one may not use anything stated metaphorically. For since definitions are the most important and most efficacious middles in disputations, it would follow, if definitions were stated in metaphorical terms, that one would have to dispute by metaphors. But this is not valid, because a metaphor is interpreted according to something which is similar; whereas it does not follow, if something is similar in one respect, that it is similar in all respects.

Lecture 17
(98a1–34)

HOW TO INVESTIGATE THE *WHY* IN SPECIAL PROBLEMS.—HOW CERTAIN PROBLEMS AGREE AS TO *PROPTER QUID*, EITHER BECAUSE THEIR MIDDLES HAVE A KIND OF UNITY OR ARE SUBORDINATED

a1. In order to formulate
a13. We are now taking
a20. Yet a further method

a23. Some connexions that require
a29. Other connexions that require

After showing how one should go about investigating the *quod quid*, the Philosopher now shows how one should investigate *propter quid*. Concerning this he does two things. First, he shows how *propter quid* should be investigated. Secondly, how diverse questions make use of a common *propter quid* (98a23). Concerning the first he does two things. First, he shows that one takes the *propter quid* by taking some common univocal item. Secondly, by taking some common analogous item (98a20). Concerning the first he does two things. First, he teaches how to take the *propter quid* by taking a common univocal item which is a definitively named genus. Secondly, by taking anything else that is common (98a13).

He says therefore first (98a1) that in order to get the *propter quid* in regard to individual problems that are proposed, it is required to consider divisions and subdivisions, and so to proceed to the individual cases by disputing, having first supposed a common genus. For example, if someone wished to consider *why* something belongs to certain types of animals, he would have to discover what items belong to every animal. Once these have been discovered, he would once more consult the divisions to determine what things follow first upon that common item which is contained under animal; for example, what things follow upon every bird. Then one would continue in this manner, always taking the first item into which a given division is immediately divided. This is the very thing that was observed above in the divisions by which one proceeds to investigate *quod quid.*

By thus proceeding it is obvious that we shall always be able to say *propter quid* certain things are present in those things which are contained under something common. Thus, if we would like to know why certain things such as being asleep and being awake are found in man and horse, we would let *animal* be that in which A, the middle, is found, and let B, i.e., the major extreme, stand for items that inhere in every animal, say, *being asleep and awake.* Then we let certain species of animals, such as *man, horse, cow,* be taken as minor extremes, namely, C, D, E. In this way it is manifest that the reason why B, i.e., *being asleep or awake,* is found in D, i.e., in *man,* is that it is due to A, i.e., because man is an *animal.* Then the same should be done in regard to the others, and the same notion must be observed in all. The reason for this procedure is that the subject is the cause of a proper attribute. Therefore, if we wish to investigate the cause why some attribute is found in certain inferiors, it is necessary to take as common the proper subject through whose definition the cause of that attribute is taken.

Then (98a13) he shows how to investigate the *propter quid* by arriving at something common which is a genus without a definite name. And he says that what has been stated above applies to those common items to which names have been assigned. However, it is not enough to consider only such items but anything else which seems to be commonly present in them, even if it is not a genus or does not have a name. After that, one must discover what this common factor follows upon, as well as what follows upon this common unnamed factor. For example, *to have horns* is something common, but it neither has a name nor is it a genus. Furthermore, two things follow upon this common factor: one of these is that every horned animal, because it must chew its cud, has several stomachs; one of which, existing farther in and called *echinus,* is hard and prickly, as it is stated in *The History of Animals* II. Another item which follows upon horned animals is that they do not have teeth in both jaws, but only in the lower one, because the dental matter is converted into horns. Again one must consider which animals are apt to have horns, namely, cows and deers. For in that way it will be clear why these animals have those properties, namely, because they have horns.

Then (98a20) he shows how to investigate *propter quid* by arriving at some common analogous item. And he says that another method of investigating *propter quid* is to select something common according to analogy, i.e., proportion. For it is possible to take something analogous which is not the same according to species or genus: for example, the bone (called *sepion*) of squid, the spine of fish and the backbone of land animals. For all these agree by proportion, because spine and backbone are related to fish and land animals in the same way. Now because of this unity of proportion certain things follow upon this common analogous item, just as if they shared in one generic or specific nature; for example, to be covered with flesh.

Then (98a23) he shows how many problems concur as to *propter quid*. First, as to having one middle. Secondly, as to the order of the middles (98a29).

He says therefore first (98a23) that some problems are the same, namely, inasmuch as they agree as to *propter quid*. In one way, because they have the same middle: thus many things are demonstrated by the middle which is *antiperistasis*, i.e., counter-resistance or reverberation. On the other hand, some middles are the same not absolutely but in genus, and these are diversified by certain differences which are based either on the diversity of subjects or on the diversity of their ways of coming to be. For example, if it is asked why an echo comes to be, or why something appears, namely, in a mirror, or why a rainbow is formed. For they are the same problem as to the middle *propter quid*, which is generically the same, since all are caused by a reverberation. However, the reverberations differ specifically. For an echo comes to be through the reverberation of air set in motion by a sounding body toward a concave body; an image in a mirror comes to be by the fact that the modification of the medium is rebounded at the mirror; but the rainbow is formed by the rays of the sun being reflected back by moist vapors.

Then (98a29) he shows how problems agree as to *propter quid* by reason of the subordination of the middles. And he says that there are certain other problems which differ from one another in point of having diverse middles, one of which is under another. And he gives the example that someone wonders why the Nile overflows more near the end of the month, i.e., of the lunar month. For the reason is that there is more rain near the end of the month. And the reason for this is taken from another middle, namely, because the moon which controls moisture is waning then. Consequently, as its light wanes the vapors in the air condense more; and this causes rain. And so it is plain that those two middles are related to one another in the sense that one of them is under the other.

Lecture 18
(98a35–b40)

CO-EXISTENCE OF CAUSE AND CAUSED

a35. The question might be
b2. For, one might argue
b4. and each capable of proof
b16. If, however, they cannot

b22. Moreover, that the
b25. On the other hand
b32. We may, however, suggest

After showing how one should investigate *propter quid,* the Philosopher now raises two questions in regard to *propter quid.* The first of these concerns the co-existence of cause to caused. The second pertains to the unity of cause (99a1) [L. 19]. Concerning the first he does three things. First, he proposes the question. Secondly, he raises an objection (98b2). Thirdly, he solves the question (98b25).

He says therefore first (98a35) that in regard to cause and caused, it is possible to wonder when one of them exists, does the other also exist? However, this question should not be interpreted as referring to co-existence in time but of succession, such that if one is posited, does the other follow regardless of whether they are concurrent in time, or before and after. And he gives two examples. In one of them, the cause precedes the caused in time: for the cause why the leaves of a tree fall off is that it has broad leaves; for the possession of broad leaves and their falling are not simultaneous in time. In the other example, the cause and the caused are simultaneous in time; as the interposition of the earth is simultaneous in time with the eclipse of the moon. The question, therefore, is whether upon the one of them the other follows.

Then (98b2) he objects to the question proposed and shows that cause and caused are always together as to succession: and he gives two reasons for this. The first one is based on the notion of cause and caused. And he says that every caused thing must have some cause. Hence, if something is posited as caused and it is not simultaneously posited that such and such is its cause, it follows that something else is its cause. For example, from the fact that the earth is between, it follows that the moon is eclipsed; and from the fact that a tree has broad leaves, it follows that its leaves fall off. Therefore, if there is no other cause, it follows that this caused is simultaneous with its cause.

Then (98b4) he gives the second reason which is based on the fact that cause and caused are demonstrated the one by the other. Concerning this he does three things. First, he states the reason. Secondly, he dismisses the

228

error that could follow (98b16). Thirdly, he proves what he had presupposed (98b22).

In regard to the first he says (98b4) that it is also manifest that cause
and caused follow upon one another simultaneously, if it is true that either
can be demonstrated by the other: because the conclusion of a demonstration follows of necessity from the middle. But the fact that either can
be demonstrated by the other is shown by the following example: Let
leaf falls off be A, the major extreme; *to have a broad leaf* be B, the
middle; and *vines* be C, which is the minor. Thus, therefore, A is in B,
because whatever has broad leaves, its leaves fall off; but B is in C,
because every vine has broad leaves. And so it is concluded that A is in C,
because every vine loses its leaves. Now in this whole process the cause is
taken as middle; consequently, the caused is demonstrated by the cause.

But it is also possible conversely to demonstrate the cause through the
caused, namely, that a vine has broad leaves because its leaves fall off.
For we may take as D, the major term, the fact of having broad leaves;
and as E, the middle, the fact that the leaves fall off; and as Z, vine,
which is the minor extreme. Thus, therefore, E is in Z, because from every
vine the leaves fall off; but D is in E, namely, that whose leaves fall off
has broad leaves. From this it is concluded that every vine has broad
leaves, which is taken as the cause accounting for the leaves falling off.

Then (98b16) he excludes an error which could follow from the foregoing, namely, that according to the same reason one of the foregoing
may be demonstrated from the other. But he rejects this, saying that if
it does not occur that the two given things are mutually causes one of the
other, namely, in the same genus of cause (since the cause is prior to that
of which it is the cause, and it does not occur that a same thing is prior
and subsequent in the same way), then since the cause of the eclipse
of the moon is the fact that the earth is between, it is not possible that the
eclipse of the moon is the cause of the earth's being between. Therefore,
if a demonstration through cause is a demonstration *proper quid,* whereas
one which is not through the cause is demonstration of the *quia,* as was
established in Book I, it follows that one who demonstrates through the
eclipse of the moon that the earth is between, knows *quia* not *propter
quid.*

Then (98b22) he proves what he had supposed, namely, that the interposition of the earth is the cause of the eclipse and not the converse. And
he says that it is obvious that the eclipsing of the moon is not the cause
of the earth's being between, but it is rather the converse; because in
explaining an eclipse it is stated that the earth is between, as has been
stated. Therefore, since *quid* and *propter quid* are the same, it is clear
that the eclipse of the moon is known through the fact that the earth is
between, as through a middle which is *propter quid;* and not conversely.

Then (98b25) he solves the proposed question, showing the cases in which it is true that cause and caused always follow upon one another, and the cases in which it is not true. Concerning this he does two things. First, he shows the cases in which it is not true. Secondly, those in which it is true (98b32).

He says therefore first (98b25) that one common thing happens to have several causes, insofar as it is found in diverse things; as to be worthy of blame belongs to a rash person because of excess, but to a timid person because of a deficiency. Therefore, let us assume that some thing is predicated of several things chiefly and immediately, i.e., that A is predicated in a first way of B and also of C; as to be blameworthy is predicated of excessiveness and deficiency. Let us further assume that these two, namely, C and B, are predicated of D and E; as excessiveness of rash, and deficiency of timid. Therefore, A will be predicated of D and of E, because both the rash and the timid are blameworthy. But the cause of A's being in D is B; for a rash person is blameworthy because of excess. But the cause of A's being in E is C; for a timid person is blame-worthy because of defect. It is clear, therefore, that since the cause exists, the thing must exist: because whether A is excess or defect, it is necessary that something be blameworthy. On the other hand, if the thing exists, it is necessary that one of the causes exist, although it is not necessary that both causes exist. For example, supposing that something is blame-worthy, it is not necessary that it be due to excess, but it is necessary that it be due either to excess or to defect.

Then (98b32) he shows in which cases it is necessary that cause and caused follow one another simultaneously. And he says that if something be asked in a universal way, and if both the cause and that whose cause is sought be taken in a universal way, then it is required that the effect always follow upon the cause, and the cause upon the effect. Thus the fact of losing leaves does not belong in a first way to several things as it did in the above example, but it belongs determinately to one common first thing; although of that common thing there are many species, to which it belongs universally that their leaves fall off: say, if we took either plants or this type of plant, namely, the type that has broad leaves. Hence, in all of these it is required to take an equal middle, so that the cause and that of which it is the cause are converted. Thus we might inquire why trees lose their leaves: if the cause of this is taken to be the fact that the moist element has hardened and made easier to dry out, it will follow that if the effect exists, the cause also exists; for example, if the tree has its leaves falling off, it is required that there be a hardening of its moist element. Conversely, it is required that if the cause is posited, then the effect is posited in such a thing: thus if the hardening of the sap exists, it follows not of anything at random but of the tree, that the leaves fall off.

Lecture 19
(99a1–b18)

WHETHER UPON UNITY OF CAUSE FOLLOWS UNITY OF EFFECT, AND VICE VERSA

HOW CAUSE AND EFFECT FOLLOW UPON ONE ANOTHER

a1. Can the cause of an
a2. Perhaps it is impossible
a4. Now it is possible
a17. The truth is that cause,

a30. If an explanation
b7. If immediate premises
b15. As regards syllogism

Having settled the question he raised, namely, whether upon the existence of the effect the existence of the cause follows, and conversely; the Philosopher now inquires whether unity of cause follows upon unity of effect, and conversely. Concerning this he does two things. First, he shows how one cause is inferred from one effect. Secondly, from this he shows the sequential connection of cause and effect (99a17). In regard to the first he does three things.

First (99a1) he proposes the question, which is this: Does it occur that of the same effect there is not the same cause in all cases but different ones, or does this not occur? For it seemed to be supposed in solving the previous question that in various cases there can be various causes of one effect.

Secondly (99a2), he solves the question by distinguishing. For it occurs that something is assigned as the cause of some effect in three ways: in one way, by taking the *per se* cause and then concluding the effect demonstratively; in another way, by taking a sign; in a third way, by taking an accident. Therefore, if one takes as cause that which is *per se* the middle of demonstration, there can be but one cause of one effect in all cases. And he proves this on the ground that a *per se* middle in demonstrations is a formality of the ultimate, i.e., the definition of the major extreme, which, if it needs to be demonstrated of the subject, will be demonstrated by the definition of the subject, as we have established above. Now it is obvious that of one thing there is one definition. Hence it is necessary that of one effect there is no cause but the one which is the middle of demonstration.

However, if one does not take as the inferring cause that which is *per se* the middle of demonstration, but some sign or accident is used as the middle, then it does happen that of one effect several causes, as it were, are taken in diverse things, as is clear in the example given earlier. For

231

the *per se* cause why something is blameworthy is that it is not according to reason. But to be excessive or defective is a sign of that which is not according to reason.

Thirdly (99a4), he elucidates his solution by showing that the members of the division he cited are possible. And he says that it is possible to consider both that which is the cause and that of which it is the cause, *per accidens:* thus a musician is *per accidens* the cause of a house whose *per se* cause is a builder, who in turn is *per accidens* the cause of its being a haven for thieves, if this happens to occur in the house. Indeed, these problems even seem to be *per accidens*. But if cause and caused are not taken *per accidens,* it is required that the middle taken as cause be of the same order as the effect whose demonstration is sought.

Hence if certain things are equivocal, then the common middle which is taken will also be equivocal; if they are not equivocal but agree as it were in genus, then the middle too will be common according to genus. Thus the fact that proportionals alternate, i.e., are commutatively proportional, is found univocally in many things, say in numbers and in lines, in which they have a cause which is in one sense different and in one sense the same: different, indeed, according to species, inasmuch as a line is one thing and a number another thing; but the same according to genus, inasmuch as lines as well as numbers agree in having such increments from which commutative proportion is demonstrated of them.

The other examples he gives concern equivocal things. He says that the cause of being similar is one thing in colors and another in figures, because similarity is predicated equivocally of the two. For in figures, to be similar consists in nothing more than that the sides have anology, i.e., that the sides are proportional and the angles equal. But in colors, similarity consists in the fact that they cause the same alteration in the sense, or something else of this sort.

Thirdly, however, he says concerning things which agree according to analogy that in their case it is also required that the middle be one according to analogy, as when it was stated above that both a rainbow and an echo are reverberations.

Then (99a17) he shows how in the light of the foregoing, causes follow one upon the other. Concerning this he does three things. First, he shows what sort of sequential connection there is between cause and effect. Secondly, he orders this connection in a syllogistic figure (99a30). Thirdly, he raises a doubt from the foregoing (99b7).

He says therefore first (99a17) that the type of connection found between cause and caused and the subject in which that caused inheres is such that if one were to take in a particular case that of which the cause is sought, it will be in more than the cause or subject. Thus, to have its exterior angles equal to four right angles belongs to every triangle for a single reason, namely, because its three exterior angles added to its three interior angles are equal to six right angles. Therefore, since the three interior angles are equal to two right angles, it follows that the three exterior angles are equal to four right angles. However, a rhombus also has four exterior angles equal to four right angles, but for another reason. For its exterior angles plus its interior angles equal eight right angles, but the four interior angles of a rhombus are equal to four right angles; therefore, the four exterior angles are equal to four right angles. Therefore, to have its exterior angles equal to four right angles extends to more things than either triangle or rhombus does; but if the latter are taken together, they are equal to the former. For all figures, which agree in having their exterior angles equal to four right angles must similarly agree as to their middle, which is the cause of being equal to four right angles. And he proves this, as in the previous case, on the ground that the middle is the definition of the major extreme. And this is why all sciences come to be in virtue of a definition.

He proves this also with an example from natural things. For the fact that its leaves fall follows on being a vine, but it extends to more, because it is true of several other things; it also follows upon being a fig tree, and extends to more. But it does not extend to more than the sum total of things in which it is found, but it is equal to their sum. Therefore, if someone desires to discover what is the first middle in relation to all, it will be the definition of the fact that the leaves fall: and this definition will be the first middle in respect to the others, since all the others are such. And again, some other middle will be discovered for this, say that the sap hardens by drying, or something of that sort. Hence, if it be asked what it is to have leaves fall off, we will say that it is nothing more than "the seminal sap hardening at a point of contact," i.e., where the leaf meets a branch.

Then (99a30) he arranges the mode of the aforesaid connection in syllogistic form, saying that if the sequence of cause and caused be sought, it can be assigned in the following way according to the figues of syllogisms. Thus let A be in every B, and B in all things that are D, but in things additional to D. Then B will inhere universally in the things contained under D, inasmuch as that is said to inhere universally which is not converted. But a primary universal is one such that each of the inferious contained under it is not converted with it, but all of them taken together are converted with the first universal and exceed each of those which are contained under it. Thus, therefore, the cause of the fact that A inheres in the things contained under D is B. Therefore, it is required that A extend to more things than B does. If this were not so but they were equal, then why should B be the cause of inferring that A is in D, any more than A be the cause of inferring that B is in D? For either of two convertible things can be concluded from the other.

Suppose, furthermore, that A is predicated of all things in which E inheres, but is not convertible. Then it will be necessary to say that all the things contained under E form one thing, which is diverse from B. For if A were not diverse from B, how could it be true to say that A inheres in every B and not vice versa, since A is only in E and in B? And so it would follow, if E and B were not diverse, that A would not be in more than E. Therefore, suppose that A is in more things than D and than E. Then why could not a cause be found explaining why it is in all things which are in D? And this cause is B. But we must still inquire whether all the things contained under E have one cause. Let C be that cause. Thus, therefore, he concludes that a same thing turns out to have several causes, but not in the same subject according to species. Thus the cause of that which is A is both B and C; but B is the cause that A is found in the things contained under D, while C is the cause that A is found in the things contained under E. And he gives an example from natural things. Let the fact of *being long-lived* be taken as A; *quadrupeds* as D; *to have no bile,* i.e., in superfluity (which is the cause of long life in quadrupeds) as B; *birds* as E; and *to be dry,* or something of that sort, which is the cause of long life, or something of that sort in birds, as C.

Then (99b7) he raises a problem occasioned by the foregoing. For it was stated above that one does not straightway from the beginning arrive at something atomic, i.e., at the indivisible, in which is found that whose cause is being sought. But straightway many and indistinct things are found in which that one thing occurs; furthermore, there is not one middle through which this one thing can be demonstrated of all, and the causes are several. The doubt therefore is this: If some cause is to be taken of these several middles, is it to be taken on the side of the primary universal, say on the side of A, or on the side of the singulars, i.e., of those which are less common, as E and D were taken above, i.e., quadrupeds and birds?

And he answers this by saying that it is always required to take the middles which are nearer the subject, in which the cause of that common caused thing is searched for: and it is necessary to proceed thus until one reaches that which is immediate to the common caused thing. And he assigns a reason for this, namely, because that which is on the part of what is contained under something common is the cause of its being under this common thing; just as is the case if D is under B, and if C is the cause of D having B in it. And from this it further follows that C is the cause of A's being in D, and that B is the cause of A's being in C. But A is in B in virtue of itself and immediately.

Finally (99b15), he summarizes what has been said in the entire teaching of the *Analytics,* saying that it is clear from all that has been stated— both in the book of the *Prior* and in this book of the *Posterior*—concerning the syllogism and concerning demonstration, both what each is and how each is formed. Furthermore, in regard to demonstrative science it is also clear how it comes to exist in us. For this pertains to the same thing, because demonstration is a syllogism causing scientific knowledge, as has been established above.

Lecture 20
(99b18–100b17)

HOW THE FIRST PRINCIPLES OF DEMONSTRATION ARE KNOWN BY US

b18. As to basic premises
b20. We have already said
b23. But there are questions
b26. Now it is strange
b28. If on the other hand
b30. So it emerges that neither
b32. Therefore we must possess

b34. And this at least
b36. But through sense-perception
a1. and when such persistence
a4. So out of sense-perception
a14. Let us now restate
b5. Now of the thinking states

After showing how that which is the principle of demonstration in the sense of a middle comes to be known, the Philosopher now shows how the first common principles come to be known. First, he states his intention. Secondly, he pursues it (99b20). He says therefore first (99b18), that from what follows it will be clear concerning indemonstrable principles both how we come to know them and by what habit they are known. However, the plan we shall observe calls for us first to propose certain problems touching this matter. Then (99b20) he pursues his plan. Concerning this he does two things. First, he raises the problem. Secondly, he settles it (99b32). In regard to the first he does three things. First, he prefaces something from which the need for an inquiry of this kind is indicated. Secondly, he raises the questions (99b23). Thirdly, he objects to a question (99b26).

He says therefore first (99b20), that it has already been established above that nothing is scientifically known through demonstration, unless the first immediate principles are known beforehand. Therefore, in order to have scientific knowledge of demonstration, it is useful to know how the first principles are acquired.

Then (99b23) he raises three questions touching this knowledge of the principles. The first question is whether the knowledge of all immediate principles is the same or not. The second is whether there is a science of all immediate principles or of none; or is there science of some, and some other type of knowledge of the others. The third question is whether the habitual knowledge of those principles comes to exist in us after previously not existing, or have they always been in us but escaped our notice.

Then (99b26) he objects to the last question to which the others are ordered. First, he objects to the second side, saying that it is absurd to claim that we have the habitual knowledge of these principles but they escape our notice. For it is obvious that those who have knowledge of the principles have a knowledge which is more certain than that which is acquired through demonstration. But knowledge through demonstration cannot be had such that it escapes the notice of the one having it. For it was established in the beginning of this book that a person who has scientific knowledge of something knows that it is impossible for it to be otherwise. Therefore, it is far less possible for someone having a knowledge of the first principles to have it escape his notice. Yet this absurdity would follow, if habitual knowledge of this kind were in us but escaped our notice.

Secondly (99b28), he objects to the other side. For if a person states that we acquire these habits or principles *de novo* after previously not having them, we are left with the further problem of how we can know and learn such principles *de novo* without some previous knowledge existing in us: for it is impossible to learn anything save from pre-existing knowledge, as we have established above in regard to demonstration. But the reason why we cannot learn the immediate principles from pre-existing knowledge is that pre-existing knowledge is more certain, since it is a cause of certitude of the things which are made known through it. But no knowledge is more certain than the knowledge of these principles. Hence it does not seem that we can begin to know them, when previously we did not know.

Thirdly (99b30), he concludes from the above two arguments that it is neither possible always to have had the knowledge of these principles but it escaped our notice, nor possible that such knowledge is generated *de novo* in us to supplant a state of absolute ignorance in which no other habitual knowledge was possessed.

Then (99b32) he solves these questions. First, he solves the last one. Secondly, he solves the first two (100b5). In regard to the first he does three things. First, he proposes that some principle of knowing must pre-exist in us. Secondly, he shows what it is (99b34). Thirdly, he shows how from a pre-existing principle of knowing we attain the knowledge of principles (100a4).

He says therefore first (99b32), that there must be in us from the beginning a certain cognitive power that exists previously to the knowledge of principles, but not such that it is stronger as to certitude than the knowledge of principles. Hence the knowledge of principles does not come about in us from pre-existing knowledge in the same way as things which are known through demonstration.

Then (99b34) he shows what that pre-existing cognitive principle is. Apropos of this he posits three grades among animals. The first of these is something which seems to be common to all animals, namely, that they have a certain connatural faculty [i.e., potency, i.e., power] for estimating about sense-perceptible things. This faculty, which is not acquired *de novo* but follows upon their very nature, is called *sense*.

Then (99b36) he mentions the second grade, saying that although sense is found in all animals, in some of them a sensible impression remains after the sense-object is removed, as happens in all the perfect animals. But in certain others this does not occur, as in certain imperfect animals; say in those which are not capable of progressive local movement. And it might perhaps be that in regard to some animals an impression remains in regard to certain sense-objects which are more vigorous, and not in regard to those which are weaker. Therefore, those animals in which no impression of sensible objects remains at all have no knowledge except when they are sensing. Similarly, in regard to animals in which such an impression is apt to remain, if it does not remain in them in the case of certain sensible objects, they cannot have any knowledge of them except while they are sensing. But animals, in which a trace of such an impression remains, are capable of having some knowledge in the mind beyond sense; and these are the animals which have *memory*.

Then (100a1) he shows, in view of the foregoing, how the knowledge of first principles comes about in us; and he concludes from the foregoing that from sensing comes remembrance in those animals in which a sensible impression remains, as has been stated above. But from remembrance many times repeated in regard to the same item but in diverse singulars arises *experience*, because experience seems to be nothing else than to take something from many things retained in the memory.

However, experience requires some reasoning about the particulars, in that one is compared to another: and this is peculiar to *reason*. Thus, when one recalls that such a herb cured several men of fever, there is said to be experience that such a herb cures fevers. But reason does not stop at the experience gathered from particulars, but from many particulars in which it has been experienced, it takes one common item which is consolidated in the mind and considers it without considering any of the singulars. This common item reason takes as a principle of art and science. For example, as long as a doctor considered that this herb cured Socrates of fever, and Plato and many other individual men, it is *experience;* but when his considerations arise to the fact that such a species of herb heals a fever absolutely, this is taken as a *rule of the art of medicine.*

This, then, is what he means when he says that just as from memory is formed experience, so from experience or even from the universal resting in the mind (which, namely, is taken as if it is so in *all* cases, just as experience is taken as being so in certain cases.—This universal is said to be resting in the mind, inasmuch as it is considered outside the singulars which undergo change. Furthermore, he says that it is *one outside the many*, not according to an autonomous existence but according to the consideration of the intellect which considers a nature, say of man, without referring to Socrates and Plato. But even though it is one outside the many according to the intellect's consideration, nevertheless in the sphere of existents it exists in all singulars one and the same: not numerically, however, as though the humanity of all men were numerically one, but according to the notion of the species. For just as *this white* is similar to *that white* in whiteness, not as though there were one numerical whiteness existing in the two, so too Socrates is similar to Plato in humanity, but not as though there were numerically one humanity existing in the two.—) the principle of *art* and *science* is formed in the mind.

And he distinguishes between art and science, just as he did in *Ethics* VI, where it is stated that *art* is right reason in regard to things to be made. And so he says here that if from experience a universal in regard to generation is taken, i.e., in regard to anything that can be made, say in regard to healing or husbandry, this pertains to *art. Science,* however, as it is stated in the same place, is concerned with necessary things; hence if the universal bears on things which are always in the same way, it pertains to *science;* for example, if it bears on numbers or figures. And this process which has been described is verified in regard to the principles of all sciences and arts. Hence he concludes that there do not pre-exist any habits of principles in the sense of being determinate and complete; neither do they come to exist anew from other better known pre-existing principles in the way that a scientific habit is generated in us from previously known principles; rather the habits of principles come to exist in us from pre-existing sense.

And he gives as an example a battle which starts after the soldiers have been beaten and put to flight. For when one of the soldiers shall have taken a stand, i.e., begun to take a battle position and not flee, another takes his stand next to him, and then another, until enough are gathered to form the beginning of a battle. So, too, from the sense and memory of one particular and then of another and another, something is finally reached with is the principle of art and science, as has been stated.

But someone could believe that sense alone or the mere remembrance of singulars is sufficient to cause intellectual knowledge of principles, as some of the ancients supposed, who did not discriminate between sense and intellect. Therefore, to exclude this the Philosopher adds that along with sense it is necessary to presuppose such a nature of mind as cannot only suffer this (i.e., be susceptible of universal knowledge, which indeed comes to pass in virtue of the *possible intellect*) but can also cause this in virtue of the *agent intellect* which makes things intelligible in act by abstraction of universals from singulars.

Then (100a4) he elucidates something asserted in the preceding solution, namely, that the universal is taken from *experience* bearing on singulars. And he says that what was stated above, albeit not clearly—namely, how from the experience of singulars the universal is formed in the mind—must now be discussed again and explained more clearly. For if many singulars are taken which are without differences as to some one item existing in them, that one item according to which they are not different, once it is received in the mind, is the first universal, no matter what it may be, i.e., whether it pertains to the essence of the singulars or not. For since we find that Socrates and Plato and many others are without difference as to whiteness, we take this one item, namely, white, as a universal which is an accident. Similarly, because we find that Socrates and Plato and the others are not different as to rationality, this one item in which they do not differ, namely, rational, we take as a universal which is an essential difference.

But how this one item can be taken he now explains. For it is clear that sensing is properly and *per se* of the singular, but yet there is somehow even a sensing of the universal. For sense knows Callias not only so far forth as he is Callias, but also as he is this man; and similarly Socrates, as he is this man. As a result of such an attainment pre-existing in the sense, the intellective soul can consider man in both. But if it were in the very nature of things that sense could apprehend only that which pertains to particularity, and along with this could in no wise apprehend the nature in the particular, it would not be possible for universal knowledge to be caused in us from sense-apprehension.

Then he manifests this same point in the process which goes from species to genus. Hence he adds: "Again in these," namely, in man and horse, "the mind lingers in its consideration, until it attains to something indivisible in them, which is universal." For example, we consider such an animal and another one, say a man and a horse, until we arrive at the common item, "animal," which is universal; and in this genus we do the same until we arrive at some higher genus. Therefore, since we take a knowledge of universals from singulars, he concludes that it is obviously necessary to acquire the first universal principles by induction. For that is the way, i.e., by way of induction, that the sense introduces the universal into the mind, inasmuch as all the singulars are considered.

Then (100b5) he solves the first two question, namely, whether the knowledge of first principles is science, or some other habit. In regard to this he accepts, from what has been stated above, that the knowledge of principles pertains to the intellect whose function is to know the universal: for he says that the universal is a principle of science. But in regard to the intellect there are two genera of habits, and these are not related to the true in exactly the same way. For some are always true, whereas others sometimes receive what is false, as in opinion and in those cases of reasoning which can be of the true and of the false. Again, there are certain erroneous habits, namely, which bear on the false. But because principles are most true, it is clear that they do not pertain to habits which are always of the false, or even to habits which now and then receive falsity, but only to habits which are always of the true. But these are *science* and *understanding* [i.e., intuition]. (In *Ethics* VI a third one is added, namely, *wisdom:* but because wisdom, as it is stated there, comprehends within itself both science and understanding—since it is a science and the chief of the sciences—he omits it here). Therefore, leaving this one aside, no other genus of knowledge but understanding is more certain than science.

Now it is plain that the principles of demonstrations are better known than the demonstrated conclusions, as was established in Book I. Moreover, it cannot be through science that we have those principles, because science is the result of reasoning, namely, demonstrative, whose principles are the very things about which we are speaking. Therefore, because nothing can be truer than science and understanding (for wisdom is included in them), what follows from our consideration of the foregoing is that, properly speaking, the knowledge of principles is understanding.

He also proves this with another reason, namely, because a demonstration is not of necessity a principle of a demonstration; otherwise there would be an infinite process in demonstrations, and this was disproved in Book I. Since, therefore, demonstration causes science, it follows that science cannot be the principle of science, as though the principles of the sciences were made known through science. Therefore, if we have no other type of knowledge except science which is always true, it follows that understanding will be the principle of science, namely, because the principles of the sciences are made known through understanding, so far forth, namely, that this understanding which is the principle of sicence is cognoscitive of the principles from which science proceeds. But this, namely, science, is *all,* i.e., a whole, which is related to every thing (i.e., to the entire matter with which science is concerned) in the way that understanding is related to the principles of science.

OTHER TITLES FROM MAGI

Adler, Mortimer, FREEDOM (From Socrates to Sartre) .50¢
Anselm, St. WHY GOD BECAME MAN and THE VIRGIN CONCEPTION $6.00
Aquinas, Thomas,
    Commentary on Letter to the Galatians $6.00
    Commentary on Letter to the Ephesians $6.50
    Commentary on Philippians and First Thessalonians $4.50
    Commentary on Posterior Analytics $6.50
Berry, Thomas, FIVE ORIENTAL PHILOSOPHIES .60¢
Delfgaauw, Bernard, THE STUDENT HISTORY OF PHILOSOPHY $4.95
    TWENTIETH CENTURY PHILOSOPHY $4.95
Donceel, Joseph, THE PHILOSOPHY OF KARL RAHNER .50¢
Fairbanks, Henry, THE LASTING LONELINESS OF NATHANIEL HAWTHORNE $5.95
Gleason, Robert, SITUATIONAL MORALITY .50¢
Hawkins, D.J.B. APPROACH TO PHILOSOPHY $1.50
McCool, Gerald, THE THEOLOGY OF KARL RAHNER .50¢
McDonagh, Enda, FREEDOM OR TOLERANCE? $3.95
Mackey, J.P. THE GRACE OF GOD, THE RESPONSE OF MAN $3.95
    CONTEMPORARY PHILOSOPHY OF RELIGION $1.00
Marechal, Joseph, STUDIES IN THE PSYCHOLOGY OF THE MYSTICS $3.75
Maritain, J. WISDOM: A MANIFESTO .60¢
Miller, Robert, THE PHILOSOPHY OF LANGUAGE .60¢
Patka, Frederick, THE CLOWNS: ADULTS IN THEIR WORLD OF
    MAKE-BELIEVE $2.50
Peifer, John, THE MYSTERY OF KNOWLEDGE (A Realistic
    Epistemology) $2.25
Simon, Yves, THE GREAT DIALOGUE OF NATURE AND SPACE $3.75
Thompson, W.R. SCIENCE AND COMMON SENSE $2.50
Troisfontaines, Roger, WHAT IS EXISTENTIALISM? .50¢
Valentine, Ferdinand, THE ART AND TECHNIQUE OF PRAYER .50¢

241